Caring for Other People's Children:
A Complete Guide to Family Day Care
FRANCES KEMPER ALSTON

Family Day Care: Current Research for
Informed Public Policy
DONALD L. PETERS & ALAN R. PENCE, Eds.

The Early Childhood Curriculum:
A Review of Current Research, 2nd Ed.
CAROL SEEFELDT, Ed.

Reconceptualizing the Early Childhood
Curriculum: Beginning the Dialogue
SHIRLEY A. KESSLER &
BETH BLUE SWADENER, Eds.

Ways of Assessing Children and
Curriculum: Stories of Early
Childhood Practice
CELIA GENISHI, Ed.

The Play's The Thing:
Teachers' Roles in Children's Play
ELIZABETH JONES
GRETCHEN REYNOLDS

Scenes from Day Care:
How Teachers Teach and What
Children Learn
ELIZABETH BALLIETT PLATT

Raised in East Urban:
Child Care Changes
in a Working Class Community
CAROLINE ZINSSER

United We Stand:
Collaboration for Child Care
and Early Education Services
SHARON L. KAGAN

Making Friends in School:
Promoting Peer Relationships
in Early Childhood
PATRICIA G. RAMSEY

Play and the Social Context
of Development in Early Care
and Education
BARBARA SCALES, MILLIE ALMY,
AGELIKI NICOLOPOULOU, &
SUSAN ERVIN-TRIPP, Eds.

The Whole Language Kindergarten
SHIRLEY RAINES
ROBERT CANADY

Good Day/Bad Day:
The Child's Experience of Child Care
LYDA BEARDSLEY

Children's Play and Learning:
Perspectives and Policy Implications
EDGAR KLUGMAN
SARA SMILANSKY

Serious Players in the Primary Classroom:
Empowering Children Through
Active Learning Experiences
SELMA WASSERMANN

Child Advocacy for
Early Childhood Educators
BEATRICE S. FENNIMORE

Managing Quality Child Care Centers:
A Comprehensive Manual for
Administrators
PAMELA BYRNE SCHILLER
PATRICIA M. DYKE

Multiple Worlds of Child Writers:
Friends Learning to Write
ANNE HAAS DYSON

Young Children Continue to Reinvent
Arithmetic—2nd Grade: Implications
of Piaget's Theory
CONSTANCE KAMII

Literacy Learning in the Early Years:
Through Children's Eyes
LINDA GIBSON

The Good Preschool Teacher:
Six Teachers Reflect on Their Lives
WILLIAM AYERS

A Child's Play Life:
An Ethnographic Study
DIANA KELLY-BYRNE

Professionalism and the
Early Childhood Practitioner
BERNARD SPODEK, OLIVIA N. SARACHO,
& DONALD L. PETERS, Eds.

(Continued)

(*Early Childhood Education Series titles, continued*)

Looking at Children's Play: The Bridge
from Theory to Practice
  PATRICIA A. MONIGHAN-NOUROT,
  BARBARA SCALES, JUDITH L. VAN HOORN,
  & MILLIE ALMY

The War Play Dilemma: Balancing
Needs and Values in the
Early Childhood Classroom
  NANCY CARLSSON-PAIGE
  DIANE E. LEVIN

The Piaget Handbook
for Teachers and Parents
  ROSEMARY PETERSON
  VICTORIA FELTON-COLLINS

Teaching and Learning in a Diverse
World: Multicultural Education
for Young Children
  PATRICIA G. RAMSEY

The Full-Day Kindergarten
  DORIS PRONIN FROMBERG

Promoting Social and Moral
Development in Young Children
  CAROLYN POPE EDWARDS

A Teacher at Work:
Professional Development and
the Early Childhood Educator
  MARGARET V. YONEMURA

Today's Kindergarten
  BERNARD SPODEK, Ed.

Supervision in
Early Childhood Education
  JOSEPH J. CARUSO
  M. TEMPLE FAWCETT

Visions of Childhood: Influential
Models from Locke to Spock
  JOHN CLEVERLEY
  D. C. PHILLIPS

Starting School: From Separation
to Independence
  NANCY BALABAN

Young Children Reinvent Arithmetic:
Implications of Piaget's Theory
  CONSTANCE KAMII

Ideas Influencing Early
Childhood Education
  EVELYN WEBER

Diversity in the Classroom:
A Multicultural Approach
  FRANCES E. KENDALL

The Joy of Movement
in Early Childhood
  SANDRA R. CURTIS

Island of Childhood:
Education in the Special World
of Nursery School
  ELINOR FITCH GRIFFIN

FAMILY DAY CARE

*Current Research for
Informed Public Policy*

Edited by
DONALD L. PETERS
ALAN R. PENCE

Teachers College, Columbia University
New York and London

Published by Teachers College Press, 1234 Amsterdam Avenue, New York, NY 10027

Library of Congress Cataloging-in-Publication Data

Family day care : current research for informed public policy / edited
  by Donald L. Peters, Alan R. Pence.
      p.   cm — (Early childhood education series)
  Includes bibliographical references and index.
  ISBN 0–8077–3202–8 (cloth : alk. paper)
    1. Family day care—United States.   2. Family day care—Canada.
  I. Peters, Donald L.   II. Pence, Alan R., 1948–   .   III. Series.
  HV854.F34   1992
  362.7'12'0973—dc20   92–20525

ISBN 0–8077–3202–8

Printed on acid-free paper

Manufactured in the United States of America

98 97 96 95 94 93 92   8 7 6 5 4 3 2 1

Contents

Preface   vii

Chapter 1   Family Day Care: Issues and Information Needs   1
            Donald L. Peters and Alan R. Pence

Part I   **Perspectives on the Social, Economic, and**
                Historic Context of Family Day Care   7

Chapter 2   Historical Perspectives on Familial and
            Extrafamilial Child Care: Toward a History of
            Family Day Care   9
            Judith D. Auerbach and Gary A. Woodill

Chapter 3   The Changing Demographics of Family Day Care
            in the United States   28
            Sandra L. Hofferth and Ellen Eliason Kisker

Chapter 4   Family Day Care in a Socioecological Context:
            Data from the Canadian National Child Care
            Study   58
            Alan R. Pence, Hillel Goelman, Donna S. Lero,
            and Lois Brockman

Chapter 5   An Introduction to the Economics of Family
            Home Day Care   72
            W. Steven Barnett

Chapter 6   Research Perspectives on Family Day Care   92
            June Pollard and Jan Lockwood Fischer

Part II   **Perspectives on the Process of Family Day Care**   113

Chapter 7   Family Day Care for Infants and Toddlers   115
            Carollee Howes and Laura M. Sakai

Chapter 8   Family Day Care and Children with Disabilities   129
             Penny L. Deiner

Chapter 9   The Physical Setting: Ecological Features of
             Family Day Care and Their Impact on Child
             Development   146
             Susan L. Golbeck

Chapter 10   Dimensions of Parent-Provider Relationships in
             Family Day Care   170
             Douglas R. Powell and Gail Bollin

Chapter 11   Training and Professionalism in Family Day Care   188
             *Susan Kontos, Sandra Machida, Sandra Griffin,
             and Malcolm Read*

Chapter 12   Models of Family Day Care and Support Services
             in Canada   209
             Irene J. Kyle

Chapter 13   Models of Family Day Care and Support Services
             in the United States   229
             Joe Perreault

Chapter 14   Assessing Quality in Family Day Care   243
             *Richard M. Clifford, Thelma Harms, Susan
             Pepper, and Barbara Stuart*

Chapter 15   Future Policy and Research Needs   266
             Arthur Emlen and Elizabeth Prescott

             About the Editors and Contributors   **279**

             Index   **287**

Preface

The concept underlying this book began to take shape at a meeting of the American Educational Research Association when the two editors and several of the contributors came together in a session involving current issues in day care research. During the discussion two things became quite clear: (1) family day care was of major and growing public importance as a child-rearing environment but was sorely underresearched, and (2) what information was available, from a variety of research disciplines and perspectives, was not conveniently accessible to either the research community or policymakers. Further, the group felt that there was far too little sharing of information between Canadian and U.S. colleagues. A comprehensive North American review and analysis seemed particularly desirable and timely.

We therefore set out to pull together, in one volume, reviews and analyses from a variety of disciplinary perspectives that would:

1. Place family day care in a historical, demographic, social, and economic context in both Canada and the United States;
2. Synthesize current thinking on the policies, organization, practices, and effects of family day care in North America;
3. Delineate the critical issues of family day care for researchers, practitioners, and policymakers, particularly as they relate to infant and toddler development; and
4. Draw out the practical and policy issues that warrant further research and analysis.

The desire to present a breadth of perspectives is reflected in the fact that the editors are from opposite ends of the continent and represent both U.S. and Canadian universities. We have assembled a list of contributors with extensive experience in the child care field in general, and family day care in particular, as researchers, teachers, and practitioners both in Canada and in the United States. Further, the contributors, through their training and their work, represent a range of disciplines, including child development and child care, demography, developmental psychology, economics, education, family studies, and sociology. Finally, the contributors are widely dispersed geographically across both countries, permitting them to incorporate their knowledge of and perspectives on regional activities and differences.

The contributors were paired or grouped by topics or issues, and although many had never met or worked together before, they were asked to coauthor chapters or develop parallel structures for their presentations. The concept was simple, though the tasks assigned to the authors were not easy. The concept was that although Canada and the United States represent two distinct and different countries with differing political, legislative, and legal systems, there are a sufficient number of sociocultural, economic, and historical bridges between the two to make useful comparisons and contrasts possible.

The extent of our success in attaining our goals is a testament to the openness, patience, and persistence of the contributing authors and to the wonders of modern communication. We suspect that more E mail messages, faxes, and couriered mail have zipped across the continent during the preparation of this book than for any other of comparable size. We wish to express our gratitude to the authors who took up this challenge to extend their own thinking and develop strategies for working with new colleagues in a fashion seldom required of contributors to an edited volume. We hope they will agree that this process has enriched their understanding. We believe that they have made a major contribution to the understanding of family day care research for informed public policy.

FAMILY DAY CARE
Current Research for
Informed Public Policy

CHAPTER 1

Family Day Care

ISSUES AND INFORMATION NEEDS

Donald L. Peters
Alan R. Pence

Family day care is a common form of out-of-home care for millions of young children in Canada and the United States. Today, the reality of North American society is that understanding family day care is essential to understanding the context of early childhood development, particularly for infants and toddlers. By all indications, this context for development will continue to be an important one in the future.

Yet in a scientific sense we know very little about family day care, and we have been slow to synthesize what knowledge is available. Our lack of understanding of family day care is unfortunate not only because it is a major source of out-of-home care for the youngest and most vulnerable children, but also because it is the least regulated or supervised form of nonrelative care. If we are to better understand the development of young children we need to better understand the ecological context in which that development occurs. And if we are to better serve young children and their families we need to better understand what is going on in family day care. Hence, for both knowledge generation and practical policy purposes, a closer scrutiny and analysis of family day care are timely and warranted.

In this book we bring together current research and thought on family day care from both the United States and Canada in a way that may better inform research and policy decisions in both countries.

WHY DO WE KNOW SO LITTLE?

Even though family day care represents one of the most common forms of out-of-home care used by families in North America, there has been far less research conducted in this setting than in other child care settings. The lack of research is attributable in part to the "invisibility" of family day care, in part to the difficulties of conducting research in the intimacies of this "private-yet-public" setting, and in part to the lack of a synthesis of knowledge that can generate and drive programmatic research efforts.

The lack of research on family day care may also be attributable to the fact that family day care is often considered to be outside the "formal" system of early childhood education and child care. As an unregulated or marginally regulated service, typically delivered by a private entrepreneurial component of the child care economy and generally staffed by untrained caregivers, family day care is seen by many as not much different from out-of-home care by close relatives or friends. As such, it appears to be more akin to the informal social support systems that have been involved in child care for centuries in all cultures. It is, in some sense, the hidden side of child care—not publicly regulated, yet familiar to large numbers of the public. As an informal system, it has only recently begun to gain the interest of researchers and policymakers.

It is generally acknowledged that conducting research both within and across family day care homes has practical difficulties that discourage many researchers (Long, Peters & Garduque, 1984). Often cited are such problems as the difficulty of locating and obtaining the cooperation of representative samples of family day care providers, particularly those that are unlicensed (Wandersman, 1981); the high turnover rates of caregivers and families; family day care providers' reluctance to participate in research that has no apparent benefits for them, or that imposes on their already stretched-thin time or resources; and the settings themselves not being conducive to either experimentation or unobtrusive observation. These logistical difficulties impose severe limitations on the reliability and generalizability of family day care research and make such research difficult to both conduct and publish.

The research that has been done on family day care has been scattered, and its dissemination through the usual professional literature has been limited. Much of what is known about family day care is the result of either local, often narrowly focused studies or the embedding of family day care within broader studies of out-of-home care where it has been only one, and not necessarily the most important, concern of the investigators. A number of local, state, or provincial governments have funded supply-and-demand studies of the local day care market. State agencies, colleges, and universities have conducted and evaluated training programs for family day care providers. Researchers of all types have conducted specific-purpose studies with opportunity samples from their own locales. However, researchers, practitioners, and policymakers have seldom had syntheses and analyses of this literature readily available. Indeed, much of it does not make the usual journals and tends to be lost to those beyond the borders of the immediate regions studied. Even when published, the knowledge generated is scattered among the journals of many fields. Multiple perspectives, involving several disciplines, have not been brought together. The parts of our understanding have seldom been interwoven into a whole.

Without such an integration to drive research there is little opportunity to build, however incrementally, a solid knowledge base for theory construction or decision making.

ORGANIZING WHAT WE DO KNOW

Family Day Care in an Ecological Context

The ecological approach to the study of human development introduced in the mid-1970s has potential for both encouraging more systematic research and organizing our knowledge in useful ways. The movement toward more contextual thinking has moved researchers out of the laboratory and into children's everyday settings and has encouraged the acknowledgment and investigation of the many systems and systems levels that have an impact on child development (Winter & Peters, 1974; Bronfenbrenner, 1979, 1989). This approach has been increasingly applied to the analysis of early childhood education generally and to day care research specifically (cf. Goelman & Pence, 1987; Pence, 1988; Peters & Kontos, 1987). It seems to offer several benefits for an analysis of family day care, namely that it directs our attention to both the microsystem level of analysis, traditionally the realm of educators and psychologists, and broader systems (e.g., the exosystem and macrosystem) that are the traditional domains of sociologists and economists; and it helps to free us from traditional forms of thinking involving univariate, linear causality and moves us into modes that include multiple determinants, actively interactive elements, and nonlinear relationships.

The Organization of This Volume

Although no single theoretical stance has been used to organize the materials in this volume, the editors, in selecting the topics to be covered and in guiding the authors, admit to their own biases toward this ecological system perspective for viewing family day care as a child-rearing environment of great importance. Our conviction of the worthiness of this approach led us to encourage the authors to think systemically as they drew together the relevant literature on their topics, integrating concerns of individual development (of infants and young children, parents, and family day care providers as people) as well as those of the family and the day care system as they interact with other systems of society. This perspective provides some cohesion to the multiple contributions of the chapter authors without, we hope, constraining their thoughts or analyses based on their own disciplinary and theoretical perspectives.

There is another organizational theme in this volume. The heart of any analysis lies in the ability to compare and contrast. Although there is a clear intention to provide a North American perspective on family day care research, there is no attempt to gloss over national differences. Indeed, the comparisons between the United States and Canada are important. Although the two countries have much in common, there are differences that are important for both the interpretation of data and the drawing of policy implications from those data.

Commonalities between the two countries derive, in part, from their European cultural and political heritage and the shared geography of North America. The two countries have enjoyed a relatively long period of close social, economic, and political cooperation. Yet, although relationships between the two countries have, for the past 150 years, been peaceful, there are many distinct philosophical and political differences between them. These differences are partially accounted for by their different political and legislative systems, differences in the power and responsibilities assumed by Canadian provinces as compared to those assumed by states in the United States, differences in population size and distribution, and differences in philosophical and social attitude inherent in the fabric of the two countries. In the United States the primacy of individual rights, aggressive market capitalism, and a minimalist and reactive view of the role of government stand in contrast to Canada's "gentle" capitalism, respect for bureaucratic structures, and greater commitment to universal health and human service programs.

To stress the North American focus of the volume we asked the authors to restrict their reviews, as much as possible, to Canadian and U.S. studies, under the assumption that these would have the most direct translatability into policy and practice within these two countries. At the same time, by presenting Canadian and U.S. research syntheses and interpretations in juxtaposition, we believed that some of the most critical research and policy issues would become clearer from the comparisons. Prevailing attitudes toward individual versus governmental rights and responsibilities, and federal versus state or provincial rights and responsibilities, that are inherent in the two systems yield different conclusions about what may to be done by whom to solve child care problems.

The book is organized in two broad parts as a means of assisting the reader through the literature. Part I provides a series of perspectives on the history, current demographics, and economics of family day care in Canada and the United States. In essence this part looks at the macrosystem issues as they relate to family day care, embedding the current research and policy issues within a broad historical and social context.

Auerbach and Woodill set family day care in a historical context of the evolution of attitudes, ideas, and modes of child care. They remind us how these attitudes and methods of rearing children have changed over historical time and how the relationships among the players in the mother care/other care debate change, with a continually uncertain role for governmental institutions.

Hofferth and Kisker for the United States and Pence, Goelman, Lero, and Brockman for Canada review the results of recent national studies. These chapters represent what is essentially our current best knowledge of the demographics of supply and demand in family day care in North America. Singly and together, they represent a considerable refinement of our definitions of out-of-home care and significant advances in the methodologies applied to addressing these issues. They also reflect important differences between Canada and the United States in the distribution and analysis of unlicensed care.

Barnett overlays an important economic pespective on the supply-and-demand issues, reminding us of some critical underlying assumptions about how things work in the marketplace. His analyses, put forth to provoke useful thought and debate, remind us of both the human factors in economic decision making in an essentially free market and the numerous other, extrinsic factors, that complicate the shaping of supply and demand.

Pollard and Fischer provide additional insight by adding the Canadian view to economic and social issues through the integration of municipal and provincial studies and by delineating a number of perspectives through which family day care can and has been viewed in the literature.

Part II changes the focus from macro perspectives to the processes of family day care at the micro-, meso-, and exosystem levels. Each of the chapters addresses issues related to the quality of the experiences provided. Howes and Sakai provide a review of family day care for infants and toddlers enrolled in family day care and the research on the outcomes of such experiences; Deiner reviews the potential of utilizing family day care as a delivery system for services to infants with developmental disabilities and their families.

Golbeck takes a careful look at characteristics of the physical setting as an education and caring environment and provides particularly useful analyses concerning the theoretical underpinnings and measurement issues in understanding the physical characteristics of a "home" environment. Powell and Bollin focus attention on parent-caregiver relations as an important variable in quality assessment and provide insights into untangling the many dimensions of the parent-provider relationship. Kontos, Machida, Griffin, and Read address the issues of training and professionalism of child care providers as they relate to issues of quality care provision. Kyle for Canada and Perreault for the United States provide perspectives on efforts to support and regulate family day care homes. Clifford, Harms, Pepper, and Stuart direct attention to the issues involved in attempting to measure quality. They review evidence from both Canada and the United States related to the reliability and validity of currently used measures.

In the final chapter Arthur Emlen and Elizabeth Prescott, two pioneers in family day care research, combine their experience and expertise to draw together the threads of the research presented and suggest the directions for research that seem important for informing future research and policy decisions.

This introduction can do little more than provide the reader with a brief overview of our thoughts as we began our work on this book. The chapters that follow provide an important compilation of what we do know and what we have yet to learn about family day care. As such we can only hope that it usefully informs current decisions and inspires further research and analysis.

REFERENCES

Bronfenbrenner, U. (1979). *The ecology of human development*. Cambridge, MA: Harvard University Press.

Bronfenbrenner, U. (1989). Ecological systems theory. *Annals of Child Development, 6*, 187–249.

Goelman, H., and Pence, A. R. (1987). Some aspects of the relationship between family structure and child language development in three types of day care. In D. Peters & S. Kontos (Eds.), *Continuity and discontinuity in child care experience* (pp. 129–46). Norwood, NJ: Ablex.

Long, F., Peters, D. L., & Garduque, L. (1984). Continuity between home and day care: A model for defining relevant dimensions of child care. In I. Sigel (Ed.), *Advances in applied developmental psychology* (Vol. 1). Norwood, NJ: Ablex.

Pence, A. R. (Ed.). (1988). *Ecological research with children and families: From concepts to methodology*. New York: Teachers College Press.

Peters, D. L., & Kontos, S. (Eds.). (1987). *Continuity and discontinuity of experience in child care*. Norwood, NJ: Ablex.

Wandersman, L. P. (1981). Ecological relationships in family day care. *Child Care Quarterly, 10*, 89–102.

Winter, M. L., & Peters, D. L. (1974). Day care is a human system. *Child Care Quarterly, 3*, 166–76.

PART I

Perspectives on the Social, Economic, and Historic Context of Family Day Care

CHAPTER 2

Historical Perspectives on Familial and Extrafamilial Child Care

TOWARD A HISTORY OF FAMILY DAY CARE

Judith D. Auerbach
Gary A. Woodill

The history of child care in Europe and North America is a tale of competing philosophies about the nature of childhood, the sanctity of family life, the special relationship between mothers and children, and the role of the state in providing support services to families. This history is rooted in the ever-present tension between idealized notions of family and motherhood and the reality of social and economic life that renders those ideals unobtainable or undesirable for many people.

All cultures have shared the belief that in order to survive and to grow up as members of a society, young children need a certain minimal level of care and education. It has been a common view among Western societies that this care and education initially should be given by loving parents, especially by the mother. When "mother care" has been impossible for one reason or another, whatever arrangement replaces it—"other care"—is seen as second best.

Yet all societies have had some alternative arrangements for child care when mothers have been unable or unwilling to care for their own children. These alternatives include care by other relatives, care by others in the community, institutions for abandoned or orphaned children, organized child care centers, and kindergartens and preschools. Regardless of the particular social and cultural circumstances surrounding their development, all of these arrangements have been compared to mother care as the standard of optimum child care. This explains why the form of other care most popular among parents continues to be that which most closely approximates mother care—

9

that is, another woman taking care of children in her home, or what we now call family day care.

Although family day care is perhaps the most common form of extra-familial child care throughout the western world, it is also the least studied. Precisely because of its relative informality, little documented evidence of its existence is available for historical analysis. Nevertheless, historical accounts of women, family, work, and education do provide clues to family day care's various incarnations over time.

A careful reading of these accounts reveals three interrelated themes that characterize the role of family day care in the mother care/other care debate. (Scarr, 1984). The first is the nature of the relationship between parents and caregivers. This includes such issues as the role of the caregiver in the socialization of the child and cultural differences and status disparities between parents and providers.

The second theme has to do with the goal of family day care, that is, whether it is directed primarily at the care or the education of young children (or both). This includes considerations of the caregiver's qualifications as compared with mother's.

The third theme—more pronounced in contemporary discussions—is the role of the state in regulating and supporting family day care. Here the issue is at what point it is appropriate for government to intercede in what historically has been a private and relatively informal arrangement between parents and caregivers.

The following brief history of familial and extrafamilial child care elaborates these themes in an effort to provide historical perspective on a paramount element of the current child care debate: family day care. Our hope is that better knowledge about what people have done in other times and places—and why—will contribute to a reasoned discussion about what is appropriate policy in the contemporary period.

PARENT-CAREGIVER RELATIONSHIP

There are many examples in the historical record of children being given up to the care of others as a result of not being wanted or as a reflection of class notions of child rearing and the status of mothering. One of the earliest and most common forms of other care was wet-nursing, when a mother sent her child to another lactating woman to be breast-fed until it was weaned—and sometimes even longer.

Research on Roman antiquity suggests that this practice existed as early as the second century B.C. Well-to-do families often placed their children in the care of a slave or "mercenary nurse" whose duty began as wet-nursing but often was extended to the socialization of the child after weaning (Dixon, 1988). In this society, the slave nurse had no choice in her occupation; she was selected by her master or mistress primarily because she was lactating, and her relationship to the child's parents was one of uncompensated servant.

The use of slave nurses in ancient Rome indicates that the mother's presence as primary caretaker of the child was not as prized as it is in modern times, at least among certain classes. But this does not mean that the practice was popular in all circles. Philosophical opposition to the use of slave nurses was articulated by both Tacitus and Plutarch, who saw the use of nonfamilial caretakers as a sign of moral decay, an indication that parents were abdicating their responsibility and exhibiting the "decadence of an imperial society that has abandoned the virtues of ancestors who reared their own children" (Joshel, 1986, p. 3). Tacitus accused slave nurses of being ill-tempered, unchaste, and drunkardly and of possessing vulgar speech, alien manners, and superstitions. He feared that these "lower-order" attributes of the care-taker corrupted the child's mind and spirit and contributed to the loss of culture (Joshel, 1986).

There are numerous other examples in the historical record of wealthy parents entrusting the care of their children to others for a good part of their childhood. For centuries throughout Europe, it was common practice for the aristocracy and nobility to employ wet nurses, nannies, and tutors to care for children in the parents' home, and for members of other social classes to send their children—from the age of seven or eight—to other homes for appren-ticeships (Aries, 1962; Shorter, 1975; Stone, 1979). Although these arrange-ments do not constitute family day care as we know it, they do represent earlier forms of extrafamilial care in which the rearing and education of children was entrusted to individuals other than the mothers in homelike settings.

In North America, the practice of the upper class assigning child-rearing responsibility to the servant class was most evident in the antebellum South of the United States. It was common practice for slave women to raise the children of their masters. Often these women took care of black (slave) and white children at the same time while the other slave parents were at work in the fields or in the big house (Genovese, 1976; Jones, 1985). Usually older women, their duty was "to look after the children, to cook for them, and to keep them out of mischief" (Genovese, 1976, p. 507). In many cases, these women supervised older children who really looked after the younger ones (Genovese, 1976); and in many ways, the home-based and group nature of this care by slave women can be seen as an early form of family day care.

Apparently, most parents were not concerned about the socialization effects on their children of exposure to slave women and their culture. Rather, the affection and devotion slave women displayed in caring for their masters' children provided the women some basic security, by protecting them from whippings and from being sold (Joshel, 1986). Furthermore, unlike in ancient Rome, the use of slave nurses in the Old South was not criticized as a decadent practice; rather, dependence on slave nurses was freely acknowledged. This dependence gave some slave women a certain measure of authority and in some cases resulted in a role reversal between them and the plantation owners with regard to child rearing (Joshel, 1986).

In the urban centers of the northern United States in the nineteenth century, there was much more status congruity between parents and family day care providers than existed in the Old South or ancient Rome. Unfortunately, the historical record is weak on details about these arrangements. But there is evidence that many immigrant working-class women employed the services of other usually older women in the community to look after their children during the workday (Kessler-Harris, 1982). These arrangements were informal and often involved no monetary compensation; they were framed by the bonds of loyalty to the cultural community of which parents and caretakers were all part.

The practice of employing another woman to care for a working mother's children was also evident in late nineteenth-century Britain. Dubbed "childminding," this early form of family day care was scorned by writers of the day, who initially confused it with "baby farming," a practice of sending illegitimate children away to other homes where they were often grossly neglected by their caretakers (Owen, 1988). Although British childminding began as an informal practice, it eventually became part of the public child care program.

Research on contemporary family day care indicates that there is far greater social class congruity between parents and caregivers than has been the case historically. Nelson (1990) argues that contrary to popular stereotypes, family day care providers in the United States frequently are as educated as their clients and in many cases held professions similar to their clients' before deciding to start their own families.

Nevertheless, parents continue to maintain a "social distance" from family day care providers (Emlen et al., 1971). Writing about why family day care consumers prefer strangers over family or friends, Emlen suggests: "1) it affords a wider selection and opportunity to find a caregiver to fit their needs . . . and 2) selection itself gives the consumer better control over the arrangement" (1974, p. 7). In other words, even though parents look for a caregiver who is in many ways like a surrogate relative, they maintain social distance as a way to preserve family day care as the businesslike relationship it is, involving the purchase of a service.

But child care is much more than a service to parents; it is also a context and an environment in which children develop and learn. Consequently, parents wish to purchase a service that they believe will provide the best quality environment for their children. Although concern over the educational and socialization aspects of child care seems heightened in the contemporary period—in which "quality" has become the buzzword—it actually has existed for a very long time and constitutes the second theme evident in historical analyses of extrafamilial care: the extent to which child care should be focused on education as well as caregiving.

THE EDUCATION OF YOUNG CHILDREN

The European roots of beliefs about the significance of childhood education are traceable back to the fifteenth and sixteenth centuries, a period of changing sensibilities toward religion, education, childhood, human nature, and science. According to some accounts, the most precipitous event in this shift from earlier thinking was the invention of the printing press, which liberated knowledge from being the province of only an elite, privileged few (Luke, 1989). With the printing press, knowledge that had been hidden in a few places, and interpreted by a small number of scholars, could now be disseminated to the public at large—provided, of course, that the public could read.

The invention of the printing press also may be partly responsible for the creation of separate categories of adults and children (Aries, 1962; deMause, 1974; Luke, 1989; Postman, 1982). Since most young children could not read, they were separated from adults culturally and excluded from the secrets of knowledge available only after years of education.

The printing press not only enabled the creation of adult literature, but also produced school textbooks and children's literature. The first known textbook for children was designed by John Comenius, a Moravian bishop who wandered throughout Europe in the mid-seventeenth century. In 1628 he wrote *School of Infancy,* which described the "school of the mother's lap," outlining the educational context appropriate for children from birth to age six. Comenius's work underscored the seventeenth-century idea that young children should be taught by their mothers at home rather than by outside institutions.

The philosophy of child rearing and education espoused by Comenius was challenged by the enormous social change engendered by the emergence of the industrial revolution beginning in the late eighteenth century. If the printing press can be seen as starting the process of defining childhood, the exploitation of children in factories and the disruption of family life caused by industrialization and urbanization made the separation and protection of children a grim necessity. The growth of an industrial (and capitalist) economy also required a more educated population and engendered more emphasis on childhood education.

One form of early childhood education beginning in the early years of industrialization resembles what we now call family day care. This was the tradition in Europe and North America of "dame schools." Although dame schools often were run by poorly educated women in squalid accommodations (Whitbread, 1972), sometimes educated women taught young children the basics of reading and writing in their own homes for a fee (Tizard, Moss & Perry, 1976).

Other child-rearing arrangements resembling modern family day care existed in the early years of the industrial revolution, provoked in part by the worsening condition of urban poverty. For example, in 1770, Protestant pastor Jean-Frederic Oberlin's belief in the improvability of the poor led him to hire 19-year-old Sarah Banzet to take care of a group of unrelated preschool children of poor families in the Alsace region of France (Kurtz, 1976). Soon Oberlin recruited other women to take small groups of young children into their homes and to teach them Bible stories and knitting. Although this movement could be seen as contributing to the evolution of day care centers, it could also be seen as an early example of what we now call family day care.

Rescue from poverty was also the aim of Heinrich Pestalozzi, who opened an industrial school for destitute children aged six to sixteen on his farm near Zurich, Switzerland, in 1774. Although his experiment led to financial ruin, and the school closed in 1780, Pestalozzi became famous as an innovator in primary and preprimary education in the early 1800s.

Pestalozzi was very interested in the cognitive capacities of infants. He believed that children could begin learning at a very young age, but emphasized that such learning was best encouraged by mothers in their own homes. In works with such titles as *How Gertrude Teaches Her Children* and *On the Education of Infancy Addressed to Mothers*, Pestalozzi suggested that girls and mothers should be taught new progressive educational techniques that they could then use with their own children (May & Vinovskis, 1976). Pestalozzi never intended his principles to be applied to child rearing in institutional settings, but later educators and reformers did so.

With knowledge of Oberlin's pioneering work in the Alsace, other Europeans opened child care programs for different populations. Madame de Pastoret opened an *asile,* or refuge, for infants of working mothers in Paris about 1800. (Later, infant centers were known as *creches.*) The first infant "asylum" was opened in London after news of Pastoret's center spread to England.

Pastoret's center and Pestalozzi's philosophy may have been the inspiration for Robert Owen's pioneering work with children of industrial workers in Scotland. Owen's original center, established in 1816 at his factory in Lanark, represented "the first program designed specifically to meet the care and developmental needs of children of working parents in an industrialized context" (Pence, 1986, p. 6). Owen and his followers expanded his child care experiment throughout England, Scotland, and Ireland and in the utopian community Owen subsequently established in the United States at New Harmony, Indiana, where his goal continued to be both education and social reform (Deasy, 1978; May & Vinovskis, 1976; Pence, 1986).

By combining the educational and caregiving ideas of Pestalozzi and Owen, along with the far less child-centered philosophies of monitorial instruction, London reformers created what became known as the infant school system, organized under the Infant School Society formed in 1824 (May & Vinovskis, 1976). These infant schools served the double purpose of attempting to ameliorate social problems caused by industrialization and urbanization and providing children of the industrial working class a place to be while their parents and older siblings worked in the factories (May & Vinovskis, 1976).

The influence of this new European child care and education movement was felt in North America as early as the 1830s, when its followers established infant schools in the Canadian cities of Quebec, Montreal, and Charlottetown (Corbett, 1968) and in the United States in New York, Pennsylvania, and Massachusetts (May & Vinovskis, 1976; Pence, 1986). Responding to new conditions of industrialization and urbanization, these infant schools, like those in Europe, focused simultaneously on education, child development, and moral reform (May & Vinovskis, 1976).

One interesting dynamic of the North American infant school movement was the belief that infant education was the provenance of women. May and Vinovskis (1976) report an exemplary assertion appearing in *Ladies' Magazine* in April 1830, which states: "it is well observed that *'females* have many natural qualifications for instructors of infants,' which men have not—it is also true that females are competent, and might be advantageously employed in the business of education to a far greater extent than has ever yet been practiced" (p. 78). Indeed, the founders, officers, and managers of the Infant School Society were women, as were virtually all the managers of the schools themselves (May & Vinovskis, 1976). Thus, the belief in the natural ability of women as child rearers—stemming from their mother identity—extended to this form of extrafamilial child care and education.

The growing emphasis on education as an important aspect of child care also was evidenced in the development of kindergartens, which emerged in Europe in the mid-nineteenth century and spread to North America soon thereafter. Although initially geared toward children of a more affluent class than the clientele of earlier forms of extrafamilial child care, and generally structured as only part-day programs, in some aspects early kindergartens resembled what we now call family day care.

Kindergartens originated with Friedrich Froebel, who spent two years (1808–10) working with Pestalozzi at his school in Yverdon, Switzerland. Kindergartens spread throughout Germany and Western Europe by the middle of the nineteenth century and were introduced into the United States by German expatriates in the 1850s as a method of preserving German language and culture in their new country. The first U.S. kindergarten was opened in 1855 in Watertown, Wisconsin, in the home of a woman named Margarethe Schurz (Shapiro, 1983). Kindergartens soon spread throughout the United States and Canada. Given their educational emphasis, and given the fact that most were only part-day programs, kindergartens initially were not child care programs for poor and working-class children, but rather were preschool education programs for middle-class children.

The philosophy of kindergartens did not detract from the long-standing belief in mothers as the best caregivers for infants. Rather, kindergartens extended the educational theories developed by Pestalozzi, Froebel, and others as they related to the developmental capacities of children. Kindergartens usually did not accept children until the age of four or five and were designed to be supplemental to a mother's daily caregiving, not to replace it. Most were—and continue to be—part-day programs.

By the early twentieth century, another form of extrafamilial child care with an educational component emerged: the nursery school. The term originated with Margaret McMillan, who, along with her sister Rachel, established the first nursery school in London in 1911 (Bradburn, 1989). Their efforts were spawned by a British study in 1908 that indicated that children's health declined precipitously by the time they entered public school (Osborn, 1980). Believing this to be the result of the unhealthy urban industrial environment, the McMillans designed their first open-air nursery school in the London slums and emphasized play, nurturing of children, and support for parents.

Word of the British nursery schools spread to the United States and Canada by the early 1920s. The earliest North American versions were attached to research centers and universities such as Columbia University in New York, the Merrill-Palmer Institute in Detroit, and the University of Toronto, and served as laboratories for studying child development.

Although kindergartens and nursery schools are not themselves forms of family day care, we mention the circumstances surrounding their development to provide some context for the contemporary emphasis on education in extrafamilial child care, including family day care. From the late eighteenth to the late twentieth century, the growth in interest and knowledge about child development and education behind the nursery school and kindergarten movements has contributed to changing notions about what constitutes the best caregiving situation for young children in the mother care/other care paradigm.

The twentieth-century contribution to this evolution in thought is the development and popularization of psychology. Knowledge about the psychological growth and health of children has had a profound impact on how parents and substitute caregivers approach child care today.

Sigmund Freud is most commonly thought of as the founder of modern psychological theory, but his investigations into the cognitive and psychological dimensions of human development were themselves influenced by earlier thinking about the nature of the child. Historically, two conflicting views dominated: One conceived of the child as unformed, innocent, and in need of freedom to explore; the other view saw the child as inherently bad, evil, and in need of control. These divergent beliefs about children led to different prescriptions for their care and education—whether by mothers or by others—still evidenced today.

Some of the earliest work on cognitive growth reflecting the first view was conducted at the end of the eighteenth century by Jean Itard, who worked in the Deaf and Dumb Institute in Paris. There, in 1799, he came in contact with Victor, the wild boy of Aveyron. Itard, along with Madame Guerin, spent many long hours trying to teach Victor to speak and to read, testing the belief that early education has a significant effect on cognitive growth and can mitigate the effects of even the wildest nature. Although Itard and Guerin were only partly successful, their methods, along with those evolved by Itard's successor, Edouard Seguin, started a tradition that drew attention to the importance of sense training and stimulation in the development of children's cognitive abilities.

Itard and Seguin were the main inspirations for Maria Montessori's ten years of work with mentally handicapped and poor children in Rome, and her opening of the *Casa dei Bambini* in 1906. Montessori wrote many books on her method and visited the United States and Britain, lecturing on her approach to the education of young children, which stressed the use of structured activities and props to support the individually paced development of children. Her belief in the value of play and exploration for children was popular among many parents of the middle class and led to the establishment of many Montessori-method preschools in North America and Europe.

The approach of Itard, Seguin, and Montessori, which emphasized the innocent and open nature of children and the value of providing environmental and educational stimuli to promote their naturalistic development, was countered by an opposite approach that emphasized the need for rationalization and control in child rearing to mitigate the inherently savage and evil nature of children.

This second approach was epitomized in North America by the work of

G. Stanley Hall, founder of the *American Journal of Psychology* and co-founder of the American Psychological Association, who believed that children were born savages who "recapitulated human evolution, developing civilized traits as they grew" (Strasser, 1982, p. 232). Writing in the early 1880s, Hall promoted "scientific motherhood," advising mothers to keep charts and books about their children's every behavior and character and to form child study groups with other mothers to compare their children's progress. Hall did not make many converts, but his notions about the significant role of mothers in advancing child development influenced the approaches of subsequent child psychologists.

The popularization of Freud in the United States in the 1920s (following the publication of his *Three Essays on Sexuality* in 1905) added another dimension to theories of child development—the importance of the social-emotional life of children. Freud's psychoanalytic approach suggested the possibility that children's ability to develop appropriately could be compromised by early negative emotional experiences in the family. This was interpreted by others to suggest the need for greater control by mothers in the behavior and rearing of their children.

The dominant theme in child-rearing advice in the first decades of the twentieth century was the link between bad child rearing and later social problems. Experts advised mothers to take a regimented approach to raising their children by establishing rigid schedules for eating, sleeping, and toilet training, and they discouraged spoiling, overattention, and the expression of emotion or affection (Mintz & Kellog, 1988; Strasser, 1982).

These two streams of child-rearing philosophy—which became known as "permissive" and "scientific"—were to remain competitive, in some form or another, through the middle and late twentieth century. Common to both of them was an emphasis on the centrality of the mother's role in determining the psychological health and development of children. Paradoxically, this maternal centrality could work in opposite ways: Mothers could be accused both of playing too significant a role, by being overprotective and overindulgent (Hartmann, 1982), and of being negligent, by not devoting enough attention to their children or by entrusting their children to the care of others.

By the mid-twentieth century, the confusion that this dialectic produced in parents—especially mothers—was somewhat ameliorated by the publication of Dr. Benjamin Spock's *Baby and Child Care* (1946), which became a world best-seller. Dr. Spock taught parents that their actions had consequences for the development of their children, but that they needn't worry so much, for, he proclaimed, "you know more than you think you do." (Later, his famous refrain was "trust yourself.") Spock suggested that children's needs and desires were legitimate and that parental authority was important but should be exercised with some flexibility. He also emphasized the importance of a good love relationship between mothers and their children.

This calmer approach to child rearing and the role of mothers did not eliminate concern about how to enhance children's social, emotional, and intellectual growth. During the 1960s, child psychology and early childhood education were influenced by the growing popularity of Piaget's theories about cognitive development, which emphasized a four-stage process through which all children passed. Mothers and other caregivers now were expected to become increasingly aware of the cognitive and behavioral characteristics of each stage in order to monitor and encourage appropriate development among their children.

By the end of the twentieth century, popular child-rearing philosophy has come to encompass elements of all the strands described above—an awareness of the cognitive, psychological, and emotional nature of children, and the need to balance permissiveness with control to allow for both freedom of individual exploration and socially appropriate behavior.

This quick historical overview of dominant child-rearing philosophies and their theoretical underpinnings is important background for understanding the role of expectations about the socioemotional and intellectual development of children in the current mother care/other care debate and the popularity of family day care. In contemporary society, with a more educated population overall, parents seeking alternative child care arrangements try to express their expectations and preferences in their choice of provider. In the most general terms, modern parents try to replicate their idealized version of mother care for their children by finding another woman in a homelike setting who can provide both loving care and intellectual stimulation. This, coupled with the practical issues of the cost and availability of child care, leads many parents to choose family day care.

THE ROLE OF THE STATE IN FAMILY DAY CARE

Although most family day care has been and continues to be informally arranged, it increasingly is coming under the scrutiny of parents and child care advocates alike. The popularization of child development and education theories in the late twentieth century, as well as some highly publicized cases of abuse and neglect in organized child care settings, have made quality a salient concern for parents seeking extrafamilial child care of any kind. Efforts to ensure quality brings us to our third theme in the history of family day care: the role of the state.

Although there is no uniform definition of quality child care—it can vary depending on parents' educational and cultural values—the operational definition of quality care that is favored by child care advocates and professionals, and that has come to dominate in the late twentieth century, is child care that is regulated by government. But this definition is problematic in North American culture, in which family life has always been considered private and government involvement justified only when parents have somehow failed in their duties. Indeed, privatism has been the ideological brake on government-sponsored child care (Auerbach, 1988). Regulation epitomizes the tension between the state's simultaneous, but sometimes conflicting, interest in protecting children and in protecting family privacy (Nelson, 1990).

Although space does not permit a full review here, historical accounts of U.S. child care policy concur that since the early nineteenth century, government-supported child care was stigmatized as being a welfare service for the poor (Auerbach, 1988; Steinfels, 1973). Only during World War II, when the massive employment of women became connected to larger economic and security issues of the nation, did the federal government launch a large-scale child care program. But this was a singular experiment—a wartime expedient—that ended as soon as the war did (Auerbach, 1988; Frank et al., 1982; National Manpower Council, 1957). For the many mothers who continued their employment after the war, finding child care became increasingly difficult.

This wartime experience was mirrored in Britain and Canada as well (Schulz, 1978; Stapleford, 1976; Whitbread, 1972), and in all three countries family day care increased after the war to fill in the gap left by the closure of government centers. But among these nations, only Britain experienced direct government involvement in family day care. The Nurseries and Childminders Act of 1948 gave local authorities the responsibility of registering private nurseries and childminders (synonymous with family day care providers). According to Cohen (1988), the act was ineffective in regulating childminding and did little to soothe many parents' concern about placing their children in less-than-adequate care. Nevertheless, the number of spaces with registered childminders increased from 1,700 in 1949 to 47,200 in 1968. Further amendments to the act in 1968 provided tighter control over registration and gave local authorities greater flexibility to support childminders. By 1985, the number of spaces in regulated childminding grew to nearly 115,000 (Cohen, 1988).

In the United States, although there was virtually no government control of family day care until the mid-twentieth century, concern over quality was evidenced much earlier. In 1918 a Children's Bureau field-worker gave the following account of family day care in Cleveland:

> One woman occupying four dark, poorly ventilated rooms was crowding into them thirty and forty children each day; another was caring for twelve

children in equally bad surroundings; a third who had less than a tenth
vision was receiving fourteen children in her two rooms; and a fourth was
caring for eight children whom she had the habit of shutting behind two
locked doors on the second floor while she did her marketing. In all these
places the food was sent by the mothers and was given cold. (quoted in
Tentler, 1979, p. 162)

Decades later, in 1972, Mary Keyserling and the National Council of
Jewish Women published *Windows on Day Care,* an equally dismal portrait
of family day care in the United States. Although this study was methodologically problematic, it was widely circulated and it reinforced the societal belief prevalent throughout much of the nineteenth and twentieth centuries that only maternal care could adequately meet the needs of young
children.

Indeed, for most of the twentieth century, family day care was characterized along with all other forms of other care as of poor quality and, by
definition, detrimental to children's well-being. It was not until the 1960s
that either family day care or center-based day care began to be studied as
specific and different forms of other care. Work by Florence Ruderman
(1968), Arthur Emlen (1971, 1972, 1974), and Elizabeth Prescott (1972)
marked the commencement of family day care research in North America.

The starting point for both family day care and center-based care research in the mid- to late twentieth century was the question of whether
maternal employment was detrimental to children. Influenced both by the
rising number of employed women and by the growing field of child development, researchers attempted to assess the effect of having a working mother on the social, emotional, and cognitive development of children (see
Chapter 6 this volume).

The most comprehensive U.S. family day care study of the 1960s and
1970s was the National Day Care Home Study (NDCHS) sponsored by the
Department of Health and Human Services in 1977. This intensive study of
793 homes in Los Angeles, Philadelphia, and San Antonio involved detailed
analysis by child development experts of the setting and the interaction of
children and caregivers in family day care and concluded that this form of
care generally afforded a positive environment for children (DHHS, 1980–
81).

Concerns over the structure and content of extrafamilial child care as
compared to maternal care led child welfare advocates, educators, and policymakers in the United States to begin considering ways in which quality
could be ensured in different child care settings and focused attention on the
role of the state as regulator.

Although U.S. states began regulating family day care as early as 1885, when Pennsylvania passed a law prohibiting anyone from providing care to more than two children under the age of three without a license issued by certain public officials, most regulation activity did not occur until the 1960s and 1970s (Travis & Perreault, 1983). Furthermore, during this latter period, although many states initially required licensing of family day care homes, many eventually changed to requiring only registration. Between 1965 and 1982, for example, Massachusetts, North Dakota, Virginia, Texas, South Carolina, Nebraska, and Maryland all introduced licensing legislation and then subsequently made the switch to registration (Travis & Perreault, 1983). This shift may have been due in great part to declining state and federal budgets for child care licensing and enforcement, and in some states, such as Texas, resulted in an increase in identified family day care homes (Kahn & Kamerman, 1987).

In addition to registration and licensing issues, increased attention also was paid to provider training during this period. Many states required providers to obtain some sort of education and training in child development in order to be licensed or registered.

In the 1970s, to accommodate this requirement, numerous training programs for family day care providers were developed and sponsored by colleges and universities throughout the United States (Travis & Perreault, 1983). These projects provided classes and training sessions in such things as early child development, health and safety issues, and nutrition. By the 1980s, many of these projects served to recruit as well as train potential new family day care providers.

These activities related to licensing and training contributed to the development of a stronger professional identity among family day care providers during the 1970s and 1980s. Efforts were undertaken both by providers and by states, localities, and private businesses that subsidized their programs to organize communitywide networks of family day care and to form associations to represent the interests of providers.

In 1978, an estimated 30,000 caregivers serving over 120,000 children were participating in day care systems in the United States defined as "networks of homes under the sponsorship of an administrative agency" (DHHS, 1980–81). These systems—or networks—provided training and referral services. Many developed as a result of state or local requirements for federal funding of subsidized care under the Amendments to the Social Security Act (Title XX). In this scenario, the federal government could contract for slots reserved for recipients of Title XX and then require certain standards of care. This allowed local and state government agencies to set up networks to better control administrative functions, including the setting of salaries and conditions of care. Additionally, these networks developed shared libraries, toy banks, and respite care services (Kahn & Kamerman, 1987).

Also beginning in the 1980s, a number of U.S. employers interested in providing a day care benefit for their employees and for others in the community selected support of family day care networks. These employers contributed money or in-kind goods and services to develop or support existing family day care networks that supplied child care services to the companies' employees and others in the community (Auerbach, 1988).

Providers, too, began organizing themselves and creating professional associations at the local, state, and national levels to protect their interests. Travis and Perreault (1983) identify the state of Washington as having the first such association, founded in 1966. Similar organizations emerged in the early 1970s in Minnesota, Colorado, California, New York, and Tennessee, and in the late 1970s in such states as New Hampshire, Florida, Kansas, Arkansas, Wisconsin, and Pennsylvania. The National Family Day Care Association, which maintains contact with these state and local organizations, was established to advocate at the federal level on behalf of providers everywhere concerned about such issues as standards and licensing requirements, training and education, salaries and working conditions, government subsidies, and relationships with children and parents.

But in the United States, all this activity around regulation, training of providers, and the development of family day care networks and associations has not translated into a coherent national policy as expressed, for example, in the adoption of federal standards for extrafamilial child care. Although such standards were developed in the form of the Federal Interagency Day Care Requirements (FIDCR) and were implemented in many states and localities, they were never employed at the federal level (Scarr, 1984).

Canada's experience from the 1960s to the 1990s is not that different from that of the United States. In Canada, where day care is a provincial responsibility, the development of family day care followed no national pattern during this period. In the late 1960s in Ontario, Canada's largest province, staff in several day care centers in Toronto began discussions on ways to solve the crisis in demand for day care spaces brought about by economic growth and women's increased labor force participation and turned to family day care (Kyle, 1991). One organization, the Protestant Children's Homes, became an agency called Family Day Care Services. Soon after, another significant day care organization, the Andrew Fleck Child Centre in Ottawa, began to offer private family day care services.

Representatives of day care centers in Toronto also began lobbying government for changes in child care legislation, and in 1971, the Day Nurseries Act was amended to include the possibility of paying subsidies to family day care in Ontario. The Ontario government also published a set of voluntary guidelines for family day care in the early 1970s, but these were not enforced in any way. In 1978, a set of standards for family day care was passed in the Ontario legislature, but the law was not implemented until 1984.

Similar to the situation in the United States, the organization and monitoring of family day care today varies in Canada from province to province. Some provinces provide no support or training for caregivers, but do license private homes for day care and conduct annual visits; others use an agency model. In some provinces, licensing and support functions may be provided by separate agencies. British Columbia, for example, had only four support agencies for family day care before 1990. In Quebec, there are no standards for providers or for staff training, but rather a system of submitting detailed plans for recruiting and training providers, allowing for wide variability within the province (Kyle, 1991).

Although the limited family day care regulation evident in both the United States and Canada may be preferable for many parents and caregivers, it leads to some problems. From the parents' perspective, the quality of care is not regularly monitored and evaluated by an outside authority, leaving open the possibility of negligence and even abuse. From the providers' perspective, parents can take advantage of the informal relationship to pick up their children late, not pay on time, and not extend professional respect to providers (Hertz, 1986; Nelson, 1990).

Although there has been increasing movement toward professionalizing family day care providers, it faces significant resistance from both parents and providers. Professional status might enhance the pay and well-being of providers, but it would impose new requirements on them as well. Whether these would take the form of child development credentials or retrofitting homes to meet licensing regulations, such requirements are unwanted impositions to many family day care providers who are content with their informal operations. At the same time, structural or educational requirements would most likely impose greater costs on parents (Gormley, 1990). Furthermore, professionalizing providers would detract from the informal nature of their care and make their homes seem more like child care centers. It would undermine their claim to being "mother-like" (Nelson, 1990).

In order to avoid these changes, parents compromise their demands for quality in return for lower cost and greater intimacy with their providers, and providers compromise their desire for professional respect and higher income in return for nonintervention by government.

CONCLUSION

For centuries, human societies have been conflicted about how to care for children when mothers or other family members are unavailable for significant portions of the day. Parents' need to locate and compensate substitute mothers conflicts with their desire to retain the private nature of family life. In the contemporary period, this conflict has led to an inability to muster the social and governmental supports necessary to deal with growing child care needs spawned by the rapid increase in maternal employment over the past three decades. In the absence of such supports, families continue to turn to the solution they historically have been most able to construct—some form of what we now call family day care.

A historical survey of perspectives on family day care reveals the many ways parents have tried to re-create a mother-like situation for their children in extrafamilial care. It also illuminates the ways in which research and theory about the nature of children and what is necessary for their socioemotional and intellectual well-being have influenced over time relationships between parents and caregivers, the relative importance of caregiving and education, and the role of the state.

The contemporary debate about standards, licensing, regulation, and the professionalization of providers illustrates the tenacity of the historical tension between informal and formal child care and the uneasy position family day care has held somewhere between mother-care and center-care in the mother care/other care paradigm. It reflects the historical evolution of extrafamilial child care from a private arrangement between individual families and caregivers to a public relationship involving government funding and monitoring.

Although it may be some time before this tension is eased, our cumulative knowledge about the nurturing, education, and protection that children need should point us in the direction of creating healthy environments for their care, whether it takes place in the children's homes or somewhere else, by the children's parents or by someone else.

REFERENCES

Ainsworth, M. D. (1962). The effects of maternal deprivation: A review of findings and controversy in the context of research strategy. In *Deprivation of maternal care: A reassessment of its effects*. Geneva: World Health Organization.

Aries, P. (1962). *Centuries of childhood: A social history of family life*. New York: Knopf.

Auerbach, J. D. (1988). *In the business of child care: Employer initiatives and working women*. New York: Praeger.

Bland, H., & Wilkins, A. (1985). *Child care: Whose priority? A state child care fact book, 1985*. Washington, DC: Children's Defense Fund.

Bradburn, E. (1989). *Margaret McMillan: Portrait of a pioneer*. London: Routledge.

Cohen, B. (1988). *Caring for children: Services and policies for childcare and equal opportunities in the United Kingdom.* Report for the European Commission's Childcare Network. London: Family Policy Studies Centre.

Corbett, B. (1968). *The public school kindergarten in Ontario, 1883 to 1967.* Unpublished Ph.D. dissertation, University of Toronto.

Deasy, D. (1978). *Education under six.* London: Croom Helm.

deMause, L. (1974). *The history of childhood.* New York: Psychohistory Press.

Department of Health and Human Services (DHHS). (1980–81). *Final report of the National Day Care Home Study* (8 volumes, including executive summary). Washington, DC: U.S. Government Printing Office.

Dixon, S. (1988). *The Roman mother.* London: Croom Helm.

Emlen, A. C. (1972). *Family day care research: A summary and critical review.* Paper prepared for Family Day Care West: A Working Conference, Pacific Oaks College, Pasadena, CA.

Emlen, A. C. (1974). *Boundaries of the surrogate relationship in family day care: An analysis of the caregiver role.* Paper presented at the 51st annual meeting of the American Orthopsychiatric Association, San Francisco.

Emlen, A. C., Donoghue, B., & LaForge, R. (1971). *Child care by kith: A study of the family day care relationships of working mothers and neighborhood caregivers.* Corvallis, OR: DCE Books.

Frank, M., Zeibarth, M., & Field, C. (1982). *The life and times of Rosie the Riveter.* Emeryville, CA: Clarity Educational Productions.

Genovese, E. (1976). *Roll, Jordan, roll: The world the slaves made.* New York: Random House.

Hartmann, S. M. (1982). *The homefront and beyond: American women in the 1940s.* Boston: Twayne.

Hertz, R. (1986). *More equal than others: Women and men in dual career marriages.* Berkeley: University of California Press.

Jones, J. (1985). *Labor of love, labor of sorrow: Black women, work, and the family from slavery to the present.* New York: Basic Books.

Joshel, S. R. (1986). Nurturing the master's child: Slavery and the Roman childnurse. *Signs, 12* (1), 1–12.

Kahn, A. J., & Kamerman, S. B. (1987). *Child care: Facing the hard choices.* Boston: Auburn House.

Kessler-Harris, A. (1982). *Out of work: A history of wage-earning women in the United States.* New York: Oxford University Press.

Kurtz, J. (1976). *John Frederic Oberlin.* Boulder, CO: Westview Press.

Kyle, I. (1991). Personal communication, Toronto.

Luke, C. (1989). *Pedagogy, printing and Protestantism: The discourse on childhood.* Albany, NY: SUNY Press.

May, D., & Vinovskis, M. A. (1976). A ray of millennial light: Early education and social reform in the infant school movement in Massachusetts, 1826–1840. In Tamara Haraven (Ed.), *Family and kin in urban communities.* New York: Watts.

Mintz, S., & Kellog, S. (1988). *Domestic revolutions: A social history of American family life.* New York: Free Press.

National Manpower Council. (1957). *Womanpower.* New York: Columbia University Press.

Nelson, M. K. (1990). *Negotiated care: The experience of family day care providers.* Philadelphia: Temple University Press.

Nye, F. I., & Hoffman, L. W. (1963). *The employed mother in America.* Chicago: Rand McNally.

Osborn, D. K. (1980). *Early childhood education in historical perspective.* Athens, GA: Education Associates.

Owen, S. (1988). *The unobjectionable service: A legislative history of childminding.* Unpublished manuscript, National Childminding Association, Bromley in Kent, England.

Pence, A. R. (1986). Infant schools in North America, 1825–1840. In *Advances in early education and day care* (Vol. 4:1–25). Norwich, CT: JAI Press.

Postman, N. (1982). *The disappearance of childhood.* New York: Dell.

Prescott, E. (1972). *Group and family day care: A comparative assessment.* Paper prepared for Family Day Care West: A Working Conference, Pacific Oaks College, Pasadena, CA.

Ruderman, F. A. (1968). *Child care and working mothers: A study of arrangements made for daytime care of children.* New York: Child Welfare League of America.

Scarr, S. (1984). *Mother care/other care.* New York: Basic Books.

Schulz, P. (1978). Day care in Canada: 1850–1962. In K. G. Ross (Ed.), *Good day care.* Toronto: Women's Press.

Shapiro, M. (1983). *Child's garden: The kindergarten movement from Froebel to Dewey.* University Park, PA: Pennsylvania State University Press.

Shorter, E. (1975). *The making of the modern family.* New York: Basic Books.

Stapleford, E. M. (1976). *History of the day nurseries branch.* Toronto: Ministry of Community and Social Services.

Steinfels, M. (1973). *Who's minding the children: The history and politics of day care in America.* New York: Simon and Schuster.

Stone, L. (1979). *The family, sex and marriage in England, 1500–1800.* Harmonsworth, England: Penguin.

Strasser, S. (1982). *Never done: A history of American housework.* New York: Pantheon.

Tentler, L. W. (1979). *Wage-earning women: Industrial work and family life in the United States, 1900–1930.* New York: Oxford University Press.

Tizard, J., Moss, P., & Perry, J. (1976). *All our children: Preschool services in a changing society.* London: Temple Smith.

Travis, N., & Perreault, J. (1983). *A history of family day care.* Atlanta: Save the Children Foundation.

Whitbread, N. (1972). *The evolution of the nursery-infant school: A history of infant and nursery education in Britain, 1800–1970.* London: Routledge and Kegan Paul.

CHAPTER 3

The Changing Demographics of Family Day Care in the United States

Sandra L. Hofferth
Ellen Eliason Kisker

One of the most remarkable developments in the United States over the past several decades is the increased enrollment of children in out-of-home child care programs. This is a consequence of the increasing rate of maternal labor force participation as well as the increased demand by parents for early education and care programs for their young children, regardless of parental activities. For example, over the past two decades, the proportion of all U.S. children under age 18 with mothers in the labor force rose 59 percent, from 39 percent in 1970 to 62 percent in 1990. If this trend continues, by 1995 two-thirds of the nation's preschoolers and three-fourths of school-age children will have mothers who are in the labor force (Hofferth & Phillips, 1987). This dramatic increase in maternal employment has led to an increase in nonparental care for children while parents work (Hofferth, Brayfield, Deich & Holcomb, 1991). In addition, a larger proportion of those children are no longer in the care of relatives. The proportion of children of employed mothers cared for primarily by nonrelatives rose from 38 to 53 percent between 1965 and 1990 (Hofferth et al., 1991).

At the same time, there has been a rapid increase in center-based enroll-

Funding for this research was provided by the U.S. Department of Education through an Interagency Agreement with the Administration for Children, Youth and Families, U.S. Department of Health and Human Services, and by the National Association for the Education of Young Children. The opinions expressed in this chapter do not necessarily reflect the position and policy of the Department of Education, the U.S. Department of Health and Human Services, the National Association for the Education of Young Children, the Urban Institute, or Mathematica Policy Research, and no official endorsement should be inferred.

ments to enhance the development of young children regardless of whether their mothers are employed. Between 1970 and 1989, the proportion of three- to four-year-old children in nursery school[1] or kindergarten nearly doubled, from 21 percent to 39 percent (U.S. Bureau of the Census, 1991). Almost nine out of ten five-year-old children spend some time in such a preprimary program (U.S. Bureau of the Census, 1991).

WHAT IS FAMILY DAY CARE AND
WHY IS IT IMPORTANT?

Although the enrollment of children in all center-based programs now surpasses that in all family day care (Hofferth et al., 1991), family day care maintains an important position in the early education and care field, providing care in a home setting rather than an institutional setting. Family day care providers care for nonresident children from infancy through school age on a regular basis in their own homes. Although many caregivers may be caring for their own children as well as children related to them, they are generally not considered to be family day care providers unless they care for at least one nonrelated child.[2] Family day care programs may enroll children with different needs than do center-based programs, particularly younger children and school-age children. Family day care providers are generally located in the neighborhood where children live and maintain a homelike environment, which many parents prefer for younger children (Hofferth et al., 1991). In addition, family day care is important in the delivery of subsidized services to low-income children and their families (Kisker, Hofferth & Phillips, 1991; Glantz, Layzer & Battaglia, 1988).

However, unlike most center-based programs, which are required to be registered or licensed in all states, family day care consists of licensed or regulated programs, nonregulated programs that are not required to be licensed primarily because they are very small,[3] and nonregulated providers who are required to be licensed or regulated but are operating illegally, whether knowingly or unknowingly. It is generally agreed that the overwhelming majority of family day care homes are not regulated and, therefore, little is known about them on a systematic basis.

Recent legislation has increased the potential sources of federal subsidies for child care, including family day care. Important policy debates in the United States at the federal and state levels over the past several years led to the enactment in October 1990 of child care legislation (under P.L. 101-508). This legislation was designed to assist low- and moderate-income working families with their child care and other household expenses; to increase the supply and improve the quality of programs, including family day care programs; and to expand Head Start. Administrators of existing programs such as Chapter 1, Head Start, and Social Services Block Grant, State Grants for Dependent Care Planning and Development, the Family Support Act of 1988, and the newly enacted Child Care and Development Block Grant now face the important task of implementing and coordinating these new programs and policies.

The new legislation has increased the importance of understanding more about family day care at the national level, including both regulated and nonregulated care. Consequently, two national surveys, the Profile of Child Care Settings Study and the National Child Care Survey 1990, cooperated in obtaining a national picture of the supply of family day care in the United States in late 1989 and early 1990. The Profile of Child Care Settings Study obtained a nationally representative sample of regulated family day care providers from licensing lists, and the National Child Care Survey obtained a nationally representative sample of regulated and nonregulated family day care providers identified through household screening. This is the first time that survey information on regulated and nonregulated family day care providers has been available.

There are three major unanswered issues that this chapter addresses: (1) How many licensed and nonlicensed family day care homes are there in the United States, and how many children are enrolled? (2) How do characteristics of family day care differ from those of center-based programs? In what respects are they similar and in what respects are they different? (3) How do characteristics of regulated and nonregulated family day care differ from each other, particularly regarding key characteristics such as group size, child-staff ratio, and provider training?

THE DATA

The data for this study were collected from nationally representative samples of parents and family day care providers in telephone surveys conducted for the National Child Care Survey 1990 (NCCS) and the Profile of Child Care Settings (PCS) study. The designs of these two studies were coordinated, and they used the same survey instrument to collect information from family day care providers. The NCCS collected information from parents and from both regulated and nonregulated family day care providers. However, most of the family day care providers interviewed were not regulated, so the sample of regulated providers is very small. Therefore, the information for regulated providers included in this chapter was taken from the PCS study.

The following sections describe the sample design, interview completion rates and completed sample sizes, and sample weights for the NCCS and PCS study.

Sample Design

National Child Care Survey 1990. The sample design used for the NCCS was a three-stage clustered sample design. In the first stage, a random sample of 100 counties or groups of counties that are representative of counties in the United States was selected. Counties were stratified according to region, metropolitan status, and poverty level and were selected from each stratum with a probability proportional to the size of the population younger than age five. In the second stage, a random sample of 955 Mitofsky-Waksberg "primary units" (banks of 100 contiguous telephone numbers) was selected from all primary units in the 100 counties or groups of counties (Waksberg, 1978). Finally, in the third stage, a random sample of telephone numbers from the 955 Mitofsky-Waksberg primary units was selected.

All telephone numbers in the final sample were dialed and screened to determine whether the telephone was a residential telephone and, if so, whether the household contacted included any children younger than age 13 or any family day care providers. Households including family day care providers were identified as those households for which the respondent to the screening questions answered yes to the question:

> I am also interested in learning if there are any children who do not live in your household who may be cared for in your home. Are there any children who come to your home to be taken care of on a regular basis?

Regular basis was defined as coming to the home at least once a week for the last two weeks.

Profile of Child Care Settings. The sample design used for the PCS survey was a two-stage clustered sample design. The first-stage sample consisted of the same nationally representative sample of 100 counties or groups of counties selected for the NCCS. In the second stage, a stratified random sample of early education and care providers within the sample counties was drawn. The providers were sorted into strata according to type: Head Start, public school programs, all other centers, and regulated family day care providers. The current study makes use of the data for both center-based programs (the first three types) and regulated family day care providers.

Sample Sizes and Completion Rates

In the NCCS, computer-assisted telephone interviews were completed with 162 family day care providers. Approximately 47,500 households were contacted during the NCCS, and screenings were completed with 36,400 households (77 percent).

In these screening interviews 845 family day care providers were identified, leading to an eligibility rate of 2.2 percent. However, a large proportion
of the family day care providers identified in the screening interview denied
being child care providers when they were recontacted for the family day
care survey. One-fourth of the households could not be recontacted, and
three-fourths of the remaining households that originally reported being family day care providers (626) reported that they had never been child care
providers or that they were no longer child care providers. Survey staff at Abt
Associates, Inc., who conducted the surveys suggest that some of these
denials probably represent "soft" refusals but that in most cases the original
screening question was not fully understood with respondents primarily fail-
ing to focus on the words "regular basis" or the phrase "who do not live in
your household" in the screening question. Thus, interviews were completed
with 162 family day care providers, representing an eligibility rate of 0.3
percent.

Of the 162 family day care providers interviewed, 102 were regulated or
caring only for related children, usually grandchildren. The regulated providers were excluded from the analysis because more precise data are available from the PCS study. The providers caring only for related children were
also excluded from the analysis because the care they provide tends to be
extremely informal, and many of the survey questions do not apply to them.
Thus, the analysis presented in the following sections includes only the 60
nonregulated providers who were caring for at least one unrelated child.

Computer-assisted telephone interviews were completed with 583 regulated family day care providers in the PCS survey. Completion rates among
regulated family day care providers were high (87 percent). If providers who
were unlocatable are assumed to be ineligible for inclusion in the sample
frame because they were unlikely to be providing care in the sample
county—not an unlikely possibility given the intensive efforts made to locate
providers—then the response rate for regulated family day care providers
was 92 percent.

Sample Weights

The sample designs used for the NCCS and PCS study necessitated the
use of sample weights to correct for nonuniform sampling rates across strata.
The weighting methodology used for the NCCS took an approach similar to
that detailed by Massey and Botman (1988) and involved two steps. First, a
basic sample design weight was calculated; then it was adjusted for non-
response. The construction of sample weights for the NCCS is described in
more detail in Abt Associates, Inc. (1990).

Sample weights were also necessary for the PCS survey. In general,
weights for each observation were computed that equaled the inverse of the

sampling rate for the stratum from which the observation was drawn, with the stratum being defined by the type of provider and the county in which the provider was located. The construction of sample weights for the PCS survey is described in detail in Kisker et al. (1991).

Since both the NCCS and the PCS used the same first-stage sample of counties and county groups and were conducted at the same time, these two studies together represent the supply and demand for child care in the same nationally representative U.S. communities in early 1990.

THE MARKET FOR EARLY EDUCATION AND CARE

At the most basic level, the market for early childhood programs consists of the demand (quantity and characteristics of services that parents want at a given price) and the supply (quantity and characteristics of services that providers offer at a given price).

Demand for Early Childhood Programs

The National Child Care Survey 1990 is the first U.S. study in over a decade to obtain comprehensive information on the early education and care arrangements of children in two-parent families, single-parent families headed by a single mother or father, and families without a parent, therefore providing a comprehensive picture of the demand for child care and child care use patterns.[4] The employment status of the mother and age of the youngest child are critical factors influencing child care arrangements.

Families with an Employed Mother. Preschool children (defined as children zero to four years of age) with employed mothers are most likely to be cared for in nonparental arrangements. According to the NCCS, in 1990 27 percent were in center-based programs, 19 percent were in family day care, and 4 percent were in the care of a nonrelative in the child's home as their primary arrangement (Figure 3.1).[5] Nearly half (48 percent) of all preschool children whose mothers were employed were cared for either by the parents (30 percent) or by relatives (18 percent) as their primary arrangement. The remainder (2 percent) were cared for in other ways.

The NCCS data show that the majority of school-age children (5–12 years of age) with an employed mother are cared for only by their parents (38 percent) or are cared for by other relatives (17 percent) before and after school. In addition, 11 percent of school-age children with an employed mother are cared for in center-based programs, 7 percent are cared for in family day care, 19 percent participate in lessons and sports, 3 percent are

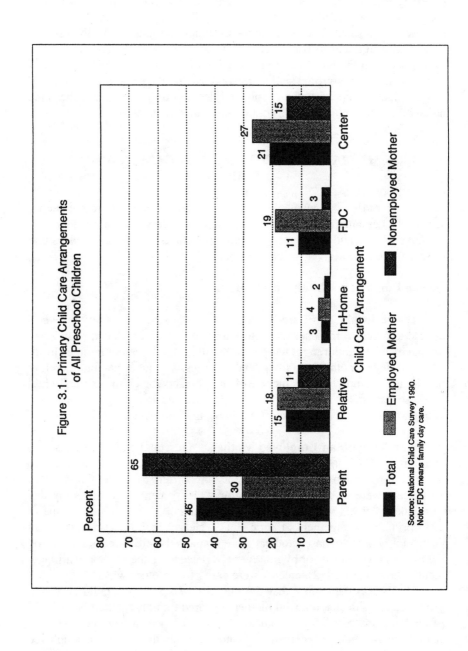

Figure 3.1. Primary Child Care Arrangements
of All Preschool Children

Percent

80
70
65
60
50 46
45
40
30 30
20 18
15
11
10 11
3 4 2
3
0

Parent   Relative   In-Home   FDC   Center

Child Care Arrangement

■ Total   ▨ Employed Mother   ■ Nonemployed Mother

19   27
11   21
15

Source: National Child Care Survey 1990.
Note: FDC means family day care.

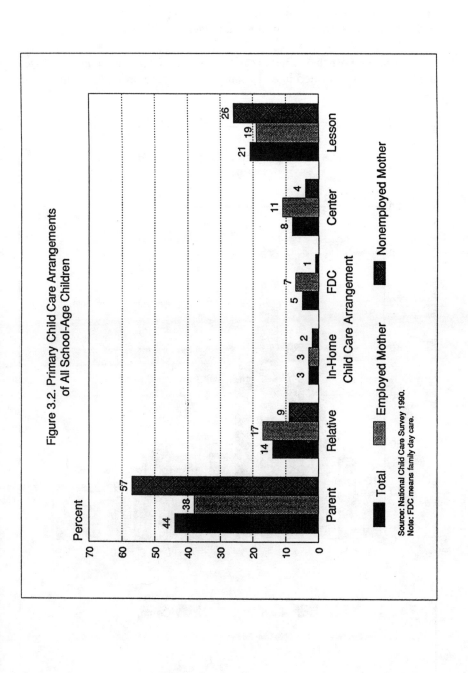

Figure 3.2. Primary Child Care Arrangements
of All School-Age Children

Percent

Parent
57
38
44

Relative
17
14
9

In-Home
3
3
2

FDC
7
5
1

Center
11
8
4

Lesson
21
19
26

Child Care Arrangement

■ Total   ▨ Employed Mother   ■ Nonemployed Mother

Source: National Child Care Survey 1990.
Note: FDC means family day care.

cared for by a nonrelative in their own homes, 3 percent care for themselves, and 2 percent are cared for in other arrangements (Figure 3.2).

Families with a Nonemployed Mother. Children of nonemployed mothers are also enrolled in early education and care programs, although in

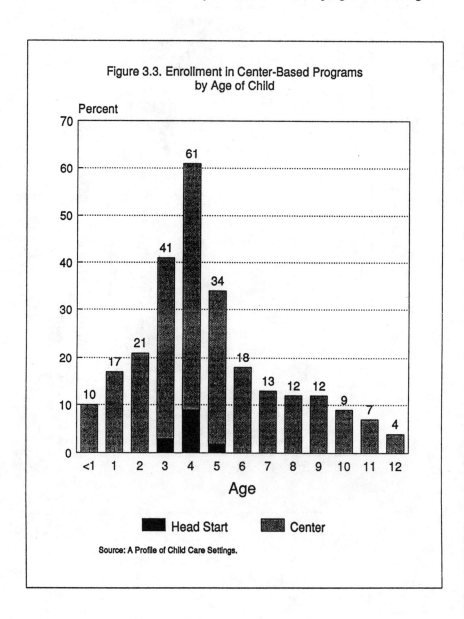

Figure 3.3. Enrollment in Center-Based Programs by Age of Child

Source: A Profile of Child Care Settings.

fewer numbers. For example, 15 percent of preschool children and 4 percent of school-age children whose mothers are not employed are enrolled in center-based programs as their primary arrangements; 3 percent of preschool and 1 percent of school-age children are enrolled in family day care (Figures 3.1 and 3.2).

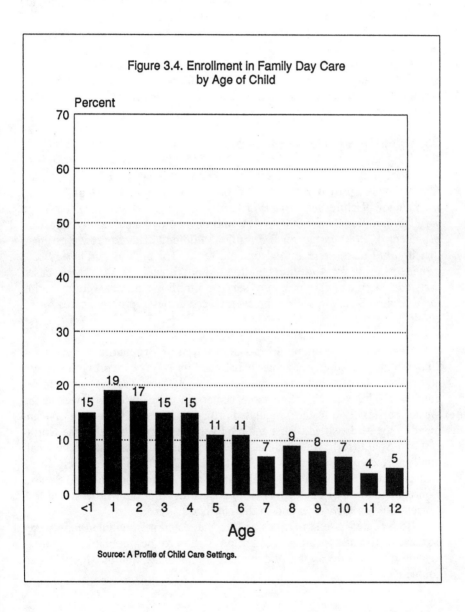

Figure 3.4. Enrollment in Family Day Care by Age of Child

Source: A Profile of Child Care Settings.

All Families. As a result of the extensive use of child care when mothers are employed and high enrollments in early education programs, a total of 14 million preschool children, more than one-quarter of all U.S. children under age 13, were cared for in either center-based programs or family day care during a typical week in 1990. Approximately 41 percent of three-year-olds, 61 percent of four-year-olds, and 34 percent of five-year-olds were enrolled in center-based programs (Figure 3.3). Only 15 percent of three-year-olds, 15 percent of four-year-olds, and 11 percent of five-year-olds were cared for in family day care settings (Figure 3.4). Ten percent of infants under age one were enrolled in center-based programs, and 15 percent were enrolled in family day care. There are no differences among toddlers aged one and two in centers versus family day care with approximately 19 percent cared for in each.

Supply of Early Childhood Programs

According to the PCS study, in 1990 approximately 118,000 regulated family day care providers serving 700,000 children were operating. Based on the number of children enrolled in family day care, we estimate that there were an additional 550,000 to 1.1 million nonregulated family day care providers in 1990 caring for 3.3 million children.[6] Therefore, we estimate that in 1990 there were a total of 668,000 to 1.2 million family day care providers caring for 4 million children. Approximately 80,000 center-based early education and care programs serving 5 million children were operating in the United States in 1990. The average center-based program cares for 62 children.

Regional and Metropolitan Distribution of Programs. Across the United States the supply of center-based and family day care programs generally mirrors the distribution of children (Table 3.1). However, relative to the number of children, there are more centers in the South and fewer in the West.[7] For family day care, regulated providers are relatively more concentrated in the Midwest and West and relatively less concentrated in the Northeast and South (reflecting regional differences in regulatory coverage; small family day care providers in the West and Midwest are more likely to be subject to regulations than are smaller providers in the Northeast and South). Nonregulated family day care is more concentrated in the Midwest and less concentrated in the South and in the Northeast.

Both center-based programs and regulated and nonregulated family day care are distributed in urban areas in proportion to the population. Approximately three-fourths are located in metropolitan areas, and one-fourth are in nonmetropolitan areas.

Sponsorship. Although most family day care providers operate independently, approximately 23 percent of regulated providers and 2 percent of nonregulated providers are sponsored by a group that organizes family day care in its community. The greater prevalence of sponsorship among regulated providers probably reflects participation in the Child and Adult Care Food Program, which requires that providers be both sponsored and regulated. Among centers, 40 percent are nonprofits sponsored by another organization, 25 percent are nonprofits independent of a sponsoring organization, 29 percent are independent centers run for profit, and 6 percent are run by for-profit chains.

PROGRAM CHARACTERISTICS

Parents look for availability, cost, and quality when they seek a child care arrangement. According to the NCCS, approximately 60 percent of parents who used centers or family day care said that some aspect of care quality was most important in their choice of the current arrangement. Availability, location, or hours were mentioned by 22 percent of those using family day care and 29 percent of those using centers; less than 10 percent (6 percent of center users and 8 percent of family day care users) mentioned cost as the most important consideration.

Availability is affected by admissions policies and services offered as well as by the number of openings: Do programs accept infants and toddlers? Are they open full or part days? Do they accept children with disabilities? Do they care for sick children? Cost is reflected not only in fees but also whether the programs accept children from low-income families: What do they charge? Do they enroll publicly subsidized children? How much are staff paid? Finally, the group size, ratio of children to staff, and training of the providers serve as indicators of quality: Do these key characteristics suggest that the services provided are of high quality? In the following sections we examine the key similarities and differences between center-based and family day care programs, and between regulated and nonregulated family day care.

Availability of Care

Both centers and family day care providers recruit children primarily by word of mouth, and this is consistent with parents' reports. Centers are more likely to advertise in the media than regulated family day care homes (58 percent versus 31 percent); however, both are more likely to advertise than nonregulated family day care providers (13 percent). Although 95 percent of regulated family providers take at least some steps to recruit children, only

Table 3.1. Distribution of Children, Programs, and Fees by Region and Urbanicity

	Percent Distribution of Children and Programs				Average Hourly Fees		
	Children <5	Center-Based Programs	Regulated FDC	Nonregulated FDC	Centers[a]	Regulated FDC	Nonregulated FDC[a]
U.S.	100%	100%	100%	100%	$1.59	$1.61	$1.48
Region							
Northeast	19	18	14	16	2.18	1.96	1.83
South	35	41	21	30	1.29	1.29	0.89
Midwest	24	23	29	30	1.63	1.42	1.83
West	23	18	36	23	1.71	1.83	1.32
Urbanicity							
Urban	75	76	77	72	1.78	1.71	1.74
Suburban					1.55	1.65	1.66
Rural	25	24	23	28	1.31	1.37	1.07

Sources: Profile of Child Care Settings Study; National Child Care Survey 1990.

Note: FDC means family day care.

[a]Excludes programs that do not charge for care.

Table 3.2. Profiles of Early Education and Care Settings, 1990

Program Characteristic	All Center-Based Programs	Regulated Family Day Care	Nonregulated Family Day Care
Average total enrollment	62	6	2
Average percentage of children enrolled age 3 to 5	62	39	40
Average percentage of children enrolled from families receiving public assistance	17	5	13
Percentage of income from public agencies	22	na	na
Percentage of programs that charge parental fees	85	99	77
Average hourly fees (for programs that charge fees)	$1.59	$1.61	$1.48
Average hourly wages of teachers	$7.49	$4.04	$1.25
Average group size	16	7/5[a]	4/2[a]
Average child-staff ratio	8.6	5.9/3.7[a]	3.7/2.8[a]
Average percentage of teachers with a college degree	47	11	15
Average percentage of teachers with training in child development	93	64	34

Source: Profile of Child Care Settings Study; National Child Care Survey 1990
[a]See note 9.
Note: na means not available.

43 percent of nonregulated providers take any action to recruit children. Given the lower level of effort in recruiting children, it is not surprising that it takes longer for a family day care home to fill a vacancy than it does a center (23–25 days, compared with 8 days), though there is no difference between regulated and nonregulated family day care. In addition, there is a higher proportion of spaces occupied in center-based programs than in family day care, and regulated providers have a higher proportion of spaces filled than nonregulated providers.

Programs for Infants and Toddlers.   Probably one of the most important considerations in parents' choice of program is the age of the child. Family day care homes are more likely than center-based programs to accept infants and toddlers (defined as ages zero to two)—96 percent of regulated and 85 percent of nonregulated family day care providers accept such children, compared with 55 percent of center-based programs (Figure 3.5). As a consequence, a larger proportion of children in family day care than in center-based care are under three years of age and a smaller proportion are ages three to five (Table 3.2).

Full-Time versus Part-Time Programs.   In 1990, three-quarters of the demand for center-based programs and family day care was due to maternal employment, and two out of three mothers were employed full time (35 or more hours a week). Thus, according to parents' reports, half of the youngest children cared for in center-based programs and two-thirds of the youngest children in family day care are in that care full time. Overall, children spend an average of 27 hours a week in center-based programs and 30 hours a week in family day care. The amount of time spent depends on the age of the child and employment status of the mother. The youngest pre-school-age child of an employed mother spends more time (38 hours), and the youngest child of a nonemployed mother spends less time (12–14 hours) in center-based programs or family day care. The youngest school-age child spends 17 to 19 hours in a center-based program or in family day care if the mother is employed and 9 to 10 hours if she is not.

Almost all regulated family day care providers and about two-thirds of center-based programs provide full-time care (Figure 3.5). A smaller proportion of nonregulated family day care providers (65 percent) than regulated providers (94 percent) provide full-time care. Although there seems to be a good match between daily operating schedules of providers and the needs of employed parents, few programs provide care during nonstandard hours, when two out of eight mothers and two out of seven fathers work one weekend day or a nonday shift. Weekend care is more likely to be obtained in a center-based program (10 percent) than in family day care (6 percent), and evening care is more likely to be obtained in regulated and nonregulated family day care homes (13 and 20 percent, respectively) than in center-based programs (3 percent).

Programs for Children with Disabilities. Family day care homes are much less likely than center-based programs to care for children with dis-

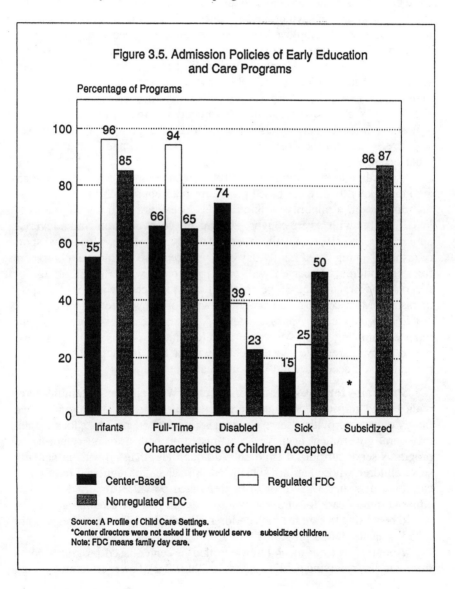

Figure 3.5. Admission Policies of Early Education and Care Programs

Source: A Profile of Child Care Settings.
*Center directors were not asked if they would serve subsidized children.
Note: FDC means family day care.

abilities. Approximately three-fourths of center-based programs (74 percent), compared with 39 percent of regulated and 23 percent of nonregulated family day care providers, reported that they care for or would accept children with diagnosed handicaps (Figure 3.5).

Care for Sick Children.   Employed parents often miss work when a child becomes sick because their regular child care providers will not care for children who exhibit symptoms of illness. According to NCCS data, 35 percent of mothers employed outside the home reported that one of their children was sick on a workday in the past month (this section focuses only on mothers instead of parents). Over half (51 percent) of those mothers stayed home to care for the sick child. Of those who did go to work when their children were sick, 21 percent reported that their partners stayed home with the sick child, over a third (36 percent) left the child with relatives, almost a quarter (23 percent) used their regular arrangements, 6 percent used self-care, 4 percent took the child with them to work, and 10 percent used other arrangements.

According to the providers' reports, regulated family day care providers are more likely than center-based programs to accept sick children, but those that do are still a minority. Approximately one-fourth will allow parents to leave children with severe coughs, 20 percent accept children with a feverish appearance, and 10 percent allow parents to leave children with unusual spots or rashes. Nonregulated family day care providers are the most likely to care for sick children; 50 percent will care for a child with a severe cough or feverish appearance, and 36 percent will care for a child with unusual spots or rashes. Most center-based programs will not allow parents to leave sick children in their care. Approximately 15 percent of center-based programs reported allowing parents to leave a child with a severe cough, 6 percent would allow parents to leave a child with a feverish appearance, and 3 percent would accept a child with unusual spots or rashes.

Programs for Low-Income Children.   What choices do families have if they need subsidies? A higher proportion of center-based programs than family day care providers serve children whose fees are paid by a local, state, or federal government agency. An estimated 40 percent of all center-based programs serve subsidized children. Although less than 20 percent actually serve children whose fees are subsidized, 86 percent of regulated family day care providers and 87 percent of nonregulated providers reported that they either currently care for children whose fees are paid by a public agency or would be willing to care for such children (Figure 3.5). This question was not asked of center-based programs.

About 17 percent of children enrolled in center-based programs come from families receiving public assistance (Table 3.2). Fewer children enrolled in family day care were from such families. Thirteen percent of children in nonregulated family day care and 5 percent of children in regulated family day care come from families receiving public assistance.

Finally, although regulated family day care providers are less likely than centers to serve subsidized children, they are more likely to serve low-income children through participation in the Child and Adult Care Food Program. About three-quarters of regulated family day care providers participate in the Child and Adult Care Food Program, compared with only one-third of center-based programs. Very few nonregulated family day care homes participate in the Child and Adult Care Food Program, primarily because eligibility criteria for the program require that family day care providers be licensed or registered where that is available.

Cost of Care

Parental fees are the major source of income for family day care and center-based providers. Ninety-nine percent of regulated family day care providers charge fees, 85 percent of center-based programs charge for care, and 77 percent of nonregulated family day care providers charge for care. Families' reports are consistent, with 91 percent of families using family day care and 82 percent of families using center-based care for their youngest children reporting that they pay for it. As a consequence, parental fees account for about three-fourths of the income of center-based providers and nearly all the income of family day care providers; the remainder of child care income comes from public agencies and other sources (Table 3.2).

Although fee structures are rather complicated in many programs, center-based programs and regulated family day care providers charge similar fees, as reported by the programs themselves. The average fee reported by directors of center-based programs that charged fees in 1990 was $1.59 an hour (Table 3.1). The average hourly fee reported by regulated family day care providers was $1.61 an hour. Fees charged by nonregulated family day care providers that charge fees are lower, averaging $1.48 an hour in 1990. There was a substantial amount of variation in the fees charged by region—a good proxy for differences in the cost of living. For example, fees were relatively higher in the Northeast and West than in the South and Midwest. They were also higher in urban and suburban areas than in rural areas (Table 3.1).

Parents' reports of their actual expenditures for center-based programs and on family day care are comparable with provider reports.[8] A family with an employed mother and a preschool child spent about $1.67 an hour for care in a child care center and $1.57 an hour for care in a family day care home (including regulated and nonregulated homes).

Wages and Income of Caregivers. Parental fees are the major source of income, and wages and salaries of providers are the major expense. Annual revenues from child care taken in by regulated home-based providers averaged $10,000, and half took in less than $8,000 a year. This translates into average hourly revenues of $4.04 an hour (Table 3.2). Nonregulated providers took in $1,961 a year on average, or about $1.25 an hour. Since they are self-employed, family day care providers receive no benefits.

Center-based programs spend an average of 62 percent of their total budgets on salaries and benefits for all staff. In 1990, the average annual salary for a preschool teacher in center-based programs was approximately $11,500, and half of preschool teachers earned less than $11,000 a year. The average hourly wage earned by preschool teachers in 1990 was $7.49 (Table 3.2). Three-quarters of preschool teachers received paid sick leave, paid vacation, and education stipends. As do fees, wages and salaries vary with the cost of living across regions (not shown).

Key Characteristics of Care

The experiences of children in early education and care settings may affect their success in school and later in life (Berrueta-Clement, Schwein-hart, Barnett, Epstein & Weikart, 1984). Three characteristics of family day care settings that research has shown to be associated with positive outcomes for children can be measured in a survey: group size, child-staff ratio, and the education or training of the caregiver (Travers et al., 1980). How do these key characteristics of day care centers and family day care homes compare to state regulations and professional standards? How do these key charac-teristics of center-based programs and family day care compare with each other? How do these key characteristics of regulated and nonregulated family day care programs compare?

Group Size. As expected, group sizes are considerably smaller in family day care homes than in center-based programs, and smaller in non-regulated than in regulated family day care. The average group size in family day care is about three to four children, compared with a group size of 16 children in center-based care. The average group size is small for both regulated and nonregulated family day care providers, with ranges from four to seven children in regulated family day care and two to four children in nonregulated family day care.[9]

Child-Staff Ratios. Consistent with differences in group sizes, child-staff ratios are higher for center-based programs than for family day care homes. Child-staff ratios average from three to one to six to one in family day care and about nine to one in center-based programs (Table 3.2). Regulated family day care providers average four to six children per caregiver, and nonregulated providers average three to four children per caregiver.

Education and Training of Providers. Although family day care homes fare favorably in comparison to center-based programs on measures of group size and child-staff ratio, they compare less favorably both on formal education and on training specifically related to young children, such as in early childhood education or child development. About half (54 to 55 percent) of regulated and nonregulated family day care providers have some education after high school, compared with 86 percent of teachers in centers. Approximately 11 percent of regulated and 15 percent of nonregulated providers have completed college or have a graduate degree. In contrast, approximately half of center-based teachers have a college or graduate degree.

In the PCS study, 93 percent of center teachers were reported to have had some "special child care or early childhood education training," compared with 46 percent of family day care providers. Regulated family day care providers are much more likely to have had such training (64 percent compared with 34 percent). The specific amount and length of training were not asked.

Goals of the Program. Center-based programs and family day care do not differ in their stated goals. All center-based programs and family day care providers reported that providing a warm and loving environment was one of their goals, and 56 percent of centers and 76–78 percent of family day care providers reported that to be their major goal. The majority of providers agreed that promoting children's development was one of their goals. However, a higher proportion of centers (33 percent) than family day care providers (9 to 13 percent) reported child development and school preparation as their *primary* goal. Only a very small proportion of all providers (under 5 percent of centers and regulated providers, 13 percent of nonregulated providers) reported providing care while parents work as their major goal. There were no significant differences in the main goals of regulated and nonregulated providers.

TRENDS IN SUPPLY AND DEMAND

Number of Programs and Enrollments

Based on comparisons of the PCS findings with those of earlier studies, the number of early education and care programs has increased substantially since the mid- to late 1970s. However, this is due primarily to the increase in supply of center-based programs. In regulated family day care, the estimated number of providers did not increase between 1976 and 1990; however, enrollment increased by 53 percent over the period.[10] Consistent with the fact that total enrollment increased more than the number of providers, the average number of nonresident children cared for in regulated home-based programs increased 50 percent, from four to six children. The percentage of regulated family day care providers with helpers also appears to have increased over the period, which helped to offset the increase in the number of children.

There were three times as many center-based programs in early 1990 as there were in the mid-1970s, and four times as many children were enrolled in such programs.[11] As a result, the average number of children per program increased 39 percent, reflecting the greater proportional increase in enrollment rather than in the number of programs. In spite of these increases in enrollments in center-based programs, the average number of staff increased by only 25 percent over the period—not enough to offset the increase in enrollments.

Trends based on parental reports are consistent with the reports of providers.[12] The use of family day care, determined as a percentage of children of employed mothers receiving such care, has remained constant over the period; however, the number of children in family day care has risen because of the rise in the number of employed mothers. Use of center-based programs for preschool-age children with employed mothers has increased consistently over the past 25 years, both because of the increased number of employed mothers and because the proportion using such programs has increased more than fourfold, from 6 percent in 1965 to 28 percent in 1990 (Figure 3.6). Accompanying the increase in the proportion enrolled in center-based programs has been a decline in the proportion cared for by in-home providers and relatives. Parental care as a primary arrangement for employed mothers appears to have grown somewhat over the past 15 years, reflecting increased time spent by both fathers and mothers in caring for their preschool-age children.

The characteristics of children enrolled in family day care and early education and care programs have not changed. There has been a shift toward caring for younger children in center-based settings, but infants and toddlers still constitute a small proportion of the total enrollment in these settings.

Cost of Programs

Average hourly fees reported by family day care providers have risen only slightly. When adjusted for inflation, average hourly fees rose by about 7 percent among regulated family day care providers and by about 11 percent among nonregulated family day care providers. Adjusted for inflation, fees reported by center-based programs have changed relatively little since 1976–77 (earlier measurements were not precise enough to determine the specific percentage of change).

Similarly, there have been only small increases in average hourly expenditures on center-based programs and family day care for the youngest preschool-age children as reported by parents. Adjusted for inflation, average hourly expenditures on family day care rose 5 percent between 1975 and 1990, and average hourly expenditures on center-based care rose 19 percent over the same period (Figure 3.7).

In contrast, other forms of care have become more expensive. After adjusting for inflation, hourly expenditures for in-home providers increased sharply from 1975 to 1990, rising by 180 percent over the period. Cost of care by a relative rose by 7 percent over the period, among those who are paid.

Trends in Wages and Income of Caregivers

The data suggest a substantial decline in the real wages of caregiving staff in center-based and home-based programs over the past 15 years, despite their increased levels of education and training. Adjusted for inflation, the average salary of center-based program teaching staff appears to have declined by almost one-quarter between the mid-1970s and 1990.

The total household incomes of family day care providers rose 30 percent in real terms since the mid-1970s. However, since regulated family day care providers charge only sightly more than they did 15 years ago and their average income from child care has remained virtually unchanged, their income from child care has declined as a percentage of total household income (from about 44 to 35 percent). Nonregulated family day care providers make 17 percent less in 1990 than they did in 1976–80, and only about one-fourth of their income comes from child care.

Key Characteristics of Programs

Trends suggest that the quality of care in both center-based and home-based settings has improved, as measured by the increased education and training of providers. The average levels of education and training received by both regulated home-based providers and center-based staff have increased substantially over the past 15 years. For example, the average schooling of family day care providers rose from only a high school education in 1976 to one year of college in 1990. Not only has the education of providers increased, but it has exceeded general increases in the level of

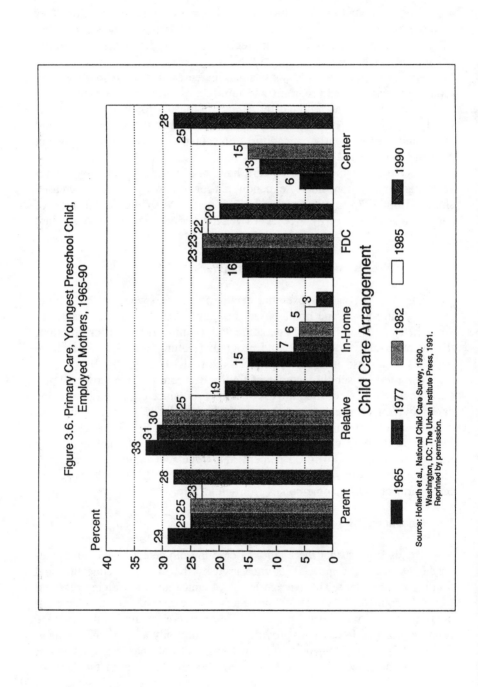

Figure 3.6. Primary Care, Youngest Preschool Child,
Employed Mothers, 1965-90

Percent

Child Care Arrangement

Parent   Relative   In-Home   FDC   Center

1965   1977   1982   1985   1990

Source: Hofferth et al., National Child Care Survey, 1990.
Washington, DC: The Urban Institute Press, 1991.
Reprinted by permission.

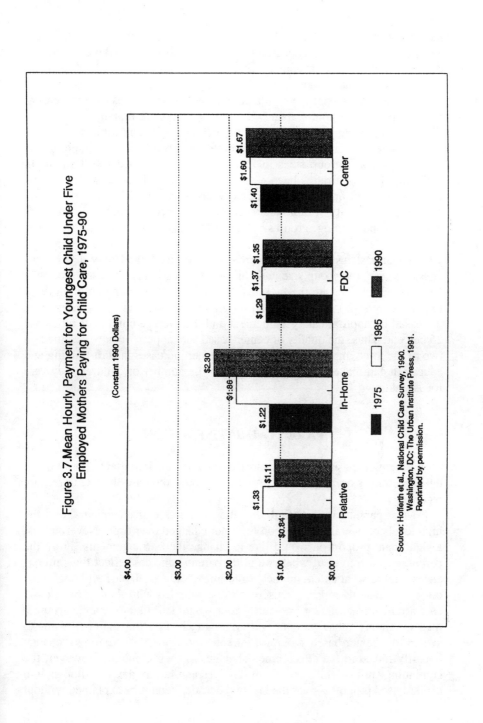

Figure 3.7. Mean Hourly Payment for Youngest Child Under Five Employed Mothers Paying for Child Care, 1975-90

(Constant 1990 Dollars)

Relative: $0.84, $1.33, $1.11
In-Home: $1.22, $1.86, $2.30
FDC: $1.29, $1.37, $1.35
Center: $1.40, $1.60, $1.67

1975   1985   1990

Source: Hofferth et al., National Child Care Survey, 1990.
Washington, DC: The Urban Institute Press, 1991.
Reprinted by permission.

education among all women. Even though all providers today, as they were 15 years ago, are better educated than the population as a whole, providers differ in their education and training. Center staff are considerably better trained and educated than family day care providers.

Average group sizes in regulated family day care homes have increased, but group sizes in nonregulated family day care have remained the same. Since nonregulated homes make up the bulk of family day care, this implies little change in average group size overall. However, it is also important to note that average group sizes in family day care homes are still small. In addition, child-staff ratios have not increased, primarily because the proportion of regulated providers with helpers has increased. Therefore, we conclude that the quality of family day care, as measured by these three indictors (education and training, group size, and child-staff ratio) has improved overall.

In contrast, as a result of increased enrollments and only a small increase in staff, the group size and child-staff ratios in center-based programs have increased. Despite the fact that the enrollment of young children (who require more staff) in center-based programs increased, average group sizes increased by approximately 16 percent and the average child-staff ratio rose 25 percent. Thus, the quality of center-based care appears to have declined on two of the three important indicators. Whether increases in staff training and education can make up for the increase in the number of children they care for is unknown.

PARENTAL SATISFACTION

Although these three measures of quality are important, they do not tell the entire story. How do parents feel about the care their children are receiving?

Most parents are satisfied with their child care arrangements, and the high levels of overall satisfaction have not changed over time. Nevertheless, a significant proportion would like to change their arrangements. From the parents' perspective, to what extent do parents' choices reflect their preferences, and to what extent do they represent what is available? Although nine out of ten parents report themselves to be satisfied with their current child care arrangements, about one out of four would still like to change arrangements. Among those parents who want to change, the majority want to switch to a center-based program. Parents' motivation for desiring a change is partly linked to the developmental stages of their children. However, the continuing shift of child care from relatives and family day care homes into center-based programs over the last two decades cannot be explained without positing increased parental preferences for center-based care over other types.

SUMMARY AND CONCLUSIONS

At the beginning of 1990 an estimated 668,000 to 1.2 million family day care providers were operating in the United States. Of these, approximately 550,000 to 1.1 million (82 to 90 percent) were not regulated and 118,000 (10 to 18 percent) were regulated family day care providers. These family day care providers were caring for some 4 million children.

How are centers and family day care homes similar and how are they different? Many of the services centers and family day care homes provide are similar and they charge similar fees. They differ somewhat in the ages of children they serve. Centers tend to serve children three to five years of age; family day care homes care for younger and older children. The demand for and supply of center care have increased dramatically both in absolute numbers and as a proportion of enrollment; family day care has declined in its share of the market, but enrollments have stayed stable due to the larger number of children with employed mothers.

Nonregulated family day care homes differ from regulated family day care homes in expected and predictable ways. They are smaller, they are more available (but harder to locate), they charge lower fees, they make less money at it, they care for children for fewer hours per week, and they are more likely to care for sick children and to provide evening care. Nonregulated providers are less likely to consider themselves professional providers. For example, they are more likely to say that they provide care as a favor for relatives or friends than are regulated providers. In other respects they are very much like regulated family day care providers.

This may surprise many readers, as nonregulated family day care is often assumed to be inferior at best and dangerous at worst. However, as we have pointed out, most family day care providers are not operating illegally. In almost half the states small family day care homes are not even required to be licensed or to register. We found that the majority of nonregulated providers are small, confirming our expectations. However, we caution the reader that, although the results appear consistent with what is expected and with the results of other recent work (Nelson, 1990), the characteristics of providers who failed to identify themselves may differ from those that did (e.g., they may have more children), and the results may be biased. Unfortunately, it is not possible to identify this bias.

It is ironic that family day care has been improving in measurable ways but its share of the child care market has been declining and enrollments have remained stable. Regulated providers' earnings are low, and nonregulated family day care providers make even less. We suspect that the supply of family day care will depend on the availability of more lucrative alternatives in the paid work force. For many mothers, family day care is a temporary way to earn additional income while caring for their own young children. It may be only a temporary solution for parents as well (see Nelson, 1990, for a discussion of the complex reciprocal relationship between caregiver and parent). Given the overwhelming preference for center-based programs among those who want to change their child care arrangements, nonregulated family day care does not seem likely to be a widespread, long-term source of care, though regulated care may be. This implies that the groups of children in which it currently specializes—infants, toddlers, and school-age children—may be a source of increased growth for center-based programs, as they apparently have been in recent years.

NOTES

1. A nursery school is defined as a group or class that is organized to provide educational experiences for children during the year or years preceding kindergarten and includes instruction as an important and integral phase of its program of child care. Day care center care may or may not be included, depending on whether the respondent considers it "educational." Head Start is included under nursery or kindergarten as appropriate.

2. In the United States, child care regulations do not apply to providers caring only for related children. However, recent changes in legislation that permit subsidies for relatives may require some of these relatives to register or become licensed.

3. Twenty-one states exempt family day care providers caring for three or fewer children from regulation or registration.

4. There are too few single-father and no-parent families for separate analysis; they are, however, included in the totals.

5. Since children may be in multiple programs, and since some experiences may consist of relatively brief periods with a provider, if a child was cared for by someone other than the responding parent, we asked which arrangement was primary, that is, which one took care of the child for the most time during a week. Otherwise parental care was coded as primary, so that every child has at least one arrangement. This provides an exhaustive and mutually exclusive count of children's primary arrangements.

6. See Hofferth and Kisker (1991) for a description of how the number of nonregulated family day care homes was estimated. The range of estimates is based on alternative assumptions about the average number of children cared for by a provider.

7. We also examined the distribution of spaces relative to the distribution of

children. The distributions are similar to the distributions of programs for centers and regulated family day care, so the conclusions are identical. The distributions differ somewhat for nonregulated family day care; however, these differences may be due to sampling error in this small sample.

8. These are actual out-of-pocket expenditures. Reimbursements that may occur later, such as income tax payments reduced by the child and dependent care credit or the dependent care assistance plan, or income disregarded in Aid for Families with Dependent Children (AFDC), are not taken into account.

9. The higher estimate is the actual number of children cared for together, including the provider's children, and represents a maximum group size. The lower estimate adjusts for the number of hours the children are in care, representing an average defined by the sum of the hours in care across children divided by the number of hours the provider cares for children.

10. To make comparisons of family day care over time, a subsample of the PCS study was selected that was as comparable as possible to the 1976–80 National Day Care Home Survey (Fosburg, Singer, Goodson, Warner, Irwin, Brush & Grasso, 1981). As in the earlier study, family day care homes that enrolled at least one child between 12 and 60 months of age for pay and for at least 20 hours a week were selected from metropolitan areas.

11. To make these comparisons for center-based programs, a subsample of the PCS data was selected and compared with results from the 1976–77 National Day Care Survey (Coelen, Glantz & Calore, 1979). As was the earlier study, this subsample was restricted to programs operating at least 25 hours a week for 9 months a year, with a licensed capacity of 13 or more children and enrollments including 50 percent or less handicapped children. Since these trends were computed based on a subset of programs, the absolute values may differ slightly from the values based on all programs.

12. To examine trends over time based on parental reports, data from the NCCS were compared with data from earlier nationally representative U.S. surveys conducted by the U.S. Bureau of the Census and other organizations. The specific sources are cited in the appropriate figures.

REFERENCES

Abt Associates (1990). *Final report on survey methods: National Child Care Survey 1990, main study and low-income substudy.* Cambridge, MA: Abt Associates.

Berrueta-Clement, J. R., Schweinhart, L., Barnett, W., Epstein, A., & Weikart, D. (1984). *Changed Lives: The effects of the Perry Preschool Program on Youths through age 19.* Ypsilanti, MI: High Scope Press.

Coelen, C., Glantz, F., & Calore, D. (1979). *Day care centers in the U.S.: A national profile 1976–1977.* Cambridge, MA: Abt Associates.

Fosburg, S., Singer, J., Goodson, B., Warner, D., Irwin, N., Brush, L., & Grasso, J. (1981). *Family day care in the United States: Summary of findings.* Washington, DC: U.S. Department of Health and Human Services.

Glantz, F. B., Layzer, J. A., & Battaglia, M. (1988). *Study of the Child Care Food Program*. Cambridge, MA: Abt Associates.

Goelman, H., & Pence, A. (1987). Effects of child care, family and individual characteristics on children's language development: The Victoria Day Care Research Project. In D. A. Phillips (Ed.), *Quality in child care: What does research tell us?* (pp. 89–104). Washington, DC: National Association for the Education of Young Children.

Hofferth, S. (1988). Child care in the United States. In *American families in tomorrow's economy* (pp. 168–87). Proceedings of hearing before the Select Committee on Children, Youth, and Families, 1 July 1987.

Hofferth, S., Brayfield, A., Deich, S., & Holcomb, P. (1991). *National Child Care Survey 1990*. Washington, DC: Urban Institute.

Hofferth, S., & Kisker, E. (1991). *Family day care in the U.S., 1990*. Washington, DC: Urban Institute.

Hofferth, S., & Phillips, D. (1987). Child care in the United States, 1970 to 1995. *Journal of Marriage and the Family, 49,* 559–71.

Kisker, E., Hofferth, S., & Phillips, D. (1991). *A profile of child care settings: Early education and care in 1990*. Princeton, NJ: Mathematica Policy Research.

Low, S., & Spindler, P. (1968). *Child care arrangements of working mothers in the United States*. Washington, DC: U.S. Department of Health, Education and Welfare, Children's Bureau; and U.S. Department of Labor, Women's Bureau.

Massey, J., & Botman, S. (1988). Weighting adjustments for random digit dialed surveys. In R. Groves et al. (Eds.), *Telephone survey methodology* (pp. 143–160). New York: John Wiley and Sons.

Nelson, M. (1990). *Negotiated care: The experience of family day care providers*. Philadelphia: Temple University Press.

Travers, J., Goodson, B., Singer, J., & Connell, D. (1980). *Final report of the National Day Care Study: Research results of the National Day Care Study*. Cambridge, MA: Abt Associates.

Unco. (1975). *National child care consumer study*. Washington, DC: Unco.

U.S. Bureau of the Census. (1982). Trends in child care arrangements of working mothers. *Current Population Reports,* Series P-117, No. 23. Washington, DC: U.S. Government Printing Office.

U.S. Bureau of the Census. (1983). Child care arrangements of working mothers: June 1982. *Current Population Reports,* Series P-23, No. 129. Washington, DC: U.S. Government Printing Office.

U.S. Bureau of the Census. (1987). Who's minding the kids? Child care arrangements: Winter 1984–85. *Current Population Reports,* Series P-20, No. 9. Washington, DC: U.S. Government Printing Office.

U.S. Bureau of the Census. (1988). School enrollment—Social and economic characteristics of students: October 1985 and 1984. *Current Population Reports,* Series P-20, No. 426. Washington, DC: U.S. Government Printing Office.

U.S. Bureau of the Census. (1990). Who's minding the kids? Child care arrangements 1986–87. *Current Population Reports,* Series P-20, No. 20. Washington, DC: U.S. Government Printing Office.

U.S. Bureau of the Census. (1991). School enrollment—Social and economic characteristics of students: October 1989. *Current Population Reports,* Series P-20, No. 452. Washington, DC: U.S. Government Printing Office.

U.S. Department of Labor. (1990). *Marital and family characteristics of the labor force from the March 1990 Current Population Survey.* Washington, DC: U.S. Bureau of Labor Statistics.

Waksberg, J. (1978). Sampling methods for random digit dialing. *Journal of the American Statistical Association, 73*(361), 40–46.

CHAPTER 4

Family Day Care in a Socioecological Context

DATA FROM THE CANADIAN NATIONAL CHILD CARE STUDY

Alan R. Pence
Hillel Goelman
Donna S. Lero
Lois Brockman

In Canada, as in the United States, the decades of the 1970s and 1980s have seen a dramatic increase in the need for and utilization of nonmaternal child care. In 1970, women constituted approximately one-third of the Canadian labor force; in 1988 this figure had increased to 44 percent. During that period of time the fastest growing segment of the female labor force consisted of mothers of preschool-age children. In 1976, less than one-third of mothers with children younger than three years of age and about 40 percent of mothers whose youngest children were three to five years old were in the labor force; comparable 1988 figures were 58.3 percent and 65.1 percent, respectively (Statistics Canada, 1990).

The 1980s saw the issue of child care emerge as a central political and policy issue in Canada at both the federal and the provincial levels. Federally, two different governments, the Liberals in 1984 and the Conservatives in 1986, created national-level committees to examine the question of child care in Canada. The reports from those two inquiries suggested quite dissimilar solutions to what advocates termed the child care crisis, nevertheless both committees agreed that a very significant social problem existed and that the exact magnitude of the problem was not fully understood given the lack of reliable information. Both federal reports were supportive of additional national data being collected to better understand the dynamics of child care use. In 1988 the Conservative government announced funding for a large-scale study of child care in Canada, the Canadian National Child Care Study (CNCCS) (Lero, Pence, Goelman & Brockman, 1987). This chapter is based on data from that study.

STUDY DESIGN

The CNCCS is the largest study of its kind ever undertaken in Canada. It is made up of two separate but linked components: an extensive national household survey and a review of provincial and territorial child care policies, programs, and historical developments. The survey was based on lengthy interviews with one parent in more than 24,000 families having at least one child 12 years of age or younger. Parents were asked about their labor force participation, family composition, child care use patterns, work-family concerns, and their perceptions of and preferences among child care alternatives. The result is a data set of enormous size and considerable complexity designed to address not only child care but a range of other family and employment issues as well. For the purpose of this chapter, discussion centers on child care, and more specifically on family day care issues.

The survey methodology was based on Statistics Canada's monthly Labour Force Survey, but included an augmented sample in order to yield data that would be statistically representative not only for the country as a whole but for each province. Population estimates can be derived separately for families and for children. In all, the data provide estimates for 98 percent of Canadian families with at least one child younger than 13 years of age: 2,724,300 families and 4,658,500 children. Telephone and in-person interviews conducted by trained Statistics Canada interviewers lasted 46 minutes on average; the national response rate was 84.3 percent.

Extensive child care data were collected for each child in the family in order to determine how many children participated in each kind of care arrangement in the reference week and for how many hours. Children's participation was also categorized according to the main activity of the interviewed parent (IP) while the child was in care.[1]

FINDINGS FROM THE *CNCCS*

Care Used for Any Purpose for More Than One Hour During the Reference Week

The CNCCS incorporates a number of "lenses" through which child care can be viewed. At the broadest macro level, the study provides information on care used regardless of parental purpose for more than one hour during the reference week, for the population of 4,658,500 children living in 2,724,300 families. The figures reflect that two-thirds (66.1 percent) of children in Canada experience at least one supplemental form of care in addition to care by the IP at home. The CNCCS was designed to capture as much of the breadth and complexity of child care use as possible utilizing a survey instrument. Figure 4.1 provides an indication of this broad-strokes approach to understanding child care use in Canada across a wide set of 15 possible care types.[2]

Figure 4.1 provides an overall sense of the magnitude of child care in Canada. Approximately 38 percent of all children 0 to 12 years of age spent at least one hour during the reference week in one of the 15 types of care, 19.9 percent spent at least one hour in two types of care, and 8.2 percent spent at least one hour in three or more types of care identified in Figure 4.1. From the broad perspective of Figure 4.1, is it apparent that parental care (the first three categories plus care by the IP at home) and school represent the two most frequently utilized forms of child care in Canada. What may be less apparent is that family day care provided by both relatives and nonrelatives outside of the child's home (categories including relative not at home, unlicensed family day care, and licensed family day care) represents the third most common form of care. The CNCCS did not approach family day care as a homogeneous entity, and although some might argue that care by a relative outside the child's home should not be included as a type of family day care, the authors believe that such categorizations are arbitrary and reflective of an inadequate development of typology of care discussions. From the perspective of the CNCCS it is critical that even finer definitions of care types emerge if we are to truly appreciate the ecological complexity of child care. Those factors that lead some parents to use care by a relative or nonrelative out of the home, or that encompass certain familial relationships as caregivers but not others, must be better understood. However, with regard to Figure 4.1, even when care by a relative out of the child's home (11.2 percent of all Canadian children spent at least one hour in this form of care) is excluded from the category of family day care, nonrelative family day care still constitutes a substantially important form of child care, with over 660,000 children (14.1 percent) in such care during the reference week.

Although the picture of child care in Canada presented in Figure 4.1 has some value in depicting the broad scope of child care, its utility for understanding focused policy and program issues is severely limited. Unfortunately, it is this sort of broad-strokes data that often constitutes the findings from major national polls on child care, and in Canada such polls sometimes carry influence beyond their credible ability to inform. Although data such as that contained in Figure 4.1 are effective in describing the magnitude of care use, one sees with Figure 4.2 what the addition of only one variable, time in care, can do to our image of the relative importance of various types of care. Information on the right side of Figure 4.2 is the same as that in Figure 4.1, but the left side indicates the mean number of hours children spent in each of the 15 types of care.

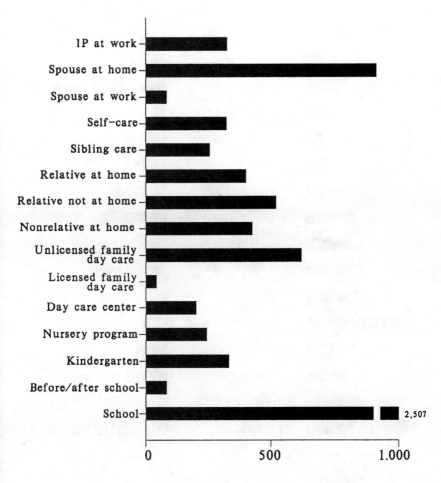

Thousands of Children

FIGURE 4.1. Number of children in various child care arrangements for at least one hour during the reference week (all ages).

In Figure 4.2 it becomes increasingly apparent that various types of care tend to fill certain socioecological niches (Bronfenbrenner, 1979). For example, although day care centers serve a much smaller population of children than care by relatives in or out of the children's homes, children cared for in centers tend to be those children requiring, on average, much longer hours of care (30.0 hours of center care per week versus 15.6 hours of care by relatives). Taking a second example, although the cate-

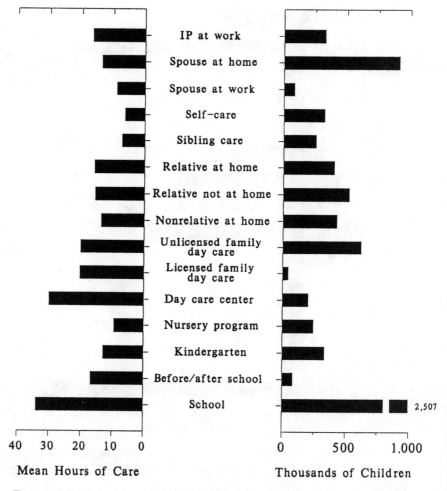

Mean Hours of Care   Thousands of Children

FIGURE 4.2.   Mean hours of care and number of children in various child care arrangements for at least one hour during the reference week (all ages).

gory "spouse at home" is second only to school in the number of children receiving that form of care, the mean hours of that type of care is only 13.6.

With such information on care use and care hours, one begins to perceive the dimly lit outlines of differing family forms and family needs behind the caregiving numbers: Presumably those families who are using only center-based care and using it for more than 30 hours a week differ in some significant ways from families who use only spouse at home care and use it for only 10 hours a week. At this preliminary stage of thinking about opaque images of families existing behind the caregiving numbers, it is impossible to state what the specific differences in families may be or in what ways various parts of the broader ecology may affect those families. But the impressions received form the basis for questions to ask, and the magnitude and complexity of the CNCCS data allow one to pursue questions far into the largely uncharted maze of children, families, work, and child care. Indeed, the exercise is one of slowly and tentatively mapping the maze; corridors lead off of corridors, family needs interact with family beliefs and lead into forms of care, which in turn are fed by other channels, other families, other needs and beliefs.

The maze, or the puzzle, of child care in Canada (and in the United States) has never been adequately mapped. Our instruments have been too weak, our conceptualizations too limited, and our data bases too small to carry us very far into this complex environment. In particular, family day care has been one of the least understood forms of care. The CNCCS is a more powerful instrument for mapping than we have had heretofore, but the mapping itself is a slow process. The remainder of the findings presented in this chapter continue the process of considering various lenses and examining different perspectives on the data.

In Figures 4.3 and 4.4, a third perspective, child age, is introduced. The age breakdowns of 0–17 months, 18–35 months, 3–5 years, 6–9 years, and 10–12 years have been used to allow some comparability with statistics that have been kept by the National Child Care Information Centre (Canada. Department of National Health and Welfare, 1972–90).

Figures 4.3 and 4.4 further accentuate the notion of ecological niches—that is, various forms of child care tend to meet certain specific child and family needs. Put in the vernacular of popular marketing, in the world of child care, one size does not fit all. Evidence of this reality is provided in Figures 4.3 and 4.4, both by age group and by hours in care.

In comparing the right-hand side of Figure 4.3 (percentage of children age five and younger cared for in the 15 care types) with the left-hand side of that figure (mean hours in care), one observation of interest is the relative disequilibrium for licensed family day care and day care centers. For both forms of care, the percentage of children who participate is quite small, but the mean number of hours of care is high compared with that of other care methods. Indeed, for infants (0–17 months) the percentage who receive

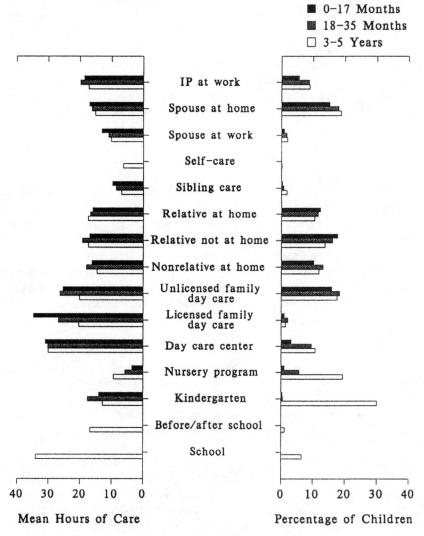

FIGURE 4.3.   Mean hours of care and percentage of preschool-age children in various child care arrangements for at least one hour during the reference week (by age groups).

licensed family day care for an hour or more during the reference week is only 2.1 percent, but that same form of care is used for the largest mean number of hours: 34.7. The general pattern of a relatively small percentage of children utilizing licensed family day care, but using such care for relatively long periods of time, holds for children 18–35 months and 3–5 years as well.

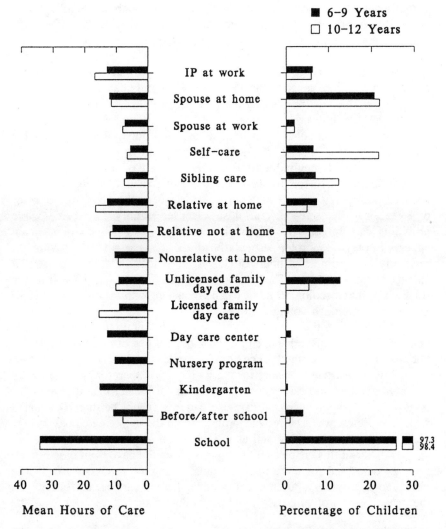

FIGURE 4.4. Mean hours of care and percentage of school-age children in various child care arrangements for at least one hour during the reference week (by age groups).

Unlicensed family day care is also significant for its relatively long mean hours of care provided, but in addition it is also notable for the relatively large percentage of children 0–3 years of age who are cared for in this setting (ranked second for children 0–17 months and first for children 18–35 months). When one combines licensed and unlicensed family day care with "relative not at home," these three forms of family day care provide care for a significantly larger percentage of children than the combined familial forms of care or group care programs such as day care centers, nurseries, and kindergartens. Family day care is important not only because of the percentages of children five and younger who use such care, but also because of the relatively long periods of time such care is used. In comparison with various familial care options noted in the 15 care types, family day care was utilized for longer periods of time during the reference week.

Figure 4.4 shows relatively less variability in hours of care than Figure 4.3, since time in school accounts for a large proportion of the caregiving day for 6–12-year-olds. For the 6–12 age groups, self-care and sibling care, which are relatively negligible for 0–5-year-olds, are quite significant forms of care, particularly for 10–12-year-olds. Relative not at home and unlicensed family day care are also fairly important forms of care, more so for 6–9-year-olds than 10–12-year-olds. Licensed family day care, while providing care for only a very small percentage of 6–12-year-olds, again appears to play a key role, particularly for 10–12-year-olds, in providing a relatively long number of hours of care for the older children who use that caregiving arrangement. The issue of licensed family day care filling a somewhat unique ecological niche can be seen here with the older children as it was with the much younger groups.

In considering the ecology of child care, it is important to bear in mind that care-use patterns are shaped not only by features of child care demand but also by child care supply. For example, in Canada many provinces have been slow to institute licensing for family day care, therefore it is generally accepted that the demand for such programs is far greater than the supply. It is important to appreciate that care-use patterns cannot be directly equated with care preference. The provision of care and the use of care are complex phenomena individually as well as in interaction.

Thus far in this chapter all the figures presented have been based on all types of care used for more than one hour during the reference week. The next section provides a different perspective on child care use by focusing on the *primary* form of care used by children during the reference week.

Primary Care

Primary care in the CNCCS is defined as the one form of supplemental care used by the child for the greatest number of hours during the reference week. As with the earlier "all care" figures, the "primary care" figures are based on care used regardless of parental purpose.

In order to orient the reader to the shift that takes place when moving from a consideration of care-use patterns reflecting all care used for one hour or more during the reference week to the pattern of care use produced when only primary care is considered, Figure 4.5 has been developed. Figure 4.5

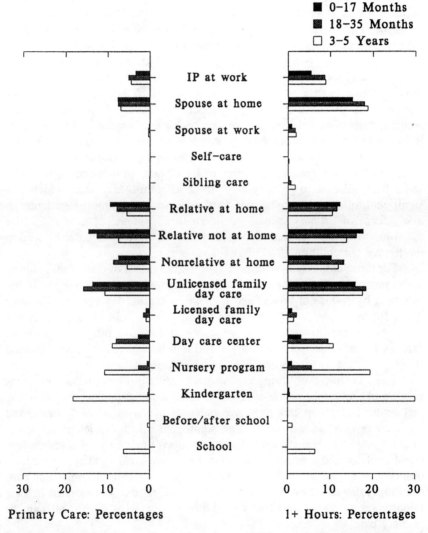

FIGURE 4.5. Percentage of preschoool-age children using various child care arrangements for at least one hour and primary care for any purpose during the reference week (by age groups).

focuses only on the three 0–5-year-old age groups, as the 6–12 age group is dominated by the school category for primary care, reducing all other forms of primary care to less than 2 percent. On the Figure 4.5 split graph the percentage of children by the age groups 0–17 months, 18–35 months, and 3–5 years who use "all care arrangements for more than one hour" is displayed on the right side, and "primary care" is shown on the left side.

The principal shift that takes place when one moves from all care used to primary care is a reduction in the percentage of children found to use each care type. The fact of a reduced percentage of users is a constant across all 15 care types—the amount of that reduction is where variability occurs. Looking first at the 0–17-month-old children, one finds that the percentages of children using some care types as their primary care are significantly reduced in comparison to the all care percentages. Of all 15 care types, family day care, both licensed and unlicensed, are reduced the least, 10 percent and 14.5 percent, respectively. Licensed day care center use is reduced 15.6 percent, followed by care by a relative not in the child's home, reduced 17.5 percent. Other care types such as spouse at home, IP at work, spouse at work, nursery care, and kindergarten care are reduced by 40 percent or more as the focus shifts from all care to primary care. In short, family day care, which is a significant form of all care regardless of purpose, is even more significant as a key form of primary care for children 0–17 months of age. A similar transition toward the increasing importance of family day care can be seen in the figures for children 18–35 months of age.

For those children 3–5 years of age, a different set of care types is found to be most significant for all care. Kindergarten, then nursery programs, followed by spouse at home, and unlicensed family day care are the four major forms of care on the right-hand side of Figure 4.5 (all care). However for primary care, kindergarten, although still the most often used form of care, has a much reduced percentage and is followed closely by unlicensed family day care as the second most utilized form of care.

The "ecology" of child care is seen to shift in Figure 4.5, sometimes subtly and sometimes not so subtly. A general observation from Figure 4.5 is that center and group-care programs (such as nurseries, kindergartens, and day care centers) play a much more significant role for older preschoolers than for younger children and that the two forms of care by relatives are less significant for older preschoolers than for infants and toddlers. A second observation is that for all three 0–5 age groups, unlicensed family day care and family day care by a relative not at the child's home both increase in their importance as major forms of caregiving as one moves from all care to primary care.

Additional analyses of the CNCCS data continue: Some focus much more specifically on families and family characteristics; some on work-force participation characteristics and others on additional lenses regarding child care use, such as child care used while working or studying. Each lens, each variable, provides different insights into the complex phenomena, the honeycombed maze, of child care, and in each set of analyses the importance of better understanding one of the least understood forms of child care, family day care, is underscored.

SUMMARY AND CONCLUSION

This chapter has presented small and focused aspects of data from the Canadian National Child Care Study using a number of different lenses. Those lenses enhance our understanding of child care as part of a complex and multifaceted socioecological system. A premise of this chapter has been that child care need and use models that focus only on a very limited set of care types or that examine child care only from an economic model of employment-driven need fail to capture the dynamic nature of an interactively complex child, family, employment, and social support system. That system has extremely complex historical, economic, individual, familial, and social roots, all of which interact to produce a multifaceted matrix of care need, care use, and care provision.

Data from the CNCCS support the use of a socioecological model in understanding child care. Different care types tend to address different niches in the broader ecology of family and socioeconomic life. Some forms of care that are used by very large numbers of children may also be forms of care that are used for relatively fewer hours, as is the case with nursery programs for 3–5-year-olds. On the other hand, there are also care types that are used by relatively fewer families and children but whose characteristics, such as long hours of availability, make them an essential service in the set of caregiving arrangements needed to support the diverse needs of families; licensed family day care could be identified as such an essentially important service.

Equally important to a full understanding of the ecology of care, and ones that have not been addressed in this chapter, are factors influencing the provision of care—factors such as availability, affordability, and accessibility, which are critically important components of the child care phenomenon. Care use is only one part of the child care equation; care provision is another. Factors such as care awareness and care beliefs represent additional elements necessary for a fuller understanding of child care. One should not read these figures and text without realizing that the glimpse at child care use patterns presented here does not reflect the full ecology of care. Care use is, in part, a reflection of care provision, and when various sorts of care are not equally accessible in relatively similar levels of perceived quality, care use is affected.

Family day care, more than most other forms of care, plays a ubiquitous role in the world of Canadian child care. Defined in this chapter as out-of-home care provided by either a relative or a nonrelative, spanning both licensed and unlicensed caregivers, participating in both formal and informal networks, family day care more than most forms of care is the "care for all reasons." Family day care is seen to play a critical role across the aspects of care discussed in this chapter: (1) all care used for more than one hour in the reference week; and (2) primary care. More critical in the caregiving patterns of parents with infants and toddlers, and with 6–9-year-old school-age children during nonschool hours (as was reported in the U.S. National Child Care Study as well), family day care is nevertheless a significant component in the Canadian caregiving "system"[3] across all age groups. For large numbers of Canadian families, family day care appears to fit their caregiving needs.

The fact of family day care's ubiquity suggests that just as our appreciation of child care in its many forms is expanding, so too must we begin to examine more closely the composite we refer to as family day care. Licensed/unlicensed is certainly one differentiation within family day care services, as is relative/nonrelative care. But beyond those categories (which are differentiated in this chapter), other characteristics of family day care need to be identified and examined to further extend our understanding of the ecology of child care. Motivation to provide care, numbers of children in care, presence or absence of the provider's own children, proximity to the child's home, training and educational background, antecedent friendship relationship with parents, care provided within the child's home, and "professional" identity as a care provider are but a few variables that could help further distinguish the nature of the fit between parents and caregivers and the niches that various family day care providers fill.

Our understanding of family day care is in its infancy despite the very long history of such care. One is reminded of the dictum: "That which is most difficult to see is that which lies before our eyes." In the world of child care, family day care has been ever-present, but too seldom seen.

NOTES

Acknowledgment: Major funding for the Canadian National Child Care Study was provided by the Child Care Initiatives Fund of the National Department of Health and Welfare Canada; supplemental funds were provided by the Social Sciences and Humanities Research Council of Canada and the Provinces of Ontario and New

Brunswick. The opinions expressed in this chapter are those of the authors and do not necessarily reflect the positions and policies of the funders.

1. The interviewed parent (IP) was the parent who identified herself or himself as most responsible for making child care arrangements. In cases in which both parents made decisions equally and jointly, the mother was interviewed. In 95 percent of families, the IP was the mother.

2. Because many children had more than one care arrangement during the reference week, the numbers and percentages in the "all care" figures are not additive.

3. The term *system* is used advisedly. Canada has not developed a comprehensive system of child care, and no legislation specific to child care exists nationally, although all provinces and territories do have legislation.

REFERENCES

Bronfenbrenner, U. (1979). *The ecology of human development: Experiments by nature and design*. Cambridge, MA: Harvard University Press.

Canada. Department of Health and Welfare. (1972–90). *Annual status of day care reports*. Ottawa: Minister of Supply and Services.

Lero, D. S., Pence, A. R., Goelman, H., & Brockman, L. (1987). *Canadian families and their child care arrangements: A proposal for a national child care survey*. Proposal submitted to the Department of Supply and Services, Ottawa, Ontario.

Statistics Canada—Housing, Family and Social Statistics Division. (1990). *Women in Canada: A statistical report*, 2d ed. Catalogue No. 89-563E. Ottawa: Minister of Supply and Services.

CHAPTER 5

An Introduction to the Economics of Family Home Day Care

W. Steven Barnett

The United States is undergoing an important transformation in its child care arrangements. It is changing from a society in which child care was provided almost entirely by parents within the home to one in which other institutions—the market, nonprofit organizations, and government—play important roles. Family home day care has become a major source of child care as these new institutional arrangements have evolved. This chapter provides an introduction to the economics of family home day care in the context of this historic transformation.

In its first major section, the chapter sets out a brief historical description of institutional changes in child care. The next two major sections provide detailed discussions of the demand and supply of family home day care in the context of the overall child care market. Within the demand section, special attention is given to long-term demand projections, market failure, and public intervention in demand. The supply section discusses the ways in which the supply of child care generally and family home day care specifically may or may not behave as predicted by standard economic theory and considers the impact of government regulation.

HISTORICAL PERSPECTIVE

Child care is a service that is produced by family and friends as an unpaid task in the home and by a variety of persons in a variety of other institutions as a paid task. The institutions producing child care include families and their social network, churches, governments, and the market system. For most of U.S. history, the family has provided most of the resources required for child care, directly producing it in and around the home. Mothers and older children assumed the largest burden of care. Government played an important role in the care of older children through schools. Churches provided limited amounts of care.

Recent increases in the participation of women in the labor market, including mothers of even very young children, are incompatible with traditional child care arrangements. This has required that families develop new care arrangements, especially for young children who are not in school and for after-school care. The expansion of other arrangements has taken a variety of forms, one of which is the growth of family home day care. From this perspective, it should be clear that what is commonly called an increase in the demand for child care is more specifically an increase in the demand for nonmaternal care.

It is hardly surprising that the transformation with regard to employment and child care is difficult for many families. Families with children are looking for new institutional arrangements to produce a service that is of vast psychological and economic importance. In this context, much of the public policy debate around child care can be seen as revolving around the question: What should be the roles of institutions other than the family—government, church, market—in child care?

In order to understand the economics of child care and how it has been changing, it is useful to have a complete description of arrangements past and present. Such a description would include for each arrangement the number of children and hours of care, quality, cost, and percentage of costs borne by parents. Unfortunately, this information is not all available, though more of it is becoming available (e.g., Willer et al., 1991), and some new data are provided by other chapters in this volume.

Before 1960 few children under the age of five were cared for primarily outside the home. As recently as 1967, less than 25 percent of women with children under age three worked outside the home (Shank, 1988). In 1965, less than 2 percent of young children had center care and perhaps 7 percent had family home day care (including relatives) as their primary arrangements. By the mid-1980s, the production of care by children's own households had declined dramatically, and other arrangements had increased proportionately.

Although the data show tremendous change, they also show that most children under five continue to have most of their child care produced by the household and close to three-fourths of all young children are cared for by a relative. Most child care continues to be unpaid. Family home day care, if defined as all care in another home (including relative care), accounts for about 20 percent of all care arrangements. Because virtually all nonrelative care is paid, and 40 to 70 percent of relative care is paid as well (Presser,

1989a, 1989b; Leibowitz, Waite & Witsberger, 1988), paid family day care can be estimated at 15 percent or more of all primary care arrangements. Thus, family day care is clearly as much a part of the child care market as center care.

In addition to their primary care arrangements, a substantial number of children are in other nonparental care arrangements. Many three- and four-year-olds whose mothers are not employed are enrolled in out-of-home care for education and companionship, and center-based programs seem to be much more commonly used for this purpose than family home day care. Arrangements such as home play groups and family day care may be used more for this purpose for children under three, but how much is unclear.

The care of school-age children has changed less over the last several decades, but has still undergone changes. During the school year most older children are in school for much of the regular workday, fall through spring. Younger school-age children of employed mothers require other arrangements before and after school, and at other times if their mothers work evenings, nights, or weekends. In 1985, of employed mothers of children under 14, about 14 percent worked a nonday shift and 24 percent worked during the weekend (Presser, 1989a). Many children need a replacement for school care during the summer. The primary alternatives for school-age children are relatives and self-care, with some center care and relatively little family home day care.

The description of trends provides a perspective for understanding the importance of family home day care. It does not provide an explanation for the changes that have taken place or offer a sound basis for predicting the future changes and their effects on family home day care. Simple linear projections could be made based on the past changes, but such projections can easily be wrong because they are purely mechanical. By drawing on economic theory to explain the past and the present, it is hoped that a stronger basis can be developed for predicting the future, including the impacts of alternative public policies. This requires an exploration of demand and supply, which together determine the quantity, quality, and price of each type of child care arrangement.

DEMAND

Nonmaternal child care arrangements produce two products simultaneously. First, they allow the mother to engage in other activities such as work in the formal labor force by providing for the current needs of the child.

Second, they invest in the child's human capital by stimulating learning and development. This joint production is recognized in the now common usage of the term early childhood care and education. Thus, the demand for non-maternal child care is actually composed of two separate demands: one for a service that allows the mother to work, the other for a service that invests in the child.

The family's choice of child care arrangements depends on the demand for these two products of child care. Demand for care to facilitate the mother's employment would be expected to depend on such family characteristics as the mother's potential earnings, income from family members, the availability of other family members to provide care, the number of children requiring care, and values regarding parental time with children. Demand for investment in children's human capital would be expected to depend on such family characteristics as income, number and age of children, beliefs about children's learning and development, and values regarding investment in children overall and in specific domains.

Some broad generalizations, for the most part obvious, can be made. For example, parents tend to use less of any type of care as its price rises relative to others. The availability of a spouse, grandparent, teenage children, or other relatives as potential caregivers can be expected to reduce the demand for other care arrangements. The belief that formal teaching is more important for older children means that center care is favored for them. However, theory does not predict how much these factors affect demand. More precise estimates must be obtained from empirical studies.

Unfortunately, there is a distinct shortage of demand studies. Although a number of studies may appear to examine the demand for child care, they suffer from two limitations. First, most examine the expenditures and arrangements that result from the interaction of supply and demand; they do not disentangle supply and demand (e.g., Willer et al., 1991; Leibowitz, Waite & Witsberger, 1988). Second, they usually fail to distinguish demand for the two joint products.

In addition, several studies that seek to provide insights into demand are based on dated, specialized samples that are a questionable basis for current generalizations (Robins & Spiegelman, 1978; Blau & Robins, 1988; Leibowitz, Waite & Witsberger, 1988). At best they suggest that theoretical expectations are generally correct. Choice of child care arrangement is sensitive to price, income, age of children, and the presence of adults other than the mother in the household. Sound estimates of the effects of prices and income on the use of nonmaternal care arrangements, and of the relationship between maternal employment and care prices, would be extremely valuable for public policy decisions.

Demand for Family Day Care

Choice of family home day care over other child care arrangements depends on parents' evaluations of how well each arrangement meets their needs. Obviously, price is an important factor. Recent data indicating that prices are roughly comparable across arrangements suggest that many parents do not strongly value one type of arrangement over another (Willer et al., 1991). On a purely logical basis, the characteristics that would seem to differentiate family home day care from center care are:

- Its half-market, half-social nature,
- The ability to have a flexible schedule for each child,
- The familiarity and noninstitutional nature of the setting,
- Its small scale,
- Parents' ability to choose their children's provider as well as the place,
- The potential to be located in the child's neighborhood, and
- Parents' opportunity to know or know about the caregiver through their social networks (a significant percentage are relatives).

For the first characteristic an explanation may be helpful. Family home day care is only partly a market activity. Buyers and sellers do not always (or even mostly) interact impersonally to determine price, quantity, and quality. The families involved tend to have personal social relationships. They may be friends. They may come to be considered part of each other's families to some extent. These relationships may involve the caregiver's own children. Some people may consider these relationships intrinsically desirable. Some may consider them desirable because they make the caregiver more trustworthy. Because people consider themselves involved in a social relationship they may behave somewhat differently than they would if it were a purely economic relationship.

The quasi-market nature of family home day care need not imply that the standard predictions of economic theory do not apply or that family home day care is distinctly different from other economic activities. Many economic activities are partly social. Employees can feel a strong loyalty to other workers, supervisors, or the company. In retail businesses and services with frequent interaction between customers and employees or owners, social relationships may develop. This may be especially likely for small enterprises in small communities. As economists have long recognized, the economic behavior of people can be quite unbusinessnesslike and still be adequately explained by economic theory (Marshall, 1920, 1982). The evidence on family day care does not indicate that consumer behavior differs from what economists would ordinarily expect.

The special characteristics of family day care tend to make it considered more suitable for infants and toddlers and less suitable for preschoolers. The need to trust the provider, the emotional involvement of the provider with the child, and the child's limitations in dealing with the environment are all important factors for younger children. The general public view appears to be that parent-like care is more important for younger children and teacher-like care is more important for older children. To the extent that family home day care providers are similar in their values, customs, and habits, it tends to be preferred to other forms of child care, though church-sponsored care has appeal in this regard as well. Family home day care also seems to be more appealing to parents whose own schedules are flexible or variable.

Long-Term Trends

The past 40 years can be characterized as a period in which the demand for nonmaternal care increased tremendously. The proximal cause of this is the increased labor force participation of women with young children (Smith & Ward, 1985; Blau & Robins, 1988, 1989). One important factor contributing to the trend has been the rising cost of maternal care. Secular increases in earnings raised the cost of mothers' time, making it much more expensive to stay out of the labor force. Also, decreases in the number of children per family raised the relative cost per child of home care. Other potentially important factors include changing attitudes that increased women's labor force opportunities and their desire for employment and a rise in single parenting. The latter increased the percentage of families with young children for whom earned income depends entirely on the mother working and decreased the percentage of families in which a father can provide care.

Forecasts of labor force participation (Shank, 1988) as well as trends in women's education, work experience, and compensation indicate a pattern of continued growth in women's commitment to uninterrupted employment (Smith & Ward, 1989). With the trend toward later marriage and childbirth, women have acquired more education and labor market experience by the time they become mothers, which tends to increase labor market attachment (Smith & Ward, 1989). Some (e.g., Fullerton, 1987) have forecast slower growth in women's labor force participation. However, participation rates for women with young children are still substantially below those for men the same age, and many mothers of young children work only part time or part year (Zill, 1988). Thus, there is ample room for continued growth in women's participation in the labor force and in hours worked where it most influences the demand for child care.

As the overall demand for nonmaternal child care increases, the demand for family home child care tends to increase as well. Thus, continued growth in the demand for family home day care is expected. However, changes in economic and demographic factors can affect the share of the market held by family home day care by influencing the demand for it relative to other types of nonmaternal care. For example, increases in the average age of children will tend to reduce the share of family home day care, because the demand for academic and cognitive experiences for older children tends to favor centers. Demand for family day care may change because of a change in tastes, or because higher incomes increase the demand for child investment and centers are perceived as providing greater investment. What happens will depend partly on whether parents view family home day care for children under age three as providing less investment (because none is needed or it is not very productive) or as providing a more appropriate type of investment.

The aggregate demand for nonmaternal child care depends on the number of young children. If birthrates fall, the demand for child care will fall, other things being equal. Whether birthrates will fall or stabilize over the next decade is difficult to predict, but it is clear that the number of school-age children needing care will increase. How this affects family home day care will depend on the extent to which it can address the need for after-school care. Other factors that will affect future demand include the numbers of single-parent families and women's labor force participation. Current labor force participation rates are lowest for mothers of children under three, so there is the potential for greater participation, which would increase the demand for family home day care.

Demand-Side Market Failure

In most cases, the consumer demand expressed in the market is assumed to accurately represent the demand of society as a whole. Although departures from this assumption occur frequently, they tend not to be of great concern because they are usually small with little impact. However, when large departures occur, it may be desirable for private or public organizations to intervene in demand. Thus, in discussing a particular market, the identification of potential problems is of limited use. What is needed is information on the size of the problem. In the case of child care there are several potential problems with market demand, but evidence of importance is available for only one.

One clear problem with demand is that there are important externalities (benefits to society that do not accrue to the principal consumers) from investment in disadvantaged children. There is substantial evidence that the provision of quality preschool programs to children in poverty can produce long-term economic benefits in excess of costs (Barnett, in press). Economic analysis of the Perry Preschool program (Barnett, 1985) indicated that most of the economic benefits of high-quality preschool programs for disadvantaged children go to taxpayers and that it would not be in the economic interests of poor parents to pay for such programs even if their incomes allowed. Thus, public action is needed to provide a considerable additional demand for preschool investment in disadvantaged children.

It seems unlikely that externalities from investment in average and advantaged children are as large. A few studies indicate that preschool programs can contribute to improved academic ability and social behavior for such children, though the effects may be smaller than those for disadvantaged children (Clarke-Stewart, 1991; Zaslow, 1991; Osborn & Milbank, 1987). Studies have not investigated benefits beyond the early primary grades, but the most likely economic benefits would be increased earnings due to gains in the quality and quantity of education. The public would reap some gains due to increased tax payments.

However, large public-sector cost savings from additional investment in nonpoor children would not be expected. Most children have relatively low rates of grade retention, special education, crime and delinquency, unemployment, and welfare dependency. It is the avoidance of these problems that provides most of the public gain from investing in disadvantaged children. Although such benefits would not be expected to end abruptly at an arbitrarily defined poverty line, they would decline as family income rises.

Another potential problem due to externalities arises with the demand for care so that mothers can work. Paid work in the formal labor force is taxed, and unpaid household work is not. Thus, in choosing between market work and household work, mothers weigh after-tax income (net of child care and other costs) and other benefits of employment against the value of their household production, including maternal child care. From a societal perspective, the income tax biases the choice against market work because the value of market work to society as a whole is represented by the pretax wage. Thus, demand for nonmaternal care is lower than is desirable from a societal perspective.

Although it may be supposed that the magnitude of lost employment-related benefits is large, dependable empirical estimates are unavailable. Data for Sweden indicate that the public gain from mothers' employment-related benefits (Swedish tax rates are high) can approach the full costs of high-quality full-day programs (Gustafsson & Stafford, 1988). Some data for the United States indicate that maternal labor force participation can be quite responsive to public subsidization of child care (Blau & Robins, 1988). However, the evidence is too limited to draw strong conclusions.

Another demand-side problem may arise from the failure of consumer demand expressed in the market to adequately represent the interests of all family members. One abstraction that economists tend to make is that the demand of parents or families for goods and services can be modeled as though there were no important differences in demand between fathers and mothers, or between parents and children. Much of the time this is useful, but in the case of child care, it may be misleading for two reasons: Men and women may differ significantly in their demand for child care, and children depend on parental altruism to ensure that their interests are represented fully.

There are a variety of models of husband-wife decision making that could be used to study the demand for child care (Manser & Brown, 1980; McElroy & Horney, 1981), but such studies have yet to be done. It seems likely that demand for nonmaternal child care may differ between men and women. This could reflect differences in their economic and social situations or in their values (Fuchs, 1989; Hunt & Hunt, 1987). This issue is important not only because women might not be adequately represented in demand, but because changes in families could lead to changes in demand. In particular, it might be predicted that a greater influence for women would lead to increases in demands for both products of child care.

Failure of parental altruism is a potential problem for all the goods and services provided to children (Becker & Murphy, 1988). Its importance is greatest when it concerns something like child care that can critically affect a child's healthy growth and development. In the United States it is generally assumed that parents act altruistically. Government intervenes only in cases of gross abuse or neglect, or by establishing minimum standards. Health and safety standards for housing and child care facilities may be partially moti-vated by the desire to prevent harm to children by a few parents who do not act in their children's interests. Recent historical work has challenged the general assumption of altruistic parents by finding that nonaltruistic behavior by parents was pervasive in nineteenth-century behavior regarding child labor and education (Parsons & Goldin, 1989). However, it is difficult to know how much of a problem this is for child care.

Even if parents act altruistically, an information problem arises in child care because parents do not fully experience the service. Children, especially very young children, cannot be relied upon to accurately report the quality of care received. This places parents at a disadvantage because they must trust the provider and rely on relatively infrequent direct checks. The value of nonparental child care would decline precipitously if parents felt the need to frequently check its quality by being present. The involvement of nonprofits in child care may be one response to this problem, with parents viewing them as more trustworthy. Family day care may have some advantages in this respect as parents can more easily acquire information about the quality of care, and the problem of relying on the provider's altruism is reduced if social bonds tie the provider and parent.

The final possible demand-side problem to be discussed is that parents may not be well-informed about the long-term effects of quality on children. In most markets, it is assumed that if consumers have the chance to make decisions fairly frequently, they become reasonably well-informed over time. Some argue that because the long-term consequences of child care for children are not easily observed by parents and wide use of nonmaternal care is relatively recent, parents are not well-informed. Thus, parents underestimate the long-term benefits of quality leading them to demand too little (e.g., Culkin, Helburn & Morris, 1990). Again, empirical evidence is sadly lacking. That child care experts believe parents underinvest in quality may simply mean that experts do not weigh family needs in the same way as parents.

Public Intervention in Demand

There are several possible responses to the demand problems discussed above. One is for philanthropic organizations and the government to add to the demand for child care by purchasing it themselves or subsidizing purchases so that parents buy more. This can be an appropriate response to the externalities problem. Government demand is considerable. The federal government alone added over $8.5 billion in demand to the market in 1988 (Besharov & Tramontozzi, 1989; Stewart, 1990; Willer, 1991; USGAO, 1989). This dropped perhaps $1 billion or more in 1989 when many parents ceased to apply for subsidies due to increased reporting requirements for the tax credit. Congressional authorization to raise Head Start spending to over $7.6 billion by 1994 would raise demand by about $5.5 billion, however, and will represent real progress toward adequate public demand for investment in disadvantaged children if the money is actually appropriated.

State and local governments provide additional public demand. Deductions or credits for child care are available in 29 states. Eight states provide tax exemptions for employer-sponsored child care. State and local funding for early childhood programs and after-school care is becoming common. A recent survey found that 36 percent of school districts had preschool programs, including 73 percent of the largest districts (American Association of School Administrators, 1988). The percentages providing extended day programs for school-age children were similar.

Contrary to popular belief, increased public provision or subsidies is not necessarily an appropriate response to the other demand problems. If parents are not sufficiently altruistic or well-informed, they might respond to public actions by decreasing other investments in their children. A more effective response might be a public information campaign to alter parental values or beliefs. This would be an especially strong option if parents are misinformed. Another possible response is regulation of care quality, though unless the action also serves to educate parents, parents will try to work around it.

These public responses to potential demand-side problems have several implications for demand for family day care. To some extent they may raise the demand for family home day care as part of a general rise in demand. However, there are likely to be effects on specific types of care as well. As noted earlier, the demand for child investment (higher quality) tends to favor centers. Family home day care tends to be further disadvantaged with respect to public demand because small scale and informality make it much more difficult to deal with administratively. Clarke-Stewart (1991) has suggested that family home day care is greatly inferior to centers for investing in preschoolers. This assertion seems overly strong given potentially contrary evidence from larger studies (Osborn & Milbank, 1987). However, it is apparent that family home care will not acquire an equal share of public demand for child investment unless it can be shown to be equally effective.

SUPPLY

Child care supply is highly diverse, with significant amounts of care provided by families, nonfamily individuals, private nonprofit organizations, public organizations, and private for-profit organizations. Each of these suppliers has advantages and disadvantages for meeting various needs for care. The suppliers also differ in cost, behavior, and extent of subsidization. Although family home day care is a large source of supply, especially if relatives providing care in their own homes are included (Wash & Brand, 1990; Willer et al., 1991), no reasonably precise estimate of the number of family home day care providers is available. The most recent estimate is 700,000 to 1.2 million (Willer et al., 1991). Most family home day care belongs to the "underground economy" and is unlicensed, unregulated, and untaxed.

To some, the supply of child care appears to be chaotic and fails to meet the needs of children and parents. Various reports have argued that there are shortages of child care, especially infant care, and mismatches between the services available and the services parents want (e.g., Kahn & Kamerman, 1987; Galinsky & Friedman, 1986; Reisman et al., 1988). Economics provides another perspective. The "invisible hand" of the market ensures that suppliers usually deliver what consumers want, as long as consumers are willing to pay what the services cost. Shortages or mismatches do not tend to persist unless there are imperfections in the market. The supply side of the child care market with its large numbers of suppliers, low costs of entry and exit, and relative lack of regulation would not appear to have serious imperfections. Thus, one would not expect shortages or mismatches with respect to parental demand.

The quantity of child care supplied has expanded tremendously and rapidly over the last two decades to keep pace with demand (Hofferth, 1989; Wash & Brand, 1990; Willer et al., 1991). At the same time, the real price of center and family home day care rose only slightly. The real price of non-parental care in the home rose greatly, for the same reasons that the price of parental care rose. Although this suggests a relatively flat long-term supply curve for center and family home day care, it is possible that a fall in quality partially explains the near stability of price. This is suggested by comparisons made by Kisker and colleagues (1991). Also, it is consistent with labor force trends. The average education level of women drawn into the labor force has declined over the past 20 years. With lower earnings and purchasing power, they would tend to have lower demand for quality.

Detailed examination of child care usage indicates that for-profit providers (including family home day care) were responsible for most of the increase in supply (Rose-Ackerman, 1986). This may reflect the dependence of private nonprofits on a limited supply of private subsidies (Rose-Ackerman, 1986; Hansmann, 1987). In this view, private nonprofit organizations depend on individuals who are willing to subsidize care through donations and lower compensation and cannot expand when the supply of these people is exhausted. Insofar as family home day care providers behave this way, further increases in supply would tend to require increased compensation.

Private nonprofit provider behavior and government provision of programs can lead to *apparent* shortages or mismatches for child care. This occurs if nonprofits and government (and possibly some family home day care providers) offer limited amounts of high-quality care at relatively low prices. Once these spaces are filled, parents must turn to lower-quality care or pay higher prices. Thus, many parents might see quality-price combinations that they would like, but cannot obtain.

Sometimes what is meant by a shortage is that high-quality care is not available at prices that everyone is willing and able to pay. This circumstance has also been seen as a market failure on the demand side (Culkin et al., 1990). However, this is not really the result of a market failure on either side. It reflects the basic facts that all goods and services are costly and resources to purchase them are limited (for society as a whole as well as individuals). In this sense, most people face shortages of some things (e.g., affordable Mercedes-Benzes), and low-income people can face shortages of many basic goods (food, health care, housing, and nonmaternal child care). The problem is one of limitations on income and its distribution across families rather than market failure.

Family Home Day Care Supply

Family home day care is a substantial industry, whether or not those who provide care for children of relatives are included. Its size makes family home day care an important source of employment as well as care. Family home day care probably provides more jobs than elementary school teaching, and may employ 2 percent to 3 percent of the female labor force. The potential supply would appear to be quite large, since entry requires little specialized investment in physical capital or formal education. For these and other reasons, the family home day care market would be expected to be highly competitive.

The most recent estimates indicate that about 4 million children under age 13 received nonrelative family home day care, and the average fee charged was $1.48 an hour for unregulated care and $1.64 an hour for regulated care (Willer et al., 1991). Relatively little is known about quality. Like price and quantity, quality results from the interaction of supply and demand, but production of quality seems likely to be strongly linked to provider characteristics such as education, personality, and values, attitudes, and beliefs regarding children, child rearing, and teaching. The National Day Care Home Study (NDCHS) (Singer et al., 1980) found day care homes to be generally safe and positive environments, but provided little more specificity. Turnover might be expected to be high though no higher than for centers. In most cases monitoring of quality is up to parents, as the vast majority of providers are unregulated (Kahn & Kamerman, 1987; Willer et al., 1991).

The belief that the standard economic models do not apply to the supply of family home day care seems to be common. This belief stems from the accurate perception that family home day care is a social as well as an economic activity and the inaccurate (but widespread) view that economic theory assumes people to be selfish and motivated only by money. Thus, it is important to understand that economics recognizes that social relationships affect economic transactions, that altruism affects economic behavior, and that job choice depends on nonmonetary as well as monetary rewards. Child care is not unique in any of these regards.

Possibly family home day care is an extreme example in some respects. The role of family relationships is larger than in many other economic activities. Many people provide care in their homes for the children of relatives. Much of this care is unpaid (Presser, 1989b) and, when paid, the price may be less than the rate charged to nonrelatives. To some extent this may represent an intrafamily transfer of income from the caregiver to children and their parents. People contribute to their children's and grandchildren's well-being in a variety of ways, including monetary bequests (Becker, 1981). Grandparents might provide child care as a gift for adult children or as an investment in young grandchildren. Other explanations are that there may be higher intrinsic rewards to caring for a closely related child, and there may be reciprocal obligations for the child's parents to pay indirectly. Payment could be nonmonetary or monetary at a later time.

From the above theoretical speculations, it would be expected that the price charged for child care would increase as the strength of the social relationship declined. Thus, more distant relatives would be inclined to charge something close to the market price. Neighbors would have fairly weak incentives to charge less, though a certain amount of barter might occur so that monetary payments would not reflect full payment. At the same time, some parents might pay more than the going rate in order to transfer income to relatives or neighbors. On average, parents of young children tend to be in relatively weak financial positions, so transfers to providers would not be expected to be extensive.

As with other aspects of family day care, data on earnings are severely limited. However, no one would deny that the earnings of even unrelated family home day care providers are low compared to those of people employed outside the home. In the NDCHS (Singer et al., 1980), the average income reported by providers was below the minimum wage. Another study found the net income reported by licensed and unlicensed providers to be substantially below the earnings of child care center workers (Weiner, 1978). The most recent studies (Willer et al., 1991) report that hourly earnings are $4.04 an hour for regulated providers and $1.25 an hour for unregulated providers. This compares to an average of $7.49 an hour for teachers in centers.

In interpreting these earnings estimates, it must be recognized that the figures are based on self-reporting. To the extent that family home day care providers are less businesslike and have highly informal arrangements with consumers, there is considerable room for reporting error. It is notable that the hourly prices reported by parents for family home day care are quite similar to the prices they report for other types of care. This is what would be expected from the ordinary interaction of supply and demand in a competitive market.

Nevertheless, it seems reasonable to conclude that the monetary earnings of even unrelated providers are quite low compared to those of people in other occupations, including relatively low-paid center staff. The low pay is sometimes cited as evidence that even unrelated providers are irrational or highly altruistic and act to subsidize the care of other people's children (e.g., Culkin et al., 1990). Economic theory and what little evidence is available suggest that there are a variety of other more plausible explanations.

First, it is important to recognize that family home day care is an activity that can be jointly conducted with other household production, including the care of one's own children, and with leisure activities. Thus, it is by no means the case that earnings should be interpreted as the full return to each hour of the provider's time. For those who have young children of their own or are caring for children of a relative, the addition of one or more children may produce only modest increases in the demands on their time.

Providers may find caring for children compatible with work on other household tasks such as cooking, cleaning, and laundry, and even gardening and shopping might be done at the same time (Nelson, 1990). Indoor and outdoor leisure activities might be conducted simultaneously as well. Thus, the earnings from family home child care are only a part, perhaps a small part, of the return to the provider's time. Earnings may appear to be higher in regulated homes because they allow fewer of these other activities.

Second, the rewards from interaction with children are likely to be an important factor in the decision to become a provider. Parents may place a high value on an activity that allows them to be with their own children because they believe it is important for the children and because they obtain high intrinsic rewards from being with their children. Surveys of satisfaction from household tasks, work, leisure, and other activities consistently find the highest rated activities to be parents' interactions with their children (Juster & Courant, 1986). That some people derive great satisfaction from caring for others' children is also reasonable. Some choose to become family day care providers because they love children and enjoy caring for them (e.g., Nelson, 1990). Thus, providers may be willing to accept low monetary wages because the intrinsic rewards are high compared to those in other jobs they could obtain, as well as because it provides the opportunity to engage in other household activities simultaneously.

Third, the appropriate monetary comparison is not wages earned but net income. A comparison of net income is much more favorable to family home day care. Net earnings from formal employment are substantially reduced by income tax, social security tax, unemployment insurance, the cost of travel to and from work, work clothes, meals away from home, child care in many cases, and other work-related expenses. Many family home day care providers pay no taxes on their income and avoid many of the other costs of jobs outside the home. Although some formal jobs pay fringe benefits, many lower-paying and part-time jobs do not offer substantial fringes. Some of the joint production benefits of family home day care (e.g., time for cooking, cleaning, laundry) could be viewed instead as costs incurred due to employment outside the home. If a provider were to work outside the home instead, in addition to the obvious cost of buying child care, a family may find that it pays more for meals (e.g., buying more prepared foods or eating out) and pays others to do cleaning and other household tasks. The pace of life for the entire family can become more hectic due to increased time pressures.

Another observation sometimes interpreted as evidence that family home day care providers are unusual in their economic behavior is that providers consider the ability of parents to pay in setting fees. However, such actions are perfectly consistent with typical economic behavior. Businesses usually consider how much consumers can pay in setting their prices, and, if they can, they seek to charge consumers according to their willingness and ability to pay. It cannot be safely assumed that altruism is the motive for such behavior or what allows it to occur. It is not uncommon for doctors to have sliding fee scales based on income or to reduce fees for those who have trouble paying. Private universities offer students tuition reductions. Airlines offer senior citizens lower fares.

Evidence that family home day care providers do not charge parents as much as they say they would be willing to pay is also interpreted as evidence of altruistic behavior. However, this is exactly what economics predicts will result from a competitive market. Most consumers do not pay the maximum they are willing to pay. Otherwise, there would be no gain to consumers from their purchases. In the ordinary model of competitive supply and demand, everyone who buys a product is assumed to pay less than the maximum they would be willing to pay, except the theoretical consumer at the margin.

From the above discussion of incentives and behavior, the supply of family day care providers would be expected to depend heavily on several groups of women (men do not appear in significant numbers). One is young mothers who have preschool-age children and relatively low earnings potential in the formal labor market. A similar group consists of those who might be drawn into the market by the need to provide care for the child of a relative. Many of these women would be expected to leave the market when the children reached school age. Another group is women who value interactions and relationships with young children (and may not have young children at home) or other home activities. There may be some who find that family day care is a convenient second job to supplement their income from a full- or part-time job outside the home because it can be performed at home during off hours. Presser (1989b) found that a third of the grandmothers who provided care were employed outside the home as well. Finally, some may choose to become providers because the income can be hidden relatively easily, thereby avoiding reductions in welfare, social security, or other government payments.

Regulation of Supply

The effects of regulation on family home day care supply are limited because compliance is essentially voluntary. More comprehensive regulation might raise quality, but it would be very costly to administer given the large numbers of small providers, easy entry and exit, and invisibility of many arrangements. It is unclear that much could be gained from regulation, unless it provided incentives for providers to cooperate and raised quality without raising costs. It appears that regulation can increase some aspects of quality, but also raises cost (Singer et al., 1980) and can have negative impacts on other aspects of quality. Regulated family day care homes tend to have more children and can be more center-like in operation and atmosphere (Nelson, 1990). Some providers resist licensing because in their view it is intrusive and diminishes the sense of autonomy that is one of the rewards of their work (Nelson, 1988).

Regulation may have indirect effects on family home day care as well. State standards for health, safety, group size, and other factors related to quality may help inform the public and influence both demand and supply, but experience does not suggest that this occurs to any great extent. More important is the possibility that the difficulty of regulating family home day care providers may operate in their favor, by allowing them to be more flexible and charge lower prices than centers, which are easier to regulate. To the extent that this has happened with infant and toddler care, it may have increased the market share held by unregulated family home day care. Finally, in some cases, organizations formed to sponsor providers for the Child Care Food Program have taken on additional functions in training, purchasing of supplies, and other activities, becoming a type of professional organization or cooperative.

IMPLICATIONS

Family home day care is an important source of care for young children. Although it is difficult to predict trends in demand and supply, it seems likely that family home day care will continue to be a major source of care, especially for infants and toddlers. However, as the public and private demand for investment in learning and development continues to rise, family day care may become less common. If a way were developed to use family home day care to invest in the learning and development of preschoolers, especially the disadvantaged, demand might increase substantially. Although this has not received attention in the past, the potential for family home care to provide a better adult-child ratio than centers for the same cost suggests that it might be a profitable area for investigation.

One of the strongest implications of this chapter is that there is a tremendous need for research on the economics of early childhood care and education generally and on family home day care specifically. Many important economic aspects of the industry are relatively unresearched. The sizes of most (potential) market failures on the demand side have not been estimated. Thus, it is impossible to assess the adequacy of the government response. There is little evidence of a crisis in supply, but there are no sound estimates of the responsiveness of supply to price. Although there may be some apparent shortages, they more likely result from the behavior of nonprofits and government than from market failure.

The lack of sound national data on supply and demand is a serious limitation to the development of public policy. Recent supply-and-demand studies (Willer et al., 1991) may provide useful information on care arrangements, but they shed little new light on supply-and-demand issues. The discussion of demand and supply in the previous pages should suggest an extensive list of useful research topics, including estimation of the responsiveness of the two types of demand for child care to prices and income, the responsiveness of choice among care arrangements to relative prices, and the responsiveness of labor supply to child care prices. Information on the beliefs, attitudes, and values of purchasers and providers that included family home day care would be extremely valuable. The data problem is especially serious for family home day care because its informal and "underground" nature makes the collection of data difficult. Estimates of the supply-and-demand relationships that determine the quantity, quality, and price of family home day care based on representative samples would be a significant advance.

REFERENCES

American Association of School Administrators. (1988). *Child care and the public schools: A survey of school districts' programs, needs, and administrators' opinions on key issues.* Arlington, VA: Author.

Barnett, W. S. (1985). Benefit-cost analysis of the Perry preschool program and its policy implications. *Educational Evaluation and Policy Analysis, 7*(4), 333–42.

Barnett, W. S. (In press). Benefits of compensatory preschool education. *Journal of Human Resources.*

Becker, G. S. (1981). *A treatise on the family.* Cambridge, MA: Harvard University Press.

Becker, G. S., & Murphy, K. M. (1988, April). The family and the state. *Journal of Law & Economics, 31,* 1–18.

Besharov, D. J., & Tramontozzi, P. N. (1989). Federal child care assistance: A growing middle-class entitlement. *Journal of Policy Analysis and Management, 8*(2), 313–18.

Blau, D. M., & Robins, P. K. (1988, August). Child-care costs and family labor supply. *Review of Economics and Statistics, 70,* 374–81.

Blau, D. M., & Robins, P. K. (1989, May). Fertility, employment, and child-care centers. *Demography, 26*(2), 287–99.

Clarke-Stewart, K. A. (1991). A home is not a school: The effects of child care on children's development. *Journal of Social Issues, 47*(2), 105–24.

Culkin, M., Helburn, S. W., & Morris, J. R. (1990). Current price versus full cost:

An economic perspective. In B. Willer (Ed.), *Reaching the full cost of quality in early childhood programs*. Washington, DC: National Association for the Education of Young Children.

Fuchs, V. R. (1989). Women's quest for economic equality. *Journal of Economic Perspectives, 3*(1), 25–41.

Fullerton, H. N., Jr. (1987, September). Labor force projections: 1986 to 2000. *Monthly Labor Review, 110*(9), 19–29.

Galinsky, E., & Friedman, D. (1986). *Investing in quality childcare*. A report for AT&T.

Gustafsson, S., & Stafford, F. (1988). *Day care subsidies and labor supply in Sweden*. Working paper, Arbetslivcentrum, Stockholm.

Hansmann, H. (1987). Economic theories of nonprofit organizations. In W. Powell (Ed.), *The nonprofit sector: A research handbook*. New Haven, CT: Yale University Press.

Hofferth, S. L. (1989, July). Public policy report. What is the demand for and supply of child care in the United States? *Young Children, 44*(5), 28–33.

Hunt, J. G., & Hunt, L. L. (1987). Male resistance to role symmetry in dual-earner households: Three alternative explanations (pp. 192–203). In N. Gerstel and H. E. Gross (Eds.), *Families and work*. Philadelphia: Temple University Press.

Juster, F. T., & Courant, P. N. (1986). Integrating stocks and flows in quality of life research. In F. M. Andrews (Ed.), *Research on the quality of life* (pp. 147–70). Ann Arbor: ISR, University of Michigan.

Kahn, A., & Kamerman, S. (1987). *Child care: Facing the choices*. Dover, MA: Auburn House.

Kisker, E., Hofferth, S. L., Phillips, D., & Farquhar, E. (1991). *A profile of child care settings: Early education and care in 1990*. Washington, DC: U.S. Government Printing Office.

Leibowitz, A. L., Waite, J., & Witsberger, C. (1988). Child care for preschoolers: Differences by child's age. *Demography, 25*, 205–20.

Manser, M., & Brown, M. (1980, February). Marriage and household decision-making: A bargaining analysis. *International Economic Review, 21*, 31–44.

Marshall, A. (1920, 1982). *Principles of economics*. London: MacMillan.

McElroy, M. B., & Horney, M. J. (1981, June). Nash-bargained household decisions: Toward a generalization of the theory of demand. *International Economic Review, 22*, 333–49.

Nelson, M. K. (1988). Providing family day care: An analysis of home-based work. *Social Problems, 35*(1), 78–94.

Nelson, M. K. (1990). Mothering others' children: The experiences of family day-care providers. In J. O'Barr, D. Pope & M. Wyer (Eds.), *Ties that bind* (pp. 129–48). Chicago and London: University of Chicago Press.

Osborn, A. F., & Milbank, J. E. (1987). *The effects of early education: A report from the Child Health and Education Study*. Oxford: Oxford University Press.

Parsons, D. O., & Goldin, C. (1989, October). Parental altruism and self-interest: Child labor among late nineteenth-century American families. *Economic Inquiry, 27*, 637–59.

Presser, H. B. (1989a). Can we make time for children? The economy, work schedules, and child care. *Demography, 26*(4), 523–43.

Presser, H. B. (1989b). Some economic complexities of child care provided by grandmothers. *Journal of Marriage and the Family, 51,* 581–91.

Reisman, B., Moore, A. J., & Fitzgerald, K. (1988). *Child care: The bottom line.* New York: Child Care Action Campaign.

Robins, P. K., & Spiegelman, R. G. (1978, January). An econometric model of the demand for child care. *Economic Inquiry, 16,* 83–94.

Rose-Ackerman, S. (1986). Altruistic nonprofit firms in competitive markets: The case of day-care centers in the United States. *Journal of Consumer Policy, 9,* 304.

Shank, S. E. (1988, March). Women and the labor market: The link grows stronger. *Monthly Labor Review, 111*(3), 3–8.

Singer, J. D., Fosburg, S., Goodson, B. D., & Smith, J. W. (1980). *National day care home study: Research report (final report, vol. II).* Cambridge, MA: Abt Associates.

Smith, J. P., & Ward, M. (1985, January). Time series growth in the female labor force. *Journal of Labor Economics, 3*(1), 59–90.

Smith, J. P., & Ward, M. (1989). Women in the labor market and in the family. *Journal of Economic Perspectives, 3*(1), 9–23.

Stewart, A. C. (1990). *Child day care.* Congressional Research Service Issue Brief, 4 December 1990. Washington, DC: Library of Congress.

U.S. General Accounting Office. (1989, October). Briefing Report, Subcommittee on Human Resources, Committee on Education and Labor, House of Representatives. Child Care. Government funding sources, coordination, and service availability.

Wash, D. P., & Brand, L. E. (1990, December). Child day care services: An industry at a crossroads. *Monthly Labor Review, 113*(12), 17–24.

Weiner, S. (1978). The child care market in Seattle and Denver. In P. K. Robins and S. Weiner (Eds.), *Child care and public policy* (pp. 43–85). Lexington, MA: Lexington Books, D. C. Heath and Company.

Willer, B. (1987). *The growing crisis in child care: Quality, compensation, and affordability in early childhood programs.* Washington, DC: National Association for the Education of Young Children.

Willer, B. (1991). 101st Congress: The children's congress. *Young Children, 46*(2), 78–80.

Willer, B., Hofferth, S. L., Kisker, E. E., Divine-Hawkins, P., Farquhar, E., & Glantz, F. B. (1991). *The demand and supply of child care in 1990.* Washington, DC: National Association for the Education of Young Children.

Zaslow, M. J. (1991). Variation in child care quality and its implications for children. *Journal of Social Issues, 47*(2), 125–38.

Zill, N. (1988). *Basic facts about the use of child care and preschool services by families in the U.S.* Washington, DC: Child Trends.

CHAPTER 6

Research Perspectives on Family Day Care

June Pollard
Jan Lockwood Fischer

Research on family day care in North America reflects the difficulty in a liberal democracy of bringing into public focus an activity that is caught between the private realm of family homes on the one hand, and the public realm of government-funded, regulated child care on the other. Virtually all Canadian and U.S. research reports begin with a statement of the dearth of research and the enormous complexity of what is being studied.

A review of the research reveals several separate streams, each representing different disciplines and bringing to the subject different questions, methodologies, funding sources, and policy recommendations. Historically, each discipline has focused on different aspects of the triad forming the essential constituents of family day care—parent, caregiver, and child—and has characterized the interaction of the triad differently.

There is a trend in current research toward interdisciplinary integration of questions, methodologies, and resources (financial, organizational, and human). However, in order to highlight the different perspectives, this chapter examines the streams separately. The disciplines that have been most represented in the literature are (1) those that relate directly to public policy—economics and demography, (2) sociology and its social work or family studies application, and (3) developmental psychology and its early childhood education or family studies application.

The following sections briefly explore each of these three streams of research but dedicate a disproportionate amount of space to those aspects of the literature that have received relatively less attention in other chapters in this volume or in other dedicated reviews of the literature (Wattenberg, 1980; Esbensen, 1985; Pence, 1985; Deller, 1988; Fischer, 1989; Kontos, 1992). To this end, economics, demography, and public policy as reviewed here have a greater Canadian than U.S. emphasis; the sociology stream focuses on critical issues related to providers and parents; and the child development section provides a brief overview of themes and issues that arise in the family day care literature over time.

ECONOMICS, DEMOGRAPHY, AND PUBLIC POLICY

The supply-and-demand studies informing North American public policy on child care make use of demographic resources and an economic perspective. G. Cleveland, a Canadian economist, makes the following statement regarding the economist's perspective on child care:

> Economists see child care through [the following] set of economic research lenses. The behaviour of child care users or potential child care users is summarized in the demand for child care services. The actions of day care centres, sitters, relatives, even fathers and mothers who provide care is viewed as the supply of services to the market. Demand and supply are each influenced by a host of distinct economic factors; the result of their interaction is the price paid by the consumer of child care and the decisions of families to use particular types of care. . . . interventionist child care policy is necessary when these markets, for one reason or another, are not working well. (Cleveland, 1991)

Supply-and-demand studies related to family day care include the following:

1. Those that ask questions about the demand for child care, including studies of demographic trends related to population and parental participation in the labor force, parental preferences for forms of care, utilization rates of different forms of care, parental satisfaction with current forms of care, and parental satisfaction with availability of care.
2. Those that ask questions about the supply of child care, such as the availability of out-of-home care; job satisfaction and turnover rates of caregivers; and the occupational status of caregivers.
3. Those that ask questions about the effectiveness of government interventions to enable the child care market to function to the satisfaction of providers and users, including studies of the effectiveness of

licensing and registration and the effectiveness of agencies as supply-demand linkages.

These questions arise within a particular political context when child care is seen primarily as a responsibility of the civil society (the family, the marketplace, or voluntary organizations) rather than the state. The values upheld in child care debates are the liberal ideals of pluralism, diversity, and choice.[1] In countries where governments have designated child care as a state responsibility, there are no cited economic studies of supply and demand in child care.[2] In those countries demographic research is used to predict future needs for the government, as it is in the school systems in North America. In the United States, Canada, and the United Kingdom,[3] on the other hand, supply-and-demand studies constitute the majority of funded research on child day care.

In both Canada and the United States the majority of research from the psychology and medical perspectives is limited to licensed family day care, a small fraction of all home-based child care. The supply-demand perspective has provided us with a broader picture of the majority of home-based child care, which includes unlicensed and informal family day care and relative care.

The Canadian studies being reviewed have been selected to demonstrate the range of municipal, provincial, and national studies carried out in relation to family day care. In the United States, because of the large quantity of studies conducted at the municipal, county, and state levels as well as at the national level, we have reviewed only the national studies. The ERIC data base on family day care provides an extensive listing of the regional studies in the United States.

The first published studies in Canada came out of a concern at the municipal level regarding the supply of care in the informal sector: its form, availability, and parental satisfaction. A metropolitan Toronto project (Johnson, 1976) used structured interviews and a two-stage stratified cluster sampling technique to study 2,567 households with children under age seven. The research was funded by three government levels and was undertaken by an advocacy group and the Social Planning Council of Toronto. Based on the findings regarding parental satisfaction with their informal care arrangements, the authors concluded that there was a need for more full-time publicly funded child care centers in metropolitan Toronto.

A response in support of informal care arrangements came out of a provincial government study carried out by a private consultant group (Longwoods Research Group, 1982). This study selected 101 providers and 73 users in five cities of varied sizes in Ontario. Focus groups were used and an individual questionnaire administered. Although the study found that the demand was greater than the supply, the report was generally very positive about parental and provider satisfaction with the care provided. It suggested that education programs for both users and caregivers would enhance satisfaction.

In 1984, the Social Planning Council and Child Care Association of Winnipeg, Manitoba, also studied the general state of supply and demand of child care in the city of Winnipeg. Funded by an employment-stimulus program of the federal government, they carried out telephone interviews with 2,202 parents selected through a disproportional stratified random sampling procedure. The study conclude that "there is an imbalance between the supply of and demand for child care arrangements of an adequate quality and price" (Stevens, 1984, p. 106).

Their more specific analysis of the imbalance suggested that:

1. There was a need to increase the overall supply of child care arrangements to respond to the demand.
2. There was a need to improve the quality of the existing supply of private- and public-market child care, especially in unlicensed care; this also reflected a preference on the part of parents for licensed care.
3. Parents did not believe that licensed care in centers should be the only arrangement available; they perceived relative care as providing good quality care and licensed family day care as giving the best quality for infant and after-school care.
4. There was a need for information and referral services.
5. There was a need for more affordable spaces and a need for more government funding.

The authors of the report discuss two solutions from an economic point of view—increasing the supply or reducing the demand—and spell out the policy options. These options were seen as reflecting values and beliefs as they dealt with four issues: whether to regulate and license; how to subsidize; who to subsidize; and what types of care arrangements should be covered by subsidies. The authors' economic perspective led them to the following conclusion:

> Our analysis has convinced us that supplementary initiatives by governments are required to redress the current imbalance between the continuing demand for adequate and affordable child care and the inadequate supply. Our examination of the alternatives convinces us that the optimal solution will be that which assures parents' ability to acquire care of adequate quality at the least cost to society. It is in finding the best trade-

off between equity, quality and efficiency that the optimal solution will be found. (Stevens, 1984, pp. 119–20)

The above studies focused on the supply and demand of child care in urban centres. Attempts to study the situation in rural areas were carried out by the Ontario provincial government in 1987 (Abramovitch, 1987) and by Brophy, Penfold, Semple, Straby & Sugarman (1988). These studies emphasized the preference among parents in small towns and rural areas for family day care over center care and the need for information and referral services.

All of the studies cited above suggest some form of government intervention. Other studies have evaluated the effectiveness of various forms of government intervention. Two studies looked at licensed agencies in Quebec (Bouchard, 1982) and in Ontario (Norpark, 1988). (See Chapter 12 of this volume for a description of the nature of agencies in Canada.) Both studies found that the agencies were effective in recruiting, supporting, and training family day care providers; as a result they were perceived as providing satisfactory child care to parents and a satisfactory work context for providers. In the Norpark study, concern was expressed about the difficulties that agencies in Ontario had in meeting the original mandate to provide care for infants and toddlers, during extended hours, and in rural areas. There was also concern about their ability to continue to attract providers.

Two other studies evaluated programs for supporting unlicensed care. Calzavara (1983) evaluated an informal care registry, and Doherty Social Planning Consultants (1987) carried out a provincial government study of the provincewide initiative to provide supports for informal care. Both of these studies validated the effectiveness of the supports for the parents and informal caregivers who were using the various services of the resource centers (e.g., information and referral, toy lending libraries, parent relief, parent and caregiver drop-in programs). In Doherty's conclusions, however, it was clear that a very small percentage of all informal caregivers were using the supports and that the centers had difficulty attracting informal caregivers. The two reasons suggested for the difficulty were that caregivers feared being publicly accountable for their income from family day care and that they had difficulty organizing the children in their care to get them to center programs.

It has become increasingly clear that all these studies provide only a fraction of the supply-and-demand information needed to give a nationwide picture or to lead to a Canadian national policy. A group of academics from major universities in Canada called the National Child Care Research Network has developed an interdisciplinary, ecological framework to study national supply-and-demand data. In a preliminary study the network (Lero, Pence, Brockman, Charlesworth, Canning, Esbensen, Morrison & Goelman, 1985) used parent interviews in 14 sites across Canada to develop their framework and to provide case studies of 336 families regarding their child care needs and preferences. This expanded into the Canadian National Child Care Study (Lero, Pence, Goelman & Brockman, 1988; Chapter 4, this volume) funded by the Canadian government, which used Statistics Canada data-collection resources and extensive interviews throughout the country to respond to the following questions:

1. What are Canadian families' child care needs, use patterns, and parental preferences and concerns about child care options?
2. What are the relationships between family, work, and child care variables in the broader context of economic, geographic, and sociopolitical factors that impinge on those relationships from both a policy and a theoretical perspective?

This second question goes beyond the purely economic supply-and-demand perspective and considers child care as offering support to families in a continuum that includes short- and long-term care, care by relatives and neighbors, family day care, and center-based care.

In the United States the early family day care studies (Ruderman, 1967; Willner, 1969; Keyserling, 1972) were critical of unregulated family day care and recommended more professionalized, universally accessible center-based child care because of parental preference, quality factors, and supply-demand imbalance. These studies were similar to the Johnson study in Ontario (1976) and the Jackson and Jackson study of illegal childminding in the United Kingdom (1979). Other studies in response (Bane, Lein, O'Donnell, Stueve & Wells, 1979) suggested that families, the market economy, and the informal exchange system were working well to provide child care services. The debate between these two positions culminated in a four-year national study of family day care (Divine-Hawkins, 1980; Fosburg, 1981), which concluded that generally the natural family day care system was working well but could use some improvement through expansion and support to compensate for the decrease in available relative care. The commitment to a "natural" system, including family and the marketplace with minimum government intervention, is reflected in subsequent supply-and-demand research and is represented in a recent special issue of the *Journal of Social Issues* on child care policy research (Hofferth & Phillips, 1991).

Discussion of the Economic Perspective

The supply-and-demand studies represent the triad of parent, caregiver, and child as separate self-interest groups with conflicting interests that require balancing. The parent needs to get the best service for the least money, the caregiver needs to make as much money as possible while serving the client, and the child needs to receive the best quality care possible. The major focus of the economic studies is the parent as consumer with certain needs to be fulfilled; the caregiver is seen in relation to that need, and the child is barely visible.

The methodology employed in economics supply-demand research is predominantly the survey, including the use of structured interviews or questionnaires, with sample sizes representing as large a body as the related public policy is intended to serve.

The economic perspective focuses on questions of accessibility, availability, and affordability. As larger and more sophisticated samples have been collected and analyzed, it has become increasingly clear that the supply-and-demand studies alone leave unanswered questions:

1. What is *quality* care? Supply-and-demand studies do not define quality other than as it is reflected by an expression of parental preference. If quality is to relate to the experience of children and their development, it is necessary to integrate into this perspective the framework of developmental psychology.

2. How can the crisis in child care quality and quantity be solved? Increasingly the conclusion of the economic studies is that a crisis related to both quality and quantity exists, especially in large urban centers. They do not, in themselves, provide us with answers about how to solve this crisis. We need to understand the role of political ideology in framing the solution to the crisis needs. The best way to understand this is through comparative studies that let us see the differential effects of ideologies on child care policy in jurisdictions with different political ideologies in power.

3. What do the questions used in the large surveys and questionnaires mean in the daily lives of parents and providers, and how does this vary depending on class, gender, race, and ethnicity? We need to have an understanding of those lives that cannot come from quantifying and objectifying people in surveys. Sociology and especially the feminist studies in sociology are beginning to provide us with this perspective.

4. How can the needs of parents, children, and caregivers be met? Although the picture of parents, children, and caregivers as having conflicting interests may reflect the reality in a situation of scarce resources, it does not give an accurate picture of the effort that caregivers and parents make to work together to provide caring environments for children or the acknowledgment that all parts of the

triad must have their needs met in order for any one part to do so. It also does not provide us with a vision of how they might do so.

SOCIOLOGY

When researchers have focused on child care from a sociological perspective, their questions have tended to relate to family structures and systems, community structures and systems, work-family conflicts, division of labor in the home, professional and occupational roles, gender, race, and class as they affect providers and parents. Some of the studies on family day care have examined how the institution of family day care has arisen out of the natural support networks of relatives and neighbors. Others have been critical of the reliance on home-based child care for meeting the country's child care needs. The feminist perspective has seen home-based child care as an exploitation of women's roles as mothers; the socialist perspective has seen home-based child care as an exploitation of caregivers as marginalized labor. The question of whether family day care providers are an extension of the family (private domain) or part of the labor force (public domain) becomes central in this research perspective.

The positive extension of the family perspective has its roots in the early work of A. Emlen and colleagues (1971) in the United States. Emlen's position is well described in a quote by Wattenberg:

> Advocates (of family day care) say that there is still no model for the rearing of children that is superior to a caring family, and that the family day care system comes as close as possible to replicating that environment. Emlen, who did much to create visibility for family day care, expresses this point of view:
>
> > "Family day care is a creative social achievement for both the caregiver and care user. It is an adaptation of family life for the working mothers. It is a way of acquiring an extended 'family within the neighbourhood' with kith, though not with kin, while for the caregiver it involves a modest and manageable expansion and modification of family life. Family day care is workable because for neither party does it require radical departures from ordinary behavior, experience, talents or motivations." (Wattenberg, 1977, p. 212, quoting Emlen, 1972)

Relating to this vision of the private nurturing world of the family and the neighborhood, researchers have examined the natural family day care system, asking what the characteristics and roles of providers are (Peters, 1972; Wattenberg, 1977; Silver & Greenspan, 1980; Wandersman, 1981; Pepper & Stuart, 1983, 1985; Stith & Davis, 1984; Innes & Innes, 1984; Washburn & Washburn, 1985; Leavitt, 1986, in progress; Eheart & Leavitt, 1986, 1989; Cox & Richarz, 1987; Kontos, 1989; Kontos & Riessen, under review), what the relationship is between parents and providers (Hughes, 1985; Pence & Goelman, 1987a, 1987b; Leavitt, 1986; Bollin, 1991), and what the networks are that link parents and providers (Powell & Eisenstadt, 1983; Powell, 1987; Kyle, 1991).

The ideal private-world family day care provider as described by Hasegawa (1972) is a mother substitute in a home away from home, providing warmth, stability, a place where children can be themselves, and a belief in the value of her mothering role. Early research in Canada and the United States gives some support to this picture. Peters (1972) refers to stable and warm child-centered homes with happy caregivers in his study; Pepper and Stuart (1983, 1985, 1988) describe their caregivers as warm, caring, responsible, consistent, careful, organized, nurturant, and stable (Pepper & Stuart 1983, 1985; Stuart & Pepper, 1988).

Then a different picture of a mix of public and private roles begins to emerge. Wattenberg (1977) differentiates providers into traditional warm, loving women providers (private role) and modernized career providers (public role). Wandersman (1981) distinguishes between substitute mothers (private) and teachers of mini-centers (public). Innes and Innes (1984) describe three social roles of providers: mothers and grandmothers (private) and teachers (public). Washburn and Washburn (1985) use role descriptions that include two clear public roles—nursery school teacher and businesswoman—and two roles that tend to be mixes of private and public—foster mother and custodian.

As the visibility of family day care providers in the public world increases, the research becomes more critical of them. Stith and Davis (1984) found that compared with mothers, providers gave less social stimulation and were less responsive. Silver and Greenspan (1980) and Pepper and Stuart (1985) reported some characteristics of rigidity, inflexibility, and lack of intellectual curiosity in the warm, nurturing providers. Eheart and Leavitt (1986) suggested that although the intention of their providers was to provide warm, sensitive, and responsible mothering, "the loving, attentive, play-filled environment that providers intended to create for children in their care was rarely realized." They speculated that "because providers' expectations of their emotional relationship to the children in their care is based on an understanding of a mother's relationship to her own child, discrepancies arise between their intended and felt emotions." (Eheart & Leavitt, 1986, p. 157)

The mothering, nurturing role itself is then seen as a deterrent to quality care for children, and the career-minded, professional, trained, and regulated provider role is associated with higher-quality care for children (Wandersman, 1981; Eheart & Leavitt, 1986; Cox & Richarz, 1987; Kontos & Riessen, under review; Leavitt, in progress).

The ideal "natural" relationship between providers and parents as described by Hasegawa (1972) was one of cooperation, friendship, and confidence. Although Hughes (1985) and Pence and Goelman (1987a, 1987b) reported some aspects of this friendly, help-giving quality in provider-parent relationships, researchers have also reported tension, hostility, and negative judgmental attitudes (Leavitt, 1986; Pence & Goelman, 1987b; Nelson, 1989). Leavitt (1986) suggests a number of reasons for the poor communication, collaboration, and coordination she found. Failures by providers included their negative feelings about parents, their lack of training to work with parents, their inability to be articulate about the goals of their caregiving, and their own satisfaction with their expertise as mothers. Parents' failures were seen as resulting from their inappropriate blind trust in the providers and their lack of affordable alternative choices. A further source of failure in the parent-provider partnership was seen as related to the private nature of the home setting, where parents could be seen and could see themselves as intruders.

Another aspect of the ideal image of family day care is to see it as an extension of the natural neighborhood child care support networks that are available to families. Providers are neighbors who help out with caregiving. However, the breakdown of these networks in large urban communities has been documented (Powell & Eisenstadt, 1983; Powell, 1987). Kyle (1991), using the Ontario data from the National Child Care Study, found that parents turned to relatives more often than friends for unexpected long-term child care and that the parents who turned to neighbors for child care tended to have higher incomes and more education and lived in more stable neighborhoods, or rural areas and small towns. Pence and Goelman (1987b) found that most of the providers and parents in their study were strangers at the beginning of the caregiving arrangement.

Family day care providers appear to be suspended in judgment between the public world with its ideology of professional caregiving and the private world with its ideology of motherhood.

Rapp and Lloyd (1989) are critical of the "home as haven" ideology, which they found to be a belief of parents who choose family day care. This belief sees the home as:

> the spiritual and physical shelter from the competition and exploitation in
> a capitalist society, a training ground for the young and a haven in a

heartless world. . . . The central concept is that the mother is the only
individual who can adequately provide a refuge for her family and she
must accomplish this task alone. (Rapp & Lloyd, 1989, p. 427)

Nelson (1990) provides a more profound criticism of the disempowerment of both providers and mothers in the parent-provider relationship as it
currently functions in North America. On the basis of in-depth interviews
with providers and mothers, she suggests that both feel powerless. Providers
feel "dependent on the willingness of parents to follow their rules," have
"few mechanisms to ensure compliance," are "vulnerable to complaints
lodged with state officials," feel obliged to offer care to "disruptive and
difficult" children because of the need of mothers for childcare, and feel
"captive in their own homes." Parents feel "extreme dependence" on the
providers because of the difficulty in finding care, feel vulnerable to the
criticisms of providers, "resent having to comply with rules that do not meet
their needs," and "question whether they have enough information to evaluate the situation" (p. 29):

> In fact, neither side has much power. Child care is hard to find. And
> mothers are tied directly to the requirements of wage labor and the double
> burden. Providers are tied less directly, but no less firmly, to the formal
> economy and, perhaps even more securely, to the demands of the domes-
> tic domain. The abuses within the relationship are thus the result of each
> person's attempt to make the best of an unmanageable situation. In the
> absence of significant social change—in the resources available for, and
> respect accorded to, childcare; in the structure of waged work; in the
> domestic division of labor—these women unwittingly, but necessarily,
> disempower each other. (p. 29)

Discussion of the Sociological Perspective

These studies tend to be based in university research projects, to have
small samples, and to use unstructured or semistructured interviews. The
focus is on either the caregiver or the parent and the relationship between
them.

From this perspective we get the clearest picture of a set of conflicting
values about motherhood, caring, and families. What we believe to be good
about families is good about family day care; what we find destructive in
families is destructive in family day care. Current feminist discussion, as it
struggles with the relationship between women's oppression and mothering
roles, can be helpful in exploring these issues. However, what is missing in

that perspective on family day care to date is a concern about the needs of children.

PSYCHOLOGY AND EARLY CHILDHOOD EDUCATION

Family day care research from the perspective of developmental psychology has investigated the effects of out-of-home care on children's social, emotional, cognitive, language, and physical development. The application of this research to early childhood education has sparked additional inquiries about what constitutes quality care. During the past three decades, family day care research methodology has evolved to complement the questions that were being asked by psychologists and educators. Early studies often focused on the differential effects of home-based care and center care on children's development; later studies have tended to examine the separate and combined effects of family life and child care experiences on the development of children. Some of the issues and trends that have emerged during these two broad periods of family day care research are briefly examined in this section.

Initial inquiries about the effects of nonmaternal child care on children's development led to comparisons of various forms of care (see Ainsworth, Andry, Harlow, Lebovici, Mead, Prugh & Wootton, 1966; Baer, 1954; Bowlby, 1951). Relatively simple designs were used during the mid-1960s and 1970s to determine which type of care (at home with mother, own home with sitter, family day care, or center care) was "best" for young children. For example, Howes and Rubenstein (1978a, 1978b) looked at indicators of social development among 40 toddlers in family day care and center care. They reported that differences in types of care did not seem to influence the frequency and complexity of peer interactions among toddlers. They also found no difference in adult facilitative and responsive caretaking and no difference in toddler affect and dependence between family day care and center care. Similarly, Portnoy and Simmons (1978) found no differences in children's attachment patterns based on form of care among 35 preschoolers who had experienced home care, family day care, and center care during their first three years. Findings in this first period of research were fairly consistent; they indicated that out-of-home care was not usually or necessarily harmful to children's development and that day care may provide an enriched environment for some children (Belsky, 1984; Clarke-Stewart, 1982; Fosburg, 1981; Pence, 1983). Conflicting interpretations of the literature from this period and later studies have resulted in an ongoing debate about the effects of early care on children's maternal attachment and their subsequent socioemotional development and social competence (see Belsky, 1986, 1987, 1988; Clarke-Stewart, 1988, 1989; Phillips, McCartney, Scarr & Howes, 1987; Richters & Zahn-Waxler, 1988).

Additional issues began to emerge from the findings of the early studies. Howes and Rubenstein (1978b) and others suggested that variation within child day care settings may provide more substantial information about caregiving quality than the type of child day care employed. Attention shifted abruptly during the late 1970s to features within family day care settings that were thought to influence the quality of care. At that time, Steinberg and Green (1979) suggested looking beyond comparisons of settings to examine the mediating effects of parents on children in various forms of care. They advocated a perspective that would acknowledge possible interactions among the parents, children, and caregivers. Consistent with this perspective, Bronfenbrenner (1979) articulated an ecological framework for understanding how children's development is influenced by their experiences in care. He called for research designs that would reflect the overlapping and interactive ecosystems in which children develop, based on this interpretation of systems theory (Lewin, 1936). Bronfenbrenner encouraged researchers to expand the narrow range of samples and settings used during the first period of family day care research so that they could investigate real-life child care arrangements. This approach marked the beginning of a new era of family day care research, which includes studies conducted during the 1980s and early 1990s.

During this second period, researchers have addressed questions about what constitutes quality care and about the interactive effects of parents, caregivers, and children with respect to their experiences in family day care. After the development of preliminary definitions and measures of the structural, contextual, dynamic, and global indicators of quality (Phillips et al., 1987), researchers have reported that the overall quality of family day care is low in North America as it is currently organized (Fischer, 1989; Kontos, 1989; Eheart & Leavitt, 1987), that parent and caregiver variables together help determine caregiving quality (Pence, 1983), and that the quality of care affects children's development in ways that are not yet entirely clear (Howes, 1990). Current work centers on efforts to find out how quality of care mediates children's experiences, which in turn influence their development.

Researchers continue to search for connections among children, families, and child care (Kontos, 1992). Pence and Goelman (1987a, 1987b), for example, have taken a multimethodological approach in their Canadian research to discern the influence of caregiver attitudes, practices, and regulable characteristics, as well as parents' preferences and perceptions, on the quality of care relative to children's development. Kontos (1992) has attempted to find out which specific combination of family and child care factors best predicts which aspect of a child's development.

Researchers have also begun to look for consistency and clarity in the interpretations that parents, caregivers, and researchers assign children's experiences in care. For example, Eheart and Leavitt (1989) conducted extensive observations of six day care homes in central Illinois. Using phenomenological methods based on interpretive interactionism, the authors found that providers did not consistently provide a loving, attentive, play-filled environment, although they intended to. Eheart and Leavitt suggest that discrepancies between the quality of intended and observed care may be due to differences in interpretations that providers and researchers have for various words, phrases, and behaviors. They have noted that although a caregiver may consider facilitating children's play to be one of her major responsibilities, she may in fact interpret this as letting the children "just kinda run around and do what they want" (Eheart & Leavitt, 1989, p. 153). She may view play as merely the way children keep busy and entertained, and her role as one that requires little planning and intervention except, perhaps, for resolving conflicts. Eheart and Leavitt contrast this interpretation with that of a child development researcher or professional who defines play as the means by which children learn and develop. Facilitating play, to them, means "creating an environment that encourages child-initiated and child-directed activities appropriate to children's development and interests. The professional caregiver extends children's play by offering appropriate help, materials, or comments" (Eheart & Leavitt, 1989, p. 156). The authors suggest that meanings that researchers assign to children's experiences in care may differ from those constructed by the child, parent, and caregiver.

Methodology within the research arena of psychology and early childhood education has become increasingly rigorous. Simple descriptions and comparisons have been supplemented with sophisticated analyses of the separate, cumulative, and interactive effects of variables affecting children in family day care. Amid an increasing complexity of methods, there is a movement also to simplify the *process* of research by seeking better and more consistent definitions, cleaner measures, and a deeper understanding of the individuals who participate in family day care. What began as an inquiry into environmental effects on the mental health and development of individual children has become a quest for research tools and methods that are sensitive to the individual *and* normative development of children throughout North America. The ecological approach introduced in the late 1970s has moved researchers out of the lab and into children's everyday settings, and requires that they acknowledge and investigate the many systems within which children are reared (Bronfenbrenner, 1979).

To date, the scope of family day care research conducted by psychologists and educators has been essentially limited to the microsystems and mesosystems of children in care. Contemporary research designs seldom include exosystem issues (which are differentially addressed by sociologists and economists). Yet, not one of these disciplines offers a research perspective broad enough to examine ideological assumptions and incongruities that affect the care and development of children within a macrosystem.

Nearly all the studies referenced in this section were conducted under the auspices of universities by researchers within the departments of developmental psychology, child development, and education. University-related grants were the most commonly reported funding source, followed by private foundation grants and national government grants. A considerable time lag exists between research and the dissemination of results, as articles follow a lengthy path to publication, often being presented at national conferences or published in ERIC before reaching a journal audience. Most of the reports referenced here have been peer-reviewed and published in professional journals.

DIRECTIONS FOR FUTURE RESEARCH

The above discussion suggests that each discipline alone fails to adequately represent the essential interactive integrity of the parent-child-caregiver triad. Ideally these three are not economic self-interest groups with conflicting goals; caregivers are not just disempowered women judged by researchers and policymakers on dimensions of motherhood and professionalism in relation to children whose development is being jeopardized by their failures. We need to develop a vision of what a healthy triad looks like: parents who are comfortable with the balance of work and family responsibilities; caregivers who are respected and valued for their work; children who receive good care and education from loving, empowered adults. Our research and policy work needs to combine the efforts of economics and public policy, sociology, and psychology to find ways to identify, create, and support that triad.

Further feminist analyses related to caring and oppression of women could be brought to bear specifically on family day care policies and practices.

A critical missing piece in the research studies on family day care is the political, ideological dimension. A study by Deller (1988) for the Ontario Ministry of Community and Social Services on family day care policies and practices in 16 countries provides a glimpse of the extent to which political ideology affects policies in different countries. More comparative analysis both internationally and within jurisdiction in North America would enable us to become clearer about our conflicting values related to family day care and would give helpful directions for policy.

NOTES

1. See Hofferth and Phillips (1991) for a review of policy research in the United States from an economic perspective related to supply and demand.

2. See Broberg (1989) for a review of research on child care in Sweden and Melhuish and Moss (1991) for a review of research in France and East Germany.

3. See Moss (1987) for a review of childminding research in the United Kingdom.

REFERENCES

Abramovitch, R. (1987). *Rural child care*. Toronto: Ontario Ministry of Community and Social Services.

Ainsworth, M. D., Andry, R. G., Harlow, R. G., Lebovici, S., Mead, M., Prugh, D. G., & Wootton, B. (1966). *Deprivation of maternal care*. New York: Schocken Books.

Baer, M. (1954). Women workers and home responsibilities. *International Labor Review, 69*, 338–55.

Bane, M. J., Lein, L., O'Donnell, L., Stueve, C. A., & Wells, B. (1979). Child-care arrangements of working parents. *Monthly Labor Review,* pp. 50–56.

Belsky, J. (1984). Two waves of day care research: Developmental effects and conditions of quality. In R. C. Ainslie (Ed.), *The child and the day care setting* (pp. 1–34). New York: Praeger.

Belsky, J. (1986). Infant day care: A cause for concern? In *Zero to Three*. Washington, DC: Bulletin of the National Centre for Clinical Infant Programs, 7(1), 1–7.

Belsky, J. (1987). Risks remain. In *Zero to Three*. Washington, DC: Bulletin of the National Centre for Clinical Infant Programs, 7(3), 22–24.

Belsky, J. (1988). The "effects" of infant day care reconsidered. *Early Childhood Research Quarterly, 3*(3), 235–72.

Benson, C. (1985). *Who cares for kids?: A report on child care providers*. Washington, DC: National Commission on Working Women. (ERIC Doc. No. ED 271 207).

Blank, H., & Wilkins, A. (1985). *Child care: Whose priority?* Washington, DC: Children's Defense Fund.

Bollin, G. G. K. (1991). *Family day care quality and parental satisfaction*. (ERIC Doc. No. ED 330 477).

Bouchard, S. (1982). *Gardez chez soi les enfants des autres: Profile des reconnues par les agencies de service de garde en milieu familiale au Quebec en 1982*. Government du Quebec, Office des services de garde a l'enfance.

Bowlby, J. (1951). *Maternal care and mental health*. Geneva: World Health Organization.

Broberg, A. (1989). *Child care and early development*. Goteborg: University of Goteberg.

Bronfenbrenner, U. (1979). *The ecology of human development*. Cambridge, MA: Harvard University Press.

Brophy, K., Penfold, G., Semple, S., Straby, R., & Sugarman, R. (1988). Who's looking after our children: A study of child care needs in rural Ontario. *The Canadian Journal of Research in Early Childhood Education, 2*(2), 141–48.

Calzavara, L. (1983). *Day care registry: An evaluation of the East York Neighborhood Information Center: Day care registry project*. Toronto: Center for Urban and Community Studies.

Child Development Associate National Credentialing Program. (1985). *Family day care providers: Child development associate assessment system and competency standards*. Washington, DC: Author.

Clarke-Stewart, A. (1982). *Daycare*. Cambridge, MA: Harvard University Press.

Clarke-Stewart, A. (1988). "The 'effects' of infant day care reconsidered" reconsidered: Risks for parents, children and researchers. *Early Childhood Research Quarterly, 3*(3), 293–318.

Clarke-Stewart, A. (1989). Infant day care: Maligned or malignant? *American Psychologist, 44*(2), 266–73.

Cleveland, G. (1991). *Economics and child care policy*. Paper presented at the research symposium "Child care policy: What can research tell us?" Learned Societies, Queen's University, Kingston.

Cox, D., & Richarz, R. (1987). *Traditional and modernized characteristics of registered and unregistered family day care providers*. (ERIC Doc. No. 290 577).

Deller (Pollard), J. (1988). *Family day care internationally: A literature review*. Toronto: Ontario Ministry of Community and Social Services.

Divine-Hawkins, P. (1980). *Family day care in the United States. Final report of the National Home Day Care Study. Executive summary*. Washington, DC: Administration of Children, Youth and Families. (ERIC Doc. No. 211 224).

Doherty Social Planning Consultants Ltd. (1987). *A survey of child care support services*. Ontario: Ministry of Community and Social Services.

Eheart, B. K., & Leavitt, R. L. (1986). Training day care home providers: Implications for policy and research. *Early Childhood Research Quarterly, 1*, 119–32.

Eheart, B. K., & Leavitt, R. L. (1987, April). *Day care homes for infants and toddlers: The nature of care*. Poster session presented at the Society for Research in Child Development 1987 Biennial Meeting, Baltimore, Maryland.

Eheart, B. K., & Leavitt, R. L. (1989). Family day care: Discrepancies between intended and observed caregiving practices. *Early Childhood Research Quarterly, 4*(1), 145–62.

Elkind, D. (1989). Formal education and early childhood education: An essential difference. *Phi Delta Kappan, 67*(9), 631–36.

Emlen, A. (1972). *Family day care research—a summary and critical review.* Pasadena: Pacific Oaks College.

Emlen, A., Donoghue, B., & LaForge, R. (1971). *Child care by kith: A study of family day care relationships of working mothers and neighborhood caregivers.* Corvallis, OR: DCE Books.

Emlen, A. C., Donoghue, B. A., & Clarkson, O. D. (1973). *The stability of the family day care arrangements: A longitudinal study.* Corvallis, OR: DCE Books.

Esbensen, S. B. (1985). The effects of day care on children, families and communities: A review of the research findings. In *Child care: Standards and quality.* Background papers for the Task Force on Child Care. Ottawa: Status of Women, Canada.

Fischer, J. L. (1989). *Family day care: Factors influencing the quality of caregiving practices.* Ph.D. thesis, University of Illinois at Urbana-Champaign.

Fosburg, S. (1981). *Family day care in the United States. Final report of the National Home Day Care Study. Summary of findings* (Vol. 1). Washington, DC: Administration of Children, Youth and Families. (ERIC Doc. No. ED211 218)

Harms, T., & Clifford, R. (1980). *The early childhood environmental rating scale.* New York: Teachers College Press.

Hasegawa, P. (1972). *What is quality family day care?* Pasadena: Pacific Oaks College. (ERIC Doc. No. ED 096 021).

Hofferth, S. L., Brayfield, A., Deich, S., & Holcomb, P. (1991). *The National Child Care Survey, 1990.* Washington, DC: Urban Institute.

Hofferth, S. L., & Phillips, D. A. (1991). Child care policy research. *Journal of Social Issues, 47*(2), 1–14.

Howes, C. (1990). Caregiving environments and their consequences for children: The experience in the United States. In E. C. Melhuish & P. Moss (Eds.), *Day care for young children: International perspectives.* London: Routledge.

Howes, C., & Rubenstein, J. (1978a). *Influences on toddler peer behavior in two types of care.* Rockville, Maryland: National Institute of Mental Health. (ERIC Doc. No. ED 175 566).

Howes, C., & Rubenstein, J. (1978b). *Toddler social development in two day-care settings.* Paper presented at the annual meeting of the Western Psychological Association, San Francisco. (ERIC Doc. No. ED 110 164).

Hughes, R. (1985). The informal help-giving of home and center child care providers. *Family Relations, 34,* 359–66.

Innes, R. B., & Innes, S. M. (1984). A qualitative study of caregivers' attitudes about child care. *Early Child Development and Care, 15,* 133–148.

Jackson, B., & Jackson, S. (1979). *Childminder: A study in action research.* London: Routeledge and Keagan Paul.

Johnson, L. C. (1976). *Who cares? A report of the project child care survey of parents and their child care arrangements.* Toronto: Toronto Social Planning Council.

Johnson & Associates, Inc. (1982). *Comparative licensing study: Profits of state day care licensing requirements. Group day care homes and summary tables* (Vol. 6, Rev. Ed.). Washington, DC: U.S. Administration of Children, Youth and Family. (ERIC Doc. No. ED 237 223).

Keyserling, M. D. (1972). *Windows on day care.* New York: National Council of Jewish Women.

Kontos, S. (1987). The attitudinal context of family day care relationships. In D. Peters & S. Kontos (Eds.), *Continuity and discontinuity of experience in child care.* Norwood, NJ: Ablex.

Kontos, S. (1989). *Predictors of job satisfaction and child care quality in family day care.* Paper presented at the annual meeting of the American Educational Research Association, San Francisco.

Kontos, S. (1992). *Family day care: Out of the shadows and into the limelight.* Washington, DC: National Association for the Education of Young Children.

Kontos, S., & Riessen, J. (Under review). *Predictors of job satisfaction, job stress, and job commitment in family day care providers.* Department of Child Development and Family Studies, Purdue University.

Kyle, I. (1991). *Ontario parents' use of child care support and neighbourhood resources and their search for child care.* M.Sc. thesis, University of Guelph.

Leavitt, R. (1986). *Invisible boundaries: An interpretative study of parent-provider relationships.* Unpublished manuscript.

Leavitt, R. L. (In progress). *Licensing family day care: Perspective and recommendations.* University of Illinois at Urbana-Champaign.

Lero, D. (1985). Parents' needs, preferences, and concerns about child care: Case studies of 336 Canadian families. In *Child Care Needs of Parents and Families.* Background paper for the Task Force on Child Care. Ottawa: Status of Women, Canada.

Lero, D., Brockman, L., Pence, A., Charlesworth, M., Canning, P., Esbensen, S., Morrison, F., & Goelman, H. (1985). *Parents' needs, preferences, and concerns about child care: Case studies of 336 families.* Background paper for the Task Force on Child Care. Ottawa: Status of Women, Canada.

Lero, D., Pence, A., Goelman, H., & Brockman, L. (1988). *The National Child Care Survey.* Ottawa: Health and Welfare Canada.

Lewin, K. (1936). *Principles of topological psychology* (F. Heider & G. M. Heider, Trans.). New York: McGraw-Hill.

Lindbergh, A. M. (1975). *Gift from the sea.* New York: Pantheon Books.

Longwoods Research Group Ltd. (1981). *Nominal focus groups on informal day care in Ontario.* Toronto: Ontario Ministry of Community and Social Services.

Longwoods Research Group Ltd. (1982). *Informal day care in Ontario: Consultants report.* Toronto: Ontario Ministry of Community and Social Services.

Lueck, M., Orr, A. C., & O'Connell, M. (1982). *Trends in child care arrangements of working mothers* (Current Population Reports P-23, No. 117). Washington, DC: U.S. Bureau of the Census.

Melhuish, E., & Moss, P. (Eds.). (1991). *Day care for young children: International perspectives.* London: Tavistock/Routledge.

Moss, P. (1987). *A review of childminding research.* London: Thomas Coram Research Unit, University of London Institute of Education.

National Association for the Education of Young Children. (1985). *In whose hands? A demographic fact sheet on child care providers.* Washington, DC: NAEYC Information Service, Publication No. 760.

National Commission on Working Women. (1986a). *Child care fact sheet.* Washington, DC: Author.

National Commission on Working Women. (1986b). *Who cares for kids? A report on child care providers.* Washington, DC: Author.

Nelson, M. (1989). Negotiating care: Relationship between family day care providers and mothers. *Feminist Studies, 15,* 7–33.

Nelson, M. (1990). *Negotiated care: The experience of family day care providers.* Philadelphia: Temple University Press.

Norpark Computer Design. (1988). *A survey of private home day care services in Ontario.* Toronto: Ministry of Community and Social Services.

Pence, A. (1983). Day care in the 80's: An overview of research and issues. *The Journal of the Canadian Association of Young Children, 8*(1), 3–9.

Pence, A. (1985). Day care in the '80's: An overview of research and issues. *Journal of the Canadian Association for the Education of Young Children, 8*(1), 3–8.

Pence, A. R., & Goelman, H. (1985–86). The Victoria day care research project: Initial descriptive data on parents. *Canadian Children, 10*(1 and 2), 115–24.

Pence, A. R., & Goelman, H. (1987a). Silent partners: Parents of children in three types of day care. *Early Childhood Research Quarterly, 2,* 103–18.

Pence, A. R., & Goelman, H. (1987b). Who cares for the child in day care? Characteristics of caregivers in three types of day care. *Early Childhood Research Quarterly, 2,* 315–34.

Pepper, S., & Stuart, B. (1983). What is quality in family day care. *Journal of the Canadian Association of Young Children, 8,* 18–28.

Pepper, S., & Stuart, B. (1985). *Informal family day care: A study of caregivers.* Unpublished report, University of Western Ontario and University of Guelph.

Peters, D. L. (1972). *Day care homes: A Pennsylvania profile.* Center for Human Services Development, Pennsylvania State University, Report No. 18.

Phillips, D., McCartney, K., Scarr, S., & Howes, C. (1987). Selective review of infant day care research: A cause for concern! In *Zero to Three.* Washington, DC: Bulletin of the National Centre for Clinical Infant Programs 7(3), 18–21.

PMA Consulting Group Ltd. (1983). *A survey of private home day care in Ontario.* Toronto: Ontario Ministry of Community and Social Services.

Portnoy, F. C., & Simmons, C. H. (1978). Day care and attachment. *Child Development, 49,* 239–42.

Powell, D. R. (1987). Day care as a family support system. In S. Kagan, D. Powell, B. Weissbourd & E. Zigler (Eds.), *America's family support programs: Perspectives and prospects.* New Haven, CT: Yale University Press.

Powell, D. R., & Eisenstadt, J. W. (1983). Predictors of help-seeking in an urban setting: The search for child care. *American Journal of Community Psychology, 11*(4), 401–21.

Rapp, G. S., & Lloyd, S. A. (1989). The role of "home as haven" ideology in child care use. *Family Relations, 38,* 426–30.

Richters, J., & Zahn-Waxler, C. (1988). The infant day care controversy: Current status and future directions. *Early Childhood Research Quarterly, 3*(3), 319–36.

Ruderman, F. (1967). *Child care and working mothers: A study of arrangements made for daytime care of children.* New York: Child Welfare League.

Silver, B., & Greenspan, S. I. (1980). Personality characteristics of family day care mothers. *Journal of Community Psychology, 8,* 206–71.

Steinberg, L., & Green, C. (1979). *How parents may mediate the effect of day care.* Paper presented at the Society for Research in Child Development Conference, San Francisco. (ERIC Doc. No. ED 145 968).

Stevens, H. (1984). *Child care needs and realities in Winnipeg—1984: A report for the Manitoba Child Care Association.* Winnipeg: Social Planning Council of Winnipeg.

Stith, S. M., & Davis, A. J. (1984). Employed mothers and family day-care substitute caregivers: A comparative analysis of infant care. *Child Development, 55,* 1340–348.

Stuart, B., & Pepper, S. (1985). *Private home day care providers in Ontario: A study of their personal and psychological characteristics.* Unpublished report, University of Guelph.

Stuart, B., & Pepper, S. (1988). The contribution of the caregiver's personality and vocational interests to quality in licensed family day care. *Canadian Journal of Research in Early Childhood Education 2* (2), 99–109.

Wandersman, L. P. (1981). Ecological relationships in family day care. *Child Care Quarterly, 10*(2), 89–102.

Washburn, P. V., & Washburn, J. S. (1985). The four roles of the family day care provider. *Child Welfare, 64*(5), 547–54.

Wattenberg, E. (1977). Characteristics of family day care providers: Implications for training. *Child Welfare, 56,* 211–29.

Wattenberg, E. (1980). Family day care: Out of the shadows and into the spotlight. *Marriage and Family Review, 3* (3/4), 35–62.

Willner, M. (1969). Unsupervised family day care in New York City. *Child Welfare, XLVlll* (6), 342–47.

PART II

Perspectives on the Process of Family Day Care

CHAPTER 7

Family Day Care for Infants and Toddlers

Carollee Howes
Laura M. Sakai

In the United States, the children cared for in family day care are more likely to be infants and toddlers rather than preschoolers and older children (see Chapter 3). Furthermore a larger proportion of infants and toddlers who are enrolled in child care are cared for in family day care than in center care (Phillips, 1991). This trend holds despite a steady increase of infants and toddlers in center care (Phillips, 1991). In this chapter we explore the social belief systems that underlie the use of family day care. We then examine, from the perspective of research, how well family day care serves the developmental needs of infants and toddlers. Finally we discuss the implications of formal caregiver training for family day care.

BELIEF SYSTEMS

There are at least three interwoven social belief systems that support the use of family day care for young children. One system we will call the maternal belief system. This is a set of personal values about child care expressed by mothers. Maternal beliefs are often the product of personal history and appear on the surface to be idiosyncratic. We suggest, however, that these maternal beliefs are embedded in a second belief system, a larger societal belief system, about the role of the family and women in our society. This belief system includes, for example, beliefs about the relative acceptability of women in the work force. The third belief system that supports the use of family day care for infants and toddlers is the advice given to parents by experts. Both experts and parents are part of the larger society, so their beliefs are influenced by societal beliefs as well as by personal experience and scientific evidence. Expert advice, particularly if it is consistent with social beliefs, becomes, over time, part of the societal belief system. Thus mothers of young children may experience and rely on societal belief, expert advice, and personal belief systems as one integrated unit.

Maternal Beliefs

Most mothers in the United States with infant or toddler-age children are also members of the paid work force (Hayes, Palmer & Zaslow, 1990). This is a fairly recent trend. There were dramatic increases in the work-force participation of mothers with young children between 1977 and 1987, but work-force participation of mothers with infants and toddlers before the late 1970s was rare (Phillips, 1991). Thus many current mothers of young children were themselves cared for by nonworking mothers.

According to attachment theory (see Bretherton & Waters, 1985), early caregiving experiences become part of a person's internal working model of the self and others. Following this assumption, a mother's own experiences of being mothered become part of her self-concept and social orientation to others and are influential in how she chooses to care for her own children. If a person's experiences of being mothered include having her mother as her primary caregiver, it is possible that when she selects care for her own children she will unconsciously want to replicate her own experiences.

However, due to economic constraints facing today's families, staying home with an infant or toddler is not always an option (Hayes et al., 1990). Therefore many mothers who want to replicate the stay-at-home mother cannot stay home themselves but must try to find the child care form that is closest to them staying at home. In-home care from a relative or nanny often appears to be the next logical choice. For many families neither of these child care forms is truly available. Many grandmothers either live in another state or are working themselves. Nannies are expensive, hard to find, and, unless the house is very large, intrude on the mother's privacy with her family when she is not working.

In these situations family day care, in its idealized form, appears to be the most viable choice. From the point of view of the popularized mythology of American society, family day care providers are good mothers who not only stay home with their own children but open their homes to a few more children. The family day care provider becomes like a mother to the children in her care. She bakes cookies, plays games, and is always there for the child who needs an extra hug or time to talk. What could be better for the baby of a mother whose personal belief system is that mothers should stay home with their babies?

For other mothers, often mothers from working-class backgrounds, the belief that mothers should stay home with young children may not be as strong. Poor and minority women have always worked outside the home, so many of these mothers grew up expecting to work and be mothers. However, child care in poor and minority communities has traditionally been informal care. Relatives and friends cared for children in a reciprocated network of services (Stack, 1974). These informal systems may no longer serve to fill child care needs as the proportion of working mothers and grandmothers increases. A recent ethnographic study of child care arrangements in a white, ethnic (Italian and Irish), working-class neighborhood suggests that even when a relative is not available, child care by "outsiders," including center care, is to be avoided (Zinnser, 1990). Family day care in this community is embedded in a matrix of familial and neighborhood personal relationships. Family day care is seen as more like family than center care.

Societal Beliefs

Societal beliefs also support the use of family day care for our youngest children. The ideal family in American society is self-reliant, nurturing, and economically self-contained (Phillips, 1991). Within this family system, it is traditionally the mother who has a natural and exclusive responsibility for child rearing. McCartney and Phillips (1988) suggest that societal beliefs currently characterize mothers who use child care as conflicted. They argue that this portrayal allows us to protect our belief that children are best cared for by their mothers in the face of statistical evidence that most mothers of young children work. Child care is viewed as an unpleasant necessity for women who would prefer to stay home but have no choice. Within such a belief system family day care is seen as less threatening than center care because it is more like a family, more like mother care.

Expert Advice

Parents receive expert advice on child care choices from their pediatricians, from popular books and magazines on child rearing, and from the media. These expert opinions are at least one step away from the scientific studies of child care, filtered through the personal interpretations of the advice givers.

The most recent and extensive analysis of expert advice to parents was conducted by Young (1990). She conducted a content analysis of two publications, *Parents* magazine and *Infant Care*, a publication of the U.S. Children's Bureau. Both publications consistently publish information on working mothers and out-of-home care. Her thematic analysis suggests that it was the dominant opinion of both publications that it is better if mothers do not work when their children are young, and that child care centers are to be avoided because they are expensive and can be dangerous for infants.

The authors' less formal survey of popular books available to parents in the book stores of a large metropolitan area suggests similar advice. These experts concur that if mothers must work it is best to find a small family-type child care arrangement for infants or toddlers. Given that the scientific literature on this issue is far from definitive, this type of statement appears to be heavily influenced by societal and personal belief systems.

Because women's work patterns are changing, beliefs, particularly beliefs about the roles of working women, are changing. Therefore, despite the seemingly apparent consensus among beliefs, today's parents must often cope with conflicting views on child care. For example, although one dominant belief is that mothers should be the primary caregivers, there is also a growing belief in the importance of fathers. Thus fathers as well as mothers are experiencing more societal pressure to care for infants. Similarly, mothers experience both the societal pressure to stay home with infants and the societal pressure to work. When beliefs are in conflict, parents have great difficulty making child care choices. In the extreme, conflicts between belief systems can be detrimental. Parents with conflicting beliefs may create unstable child care for their children by always being dissatisfied with child care placements, creating interpersonal conflicts with providers, and making many child care changes for their children. Child care instability is linked to less optimal child outcomes (Howes & Stewart, 1987).

In summary, despite being a society in transition in patterns of women's work, there is a surface consensus among maternal beliefs, societal beliefs, and expert advice. Family day care, as the child care form most like our idealized American family, is the child care form of choice for infants and toddlers. In the next section we explore how similar family day care really is to the ideal and examine the research evidence for the claim that children fare better in family day care than in other forms of care.

HOW FAMILY IS FAMILY DAY CARE?

Fortunately there is a growing literature on family day care generated by child development researchers. Much of this research is reviewed elsewhere in this volume. In this section, we briefly review literature describing the social ecology of family day care with respect to the question: How family is family day care? In doing so we ignore some very positive and well-documented aspects of family day care, including its accessibility for families due to lower costs, flexible hours, and convenient neighborhood locations, and its potential for being part of a larger social network of friends and neighbors. These aspects interact with belief systems to influence family choice.

Family day care physically looks more like family care than center care. Family day care is conducted in an environment organized for adults as well as children (Clarke-Stewart & Gruber, 1984; Howes, 1983). Compared with child care centers, family day care homes have more items that are potentially dangerous to children, such as hot stoves, lawn mowers, and furniture with sharp edges. Family day care settings also include more off-limits areas than centers, such as the living room with the good furniture or the china closet. Family day care homes are less likely than centers to have toys and educational items to stimulate children and, especially in urban areas, family day care homes are also less likely to have outside play spaces and equipment (Clarke-Stewart & Gruber, 1984; Howes, 1983).

Perhaps because of the adult-oriented environment, family day care providers are more like mothers at home than teachers in centers in terms of restrictions and prohibitions directed toward children. Center teachers are less restrictive and prohibit fewer activities of toddlers (18–36 months old) than family day care providers (Cochran, 1977; Howes, 1983). Higher levels of prohibitions and restrictions in child care are linked to less optimal child outcomes (Howes & Hamilton, in press). These differences in behaviors also may be linked to differences in belief systems. Family day care providers may be more traditional in their beliefs about children's compliance. It may be more important to a family day care provider than to a center teacher for toddler-age children to "mind their manners."

Family day care providers usually care for a mixed age group of children. Thus the array of children in care looks more like siblings than a school classroom. The particular age mix influences children's experiences in family day care. The National Day Care Home Study (Stallings & Porter, 1980) suggests that when infants (0–18 months old) are present, caregivers spend more time with them and less time with older children. According to this study, toddler-age children appeared to receive the least attention when they were part of a heterogeneous age mix. In settings with infants and toddlers, toddlers tended to monitor infant-caregiver interactions rather than engage directly with caregivers. In settings with toddlers and preschoolers, toddlers engaged in fewer language exchanges with caregivers. However, when the number of toddler-age children increases, the providers spend more time controlling the children and less time in developmentally appropriate activities. These data suggest that the particular developmental demands of a toddler-age child may be least able to be met in a family day care setting.

Family day care providers also sound like our idealized notion of mothers. When interviewed about their jobs, many family day care providers say that they chose to do family day care because they love children and it provides them with the opportunity to stay home with their own children (Kontos, in press). They report relatively high job satisfaction and self-efficacy (Kontos, in press). In general, family day care providers appear to be satisfied with both their job choices and their competence (Kontos, in press). They believe that they are being good mothers for both the children in their care and their own children (Eheart & Leavitt, 1989).

A recent ethnographic study suggests that there are discrepancies between family day care providers' perceptions of their jobs and their actual practices. Eheart and Leavitt (1989) interviewed 31 providers about their daily activities. They then observed six representative providers over a ten-month period. Most of the providers stressed that their primary goal was to provide love and attention, to be second mothers to the children, and to provide a home atmosphere. In all observed homes there were both incidences of loving and attentive caregiving and recurrent incidences of favoritism, neglect, lack of empathy, and threats of punishment. Likewise providers reported that they ensured children's happiness by allowing them to play freely so that their days were not structured. Observations suggest that the children were bored and frustrated with little adult management of play and few age-appropriate toys or activities. Toddlers in these settings quickly became victims or created discipline problems for the providers.

We suspect that if the researchers had completed a similar study in family care as opposed to family day care similar discrepancies may have emerged. Most parents would probably answer that their goal is to provide loving and sensitive care, yet we know that parental care can include neglect and abuse as well as nurturance. Are we expecting too much when we want family day care to be better than home care?

Eheart and Leavitt (1989) suggest a contradiction between the expectation that family day care providers will act like mothers and the reality of their jobs—long hours, low pay, low status in the world, and an ever-changing group of children. For example, they point out that it may be unrealistic to expect a provider to bond with as many as the 21 different children seen in one family day care home over a six-month period. The caregivers may want to provide love and nurturing like a mother but not feel that kind of love. Katz (1981) suggests that professional caregivers of young children understand that they can nurture a child without loving that child like a mother, that teachers play important but different roles in the lives of children than do mothers. According to this analysis, family day care providers set themselves up to be like mothers, yet due to real demands and stresses, they are unable to feel the unconditional love that most mothers feel toward their young children and are unable to act as they wish they felt.

We suspect that the way out of this dilemma lies with caregiver training that helps providers realize that they can nurture the children in their care without being the children's second mother. If providers were monitoring their own behaviors according to child development standards rather than their personal interpretations of societal beliefs about good mothers, their jobs might be less stressful. Certainly a large body of data drawn from family day care as well as center care suggests that education and training in child development is linked to caregiver sensitivity (Whitebook, Howes & Phillips, 1990). However, the very belief system that may have led to the discrepancies between family day care providers' intentions and practice makes training programs problematic. If a provider believes that the most important part of her job is to act like a good mother, then she is unlikely to seek or accept training. According to our societal beliefs, good mothers are not trained to be child development professionals. They are good mothers because they love children. Often family day care providers are critical of center care for being institutional or too much like school. Family day care providers want to provide the homelike atmosphere they perceive to be missing in center day care. In order to accept child development training, providers may have to be convinced that it will enhance, not destroy, their nurturing roles as home-based providers.

Parent-provider relationships also may perpetuate the discrepancy between provider intentions and practices. As we have discussed above, many parents select family day care because it is like a family. However, one salient parental anxiety is that their children will prefer the provider to themselves. This contradiction may create tension in the parent-provider relationship.

Studies of family day care providers' attitudes toward the parents of the children they care for suggest that providers are often critical of and uncomfortable with parents (Innes & Innes, 1984). Innes and Innes suggest that family day care providers are often critical of parents for leaving their children in child care because a good mother would not go to work. If the provider who holds these beliefs is then expecting to be the good mother for these children, she may unconsciously undermine the children's relationships with their parents. These conflicts may influence the provider's ability to nurture the children. The children may be sensitive to the parent-provider tension and feel distrustful of both caregivers.

In summary, we have suggested that the family day care environment looks very much like a home in terms of physical setup and in terms of relatively high levels of restrictions and prohibitions on children's activities. Family day care homes also look like families because of the mixed age range of children. Most important, family day care looks like families in that providers intend to mother the children and create a homelike atmosphere and experience for the children. We suggest that these aspects of family day care that make it appear like a family may be the very aspects that make it difficult for providers to create the intended nurturing, developmentally appropriate experience for the children in care.

FAMILY DAY CARE VARIETY

Until this point in the chapter we have been writing as if all family day care providers were alike. In reality, family day care providers are a heterogeneous group on many dimensions. The care provided by family day care providers also varies widely in quality. High-quality family day care homes support optimal child development, and poor-quality family day care homes are detrimental to children's development (Howes & Stewart, 1987). In this study, quality was defined by adult-child ratio and scores on the Family Day Care Environmental Rating Scale (Harms & Clifford, 1989). The variety in family day care makes it difficult if not impossible to compare the care provided in family day care with the care provided in center or by mothers. The vast majority of comparison studies find no differences (Howes & Hamilton, in press). In addition, similar relationships between quality indicators and children's development appear to occur in all forms of child care. Indicators of quality that predict optimal outcomes are consistent in direction and magnitude across all forms of care (Howes & Hamilton, in press). This similarity makes our next task easier. In examining the developmental issues of the infant-toddler period and their socialization, we draw from research literature based on children in all forms of child care.

Developmental Issues in the Infant-Toddler Period

Important developmental issues for children in the infant-toddler period include attachment and the development of autonomy and self-regulation. In this section we describe each of these issues from a theoretical perspective and then discuss the socialization of these developmental issues in family day care.

Attachment.   Attachment refers to children's relationships with caregiving adults. These relationships emerge during the first year of life, although children and adults form attachments throughout life. An attachment relationship is based on children's felt security with caregivers. Within attachment theory (Bretherton & Waters, 1985), security refers to both physical and emotional security. Attachments develop with all caregiving adults, and children commonly form more than one simultaneous attachment relationship. Therefore children form attachments to their family day care providers as well as to their parents. Each attachment relationship is unique to a particular caregiver-child dyad. Thus children may have one type of attachment relationship with their mothers and another with their family day care providers.

Although all attachment relationships are sensible adaptations to a particular caregiving situation, not all attachments are adaptive in the larger society. Children develop insecure attachment relationships with caregivers who are emotionally unavailable or harsh and secure attachment relationships with caregivers who are sensitive and responsive. These relations between caregiver behavior and children's attachment security are found in both parental (Bretherton & Waters, 1985) and alternative (Howes, Phillips & Whitebook, in press) caregiver attachments.

Theoretically, internal representations of children's attachment relationships become part of children's internal models of themselves and of social relationships with others (Bretherton & Waters, 1985). Thus nurturing family day care providers can contribute to children's positive sense of self and their future relationships with others. Children with secure attachments to child care caregivers are, for example, likely to have competent peer relationships (Howes et al., in press).

Because children's attachment relationships with family day care providers are independent of their attachment relationships with their parents, family day care providers have the potential to be compensatory figures for children. Children whose parents have difficulty providing a sensitive and responsive environment may construct a secure attachment with their family day care providers. However, because attachment relationships, especially early attachments, are independent, a secure maternal attachment relationship will not buffer a child from a harsh and insensitive family day care provider.

Unfortunately, parents who are less able to provide appropriate home environments to nurture secure attachments are also less likely to enroll their children in family day care homes where the children will form secure attachments with caregivers. In a study of attachment relationships with mothers and caregivers, children (13–24 months) with insecure maternal attachments (measured in the Strange Situation) were found to be more often enrolled in family day care homes with the worst adult-child ratios (Howes, Rodning, Galluzzo & Meyers, 1988). Child care providers, at least in center-based care, who have poorer adult-child ratios are less likely to be sensitive and appropriate in their caregiving and therefore less likely to facilitate secure attachment relationships (Howes et al., in press).

The training implications for family day care providers concerning children's attachment issues are not straightforward. As we have discussed, most family day care providers believe that they are providing sensitive and responsive care. Researchers and family day care providers may not define sensitive and responsive care in the same way, or there may be discrepancies between beliefs or intentions and actual practice. If the issue is definition, then caregivers could be helped through training to redefine their goals. If the issue is discrepancies between intentions and practice, training becomes more complicated.

Maternal behavior linked to attachment appears to change not because of efforts to change mothering behaviors but because of internal reorganization of the mothers' own attachment systems (Ricks, 1985). Translating this knowledge of family day care training requires a flexible notion of training. We suspect that this major type of reorganization is unlikely to occur after a single workshop on children's attachment, but it may begin through a supportive relationship with a person modeling sensitive and responsive behaviors with both the provider and the children she cares for.

Autonomy and Self-Regulation.   In their second year of life, children face a set of conflicting developmental and environmental demands. With an increasing awareness of the self as separate and an emerging competence within optimal developmental contexts, toddler-age children make increasing demands for independence. She wants to put on her own shirt and he wants to pour his own juice. Simultaneously the caregivers, recognizing that the children have increasing control over their physical movements and are able to understand and follow simple verbal directions, begin to demand compliance and self-regulation. Caregivers say things like "No, don't touch" or "give it back to Becca."

The issues of autonomy and self-regulation have been approached from several theoretical positions. Kopp (1982) has argued that cognitive skills underlie abilities to regulate behavior and comply with caregiver demands. She suggests that under normal circumstances children follow a developmental progression toward self-regulation. Attachment theorists (Matas, Arend & Sroufe, 1978) suggest that the quality of the caregiver-child attachment relationship interacts with cognitive development in the pathway to autonomy and self-regulation. Children with secure attachment relationships are better able to freely and flexibly explore their growing competence than children who are insecure. Likewise children who are secure with their caregivers are most likely to comply with caregiver demands.

A third theoretical perspective drawn from Vygotskian theory (Schaffer & Crook, 1979) suggests that competent caregivers provide children with compliance and autonomy experiences that are appropriate to the children's zone of proximal development. The zone of proximal development is composed of behaviors just one developmental step in advance of the child. Thus the caregiver is facilitating development.

The field of early childhood education has a large body of practical knowledge that is useful in promoting autonomy and self-regulation in children. The National Association for the Education of Young Children's materials on developmentally appropriate practice (Bredekamp, 1987) can form the basis for training in this area. For example, this guideline recommends that adults recognize that toddlers test limits and express opposition to adults as part of their normal development of a healthy sense of self as a separate and autonomous individual. Therefore adults should prohibit only activities that are not safe rather than become involved in power struggles that do not relate to the children's health or well-being. Routines are used to help children achieve self-regulation. Thus everyday activities such as snack time, hand washing, or cleanup time form the context for experiences in autonomy and self-regulation.

However, as with attachment, the real issue in the training of family day care providers is not content but belief systems that interfere with seeking and receiving training. As we discussed earlier, one strong belief system within the family day care provider community is that they are most successful when they provide a homelike atmosphere. However, toddlers in family day care homes are reported to receive elevated levels of restrictions and are less involved in developmentally appropriate behaviors than other age groups. The providers' desire to protect their homes from active and adventuresome toddlers appears to interfere with experiences that promote toddlers' autonomy and self-regulation.

SUMMARY

We suspect that the "family" in family day care is a paradox. On one hand, parents may select family day care because maternal beliefs, societal beliefs, and expert advice coalesce around the notion that young children are best cared for in settings similar to traditional families. However, when parents are looking for a family they may not attend to the aspects of family day care that are more closely linked to quality. In addition, their emotional responses to having someone else be a mother to their children may interfere with the parent-provider relationship.

Likewise family day care providers intend to provide care that is based on idealized notions of good mothers and good families. Yet we have argued in this chapter that it is these very belief systems that often cause problems. Children may not receive sensitive and responsive care when the provider's intentions conflict with her feelings and the real demands of her job. Providing developmentally appropriate care for toddlers is often at odds with being a good housekeeper and creating a comfortable and appropriate adult environment.

Most significantly, from a social policy point of view, the belief system of both parents and providers that supports family day care because it is like a family may seriously interfere with training family day care providers. Family day care providers who are sensitive and responsive and who engage in appropriate activities with children care for children who are enjoying optimal development (Howes & Stewart, 1987). Experience as a mother is unrelated to these caregiving behaviors, but formal training in early childhood education is linked to optimal caregiving (Whitebook, et al., 1990). If family day care providers do not attend training sessions because they do not believe that good mothers need training, if trainers of family day care providers emphasize that good care is linked to good mother behaviors rather than to child development principles, or if family day care providers do not receive support in understanding the problematic aspects of discrepancies between beliefs, intentions, and behaviors, we jeopardize the quality of care in family day care.

We believe that family day care homes can be optimal child development environments for infants and toddlers. The small home setting can provide the exploring child with a sense of mastery and competence. The everyday activities within the home can be used to stimulate emerging cognitive and social competencies. A sensitive and responsive caregiver with a small group of infants and toddlers can facilitate the construction of secure attachments. But we also believe that reasoning that family day care is a good place for children because it is like a family creates problems for parents, for providers, and ultimately for children.

REFERENCES

Bredekamp, S. (1987). *Developmentally appropriate practice in early childhood programs serving children from birth through age eight.* Washington, DC: National Association for the Education of Young Children.

Bretherton, I., & Waters, E. (1985). Growing points in attachment theory. *Monograph of the Society for Research in Child Development* (Vol. 50).

Clarke-Stewart, A., & Gruber, C. (1984). Day care forms and features. In R. C. Ainslie (Ed.), *Quality variations in daycare* (pp. 35–62). New York: Praeger.

Cochran, M. (1977). A comparison of group day care and family child rearing patterns in Sweden. *Child Development, 48,* 702–7.

Eheart, B. K., & Leavitt, R. L. (1989). Family day care discrepancies between intended and observed caregiving practices. *Early Childhood Research Quarterly, 4,* 145–62.

Harms, T., & Clifford, R. M. (1989). *Family day care rating scale.* New York: Teachers College Press.

Hayes, S., Palmer, J. L., & Zaslow, M. J. (1990). *Who cares for America's children.* Washington, DC: National Academy Press.

Howes, C. (1983). Caregiver behavior in center and family day care. *Journal of Applied Developmental Psychology, 4,* 99–107.

Howes, C., & Hamilton, C. (In press). Child care for infants, toddlers, and young children. In B. Spodek (Ed.), *Handbook of research in early childhood Education.* New York: Macmillan.

Howes, C., Phillips, D., & Whitebook, M. (In press). Thresholds of quality: Children's social development in center based child care. *Child Development.*

Howes, C., Rodning, C., Galluzzo, D., & Meyers, L. (1988). Attachment and child care: Relationships with mother and caregiver. *Early Childhood Research Quarterly, 3,* 403–16.

Howes, C., & Stewart, P. (1987). Child's play with adults, toys, and peers: An examination of family and child care influences. *Developmental Psychology, 23,* 423–30.

Innes, R., & Innes, S. (1984). A qualitative study of caregivers' attitudes about child care. *Early Child Development and Care, 15,* 133–48.

Katz, L. (1981). Mothering and teaching: Some significant distinctions. In *Current Issues in Early Childhood Education, 2.* Norwood, NJ: Ablex.

Kontos, S. (In press). Family day care. *Monograph of the National Association for the Education of Young Children.* Washington, DC: National Association for the Education of Young Children.

Kopp, C. B. (1982). The antecedents of self-regulation. *Developmental Psychology, 18,* 199–214.

Matas, L., Arend, R. A., & Sroufe, L. A. (1978). Continuity of adaptation in the second year. The relationship between quality of attachment and later competence. *Child Development, 49,* 547–56.

McCartney, K., & Phillips, D. A. (1988). Motherhood and child care. In B. Birns & D. Hay (Eds.), *The different faces of motherhood.* New York: Plenum.

Phillips, D. A. (1991). Daycare for young children in the United States. In E. C. Melhuish & P. Moss (Eds.), *Daycare for young children: International perspectives* (pp. 161–84). London: Tavistock/Routledge.

Ricks, M. H. (1985). Social transmission of parental behavior: Attachment across generations. In I. Bretherton & E. Waters (Eds.) *Growing points of attachment theory and research. Monographs of the Society for Research in Child Development,* Vol. 50 (Serial #209), pp. 211–27.

Schaffer, H. R., & Crook, C. K. (1979). Maternal control techniques in a directed play situation. *Child Development, 50,* 989–96.

Stack, C. B. (1974). *All our kin.* New York: Harper.

Stallings, J., & Porter, A. (1980). Final report of the National Day Care Home Study (Vol. 3). In *Family day care in the United States: A research report.* Cambridge, MA: Abt Associates.

Whitebook, M., Howes, C., & Phillips, D. A. (1990). *Who cares: Child care teachers in America: Final report of the national child care staffing study.* Oakland, CA: Child Care Employee Project.

Young, K. T. (1990). American conceptions of infant development from 1955

to 1984: What the experts are telling parents. *Child Development, 61,* 17–
    28.
Zinnser, C. (1990). *Born and raised in East Urban: A community study of in-
    formal and unregulated child care.* New York: Center for Public Policy Re-
    search.

CHAPTER 8

Family Day Care and Children with Disabilities

Penny L. Deiner

This chapter focuses on the policies and practices of including children with disabilities into family day care homes. There is no absolute dividing line between the requirements of those with disabilities and those without. In general, however, a child with a disability has more extensive needs than other children and they occur more frequently and tend to interfere more with the everyday life of the child (U.S. Department of Health, Education and Welfare, 1972). Viewed in another way, these are children "who have substantial developmental delay or specific congenital or acquired conditions with a high probability of resulting in developmental disabilities if services are not provided" (Public Law 101-496, 1990). This definition in the law includes children with specifically identified conditions such as autism or Down syndrome. It also allows for more global definitions such as "developmentally delayed" without a specific diagnosis attached. Further, it allows for the inclusion of conditions that are likely to result in developmental disabilities.

Placing children with disabilities in family day care homes is not a new idea (U.S. Department of Health, Education and Welfare, 1972), but it has recently received a great deal of attention in the United States because of changing demographics, a changing philosophical environment, and a new legislative base that calls for early intervention services to help these children.

NEED

Many mothers of young children are now in the work force. Work by Emlen (1991) in a 1983 study of 33 companies found that 3.3 percent of the fathers and 2.1 percent of employed mothers identified their children as having disabilities. This constituted 85 children with disabilities out of 3,112. Of these children 12 (14 percent) were in family day care as compared to 25 percent of other children under 12. Emlen reported that 7 percent were in center-based care compared with 14 percent of other children. Data collected in 1987 using 4,422 families in the Portland, Oregon, area found 100 families identifying their children as having disabilities, or about 2.3 percent of children under age 18. In this study 22 children were in family day care or other home placements and 18 were in center-based programs. Thirty were cared for in their own homes by a relative (usually the spouse), 47 used after-school activities, and 35 cared for themselves. It should be noted that most families used multiple care arrangements, and all were noted (Emlen, 1991). Although the percentage compared to other children is small, there appears to be an increasing number of children with disabilities in family day care.

Some estimate that by the year 2000 nearly seven in ten mothers of preschool-age children will be employed outside the home (Children's Defense Fund, 1990). Between 5 and 10 percent of these children are disabled (Salkever & Connolly, 1988). Taking note of this national trend of increasing numbers of mothers of young children in the work force (Hofferth & Phillips, 1987), Fewell (1986) estimated that in 1990 there were already 1,475,303 children with disabilities under age six with mothers in the work force. This number will grow as more mothers join the work force.

Most mothers work because of economic necessity. Parents of children with disabilities face increased financial burdens (Hartley, White & Yogman, 1989). Medical treatment, equipment, and supplies are expensive. A national survey of families having children with physical disabilities (Harbaugh, 1984, in Seligman & Darling, 1989) found child care to be the largest single out-of-pocket expense. Parents of these children may hold additional jobs to make ends meet.

The work-family conflict causes stress in most single-parent and dual-career families. Stress, as a result of child care concerns, was rated the number-one problem by employees of a Boston corporation (Friedman, 1986). Such stress is likely to be exacerbated when a child has a disability.

PHILOSOPHICAL BASE FOR EARLY INTERVENTION

Early childhood intervention is programming designed to prevent or minimize long-term disabilities. It is currently based on two assumptions: that the needs of young children can be understood only within the context of the family, and that these needs are so diverse that a range of interdisciplinary services is necessary to meet these needs (Meisels & Shonkoff, 1990).

Early intervention is no longer perceived as "child saving," where professionals remove a child from the negative influence of the parents and show them what to do (Zigler, 1990). Early childhood special education is unanimously in support of early intervention. Overall, researchers agree that early intervention is both cost-effective for society and supportive of the quality of life of the children served.

The unit of intervention, however, has moved from the child to the family. This shift has resulted in a major effort to understand the impact of a child with a disability on the family system. Professionals are also studying the types of interventions and supports that are necessary for families to keep children at home. Children with disabilities are often less responsive to caregivers than are other children (Field, 1982). Some smile less frequently (Brooks-Gunn & Lewis, 1982) and give unclear signals (Barnard, 1981). A child with a disability also usually requires more caregiving for a greater length of time. The caregiving skills required are demanding of both time and energy. In general, the more severe the disability the more difficult the caregiving will be. It is assumed that a family's adjustment to a child with a disability is affected by factors such as the amount and helpfulness of available informal and formal social supports.

Increasingly, work-family issues have become part of the total caregiving picture, and the need for both child and respite care has become apparent. Broadly defined, respite care is "the temporary care of a disabled individual for the purpose of providing relief to the primary caregiver" (Cohen & Warren, 1985, p. 26). That is, families need a break from the stress of caring for a child with a disability. Respite care is part of a support system that keeps children with developmental disabilities in the community (Powell & Hecimovic, 1981). In a national survey, Wikler (1980, cited in Levy & Levy, 1986) found respite care to be one of the most needed and least available services to families.

For children who are cared for outside the home, family day care is the most likely setting, as it constitutes 40 percent of child care arrangements (U.S. Bureau of the Census, 1983). Family day care probably serves more disabled children than any other arrangement (Fewell, 1986).

Viewing families as dynamic parts of a larger social system has caused people to rethink the support systems necessary and how these are most appropriately delivered. Empowering parents to make choices in the best interests of both their children and their families has affected the systems, thoughts, and actions of professionals in the field of early childhood special education.

LEGISLATIVE BASE FOR EARLY INTERVENTION

In the United States, the move to place and educate children with disabilities in the least restrictive environment began with the passage of Public Law 93-112, the Rehabilitation Act of 1973. Section 504 of this law mandates equal opportunities for children with disabilities in schools and preschools that receive *federal* funds. Public Law 94-142, the Education for All Handicapped Children Act of 1975 (EHA), guaranteed a free appropriate education to children and youth with disabilities. In 1983 amendments to this act (Public Law 98-199) offered incentives for professionals to develop model demonstration programs for preschool special education, early intervention, and transition programs. These were identified as areas that needed attention and innovative approaches. Public Law 99-457, passed in 1986, consisted of further amendments that lowered the age of eligibility to three years and established the Infants and Toddlers Program (Part H).

Amendments to the EHA made in 1990 made even more significant changes. The law was renamed the Individuals with Disabilities Education Act (IDEA) (Public Law 101-476). The term *handicapped* has been replaced by *disability,* and "people first" language has been instituted—that is, one refers to a child with a hearing impairment, not a hearing-impaired child. Children with autism and traumatic brain injury are now covered under the law. Special programs on transition and assistive technology are included. Services for children with serious emotional disturbances and attention-deficit disorders are included.

The Americans with Disabilities Act (ADA) of 1990 (Public Law 101-336) extends civil-rights protection similar to the nondiscrimination requirements based on race, sex, national origin, and religion to children with disabilities (National Information Center for Children and Youth with Disabilities, 1991). When the ADA goes into effect (January 26, 1993), child care settings and private schools will not be able to deny children admission to their programs because they have disabilities.

In summary, the field has become family and systems focused. Children with disabilities are expected to be raised in patterns as close to "normal" as possible. This means that children with disabilities will increasingly be cared for in family day care homes in their neighborhoods.

FAMILY DAY CARE AS A SOCIAL SUPPORT

Family day care is viewed as part of the social support system that helps children with disabilities remain in their homes. Most families of young children with disabilities choose family day care homes (as opposed to center-based settings) for placement when they are available (Deiner & Prudhoe, 1990). Because family day care providers are also the proprietors of their businesses, parents do not have to get the approval of teachers and program administrators to accommodate their children's needs as they do in center-based care. Family day care provides more continuity of care for children and families than do center-based programs. Parents have less worry that teachers will be shifted from one room to another or that as teachers change shifts important information about their children will be lost. There are fewer children in the setting, lessening the concern about infection.

Families who have young children with disabilities vary in their need for child care. To be responsive to these families, the child care system must be flexible. Family day care homes can provide this flexibility. Some families need full-time child care to allow parents to work; sometimes this includes nights and weekends. Some families need full- or part-time child care for respite.

Family day care homes are often located in the family's neighborhood and have the potential for more flexible hours than center-based programs. Arrangements for part-time care may be worked out. Such family day care homes also offer the potential for expanding the informal support network of the family by the addition of other parents and the family day care provider herself (Deiner & Whitehead, 1988).

BARRIERS TO CHILD CARE FOR CHILDREN WITH DISABILITIES

Finding a caregiver for a child with disabilities is often difficult. "We are often talking about desperate situations—families swamped by bills who may lose their homes without the mother working. And who will take a sick baby all hung with tubes?" (Healy, Keesee & Smith, 1985, p. 78). Parents may have to change their plans to return to work (Fewell, 1986) or utilize care that is less than satisfactory. They may have to develop complicated "packages" of care based on early intervention, therapy, and health concerns. Parents whose children attend school programs often need care before and after school as well as in the summer. This need extends past the age when other children can be left at home independently.

Few family day care providers are willing to accept children with disabilities. A child care data base called LOCATE found only 673 family day care providers in the state of Maryland who were willing to accept children with disabilities. There were, however, wide differences in the children they were willing to accept. Over half of the family day care providers were willing to accept children with delayed development, hearing loss, learning disability, speech and language delay, or vision loss. Less than 5 percent were willing to accept children with AIDS or respiratory problems (Salkever & Connolly, 1988).

The most common reasons given for not accepting children with disabilities are focused in four major areas: personal preparation and work load, liability issues, space and curricular restraints, and concerns about their own family and the other children in care.

Many family day care providers did not want to take children with disabilities because of their own lack of training or lack of time to participate in additional training. They felt that children with disabilities required extra resources, time, and energy, and they reported feeling overworked already (Deiner & Whitehead, 1987). Some were concerned that the needs of a disabled child were more than they could handle (Salkever & Connolly, 1988).

Providers reported being concerned about liability issues—particularly issues of health, safety, and insurance (Deiner & Whitehead, 1987; Fewell & Neisworth, 1987). Inadequate space and the actual structure of some homes were of concern to some, as was adapting the curriculum to meet the needs of this group of children (Fewell & Neisworth, 1987).

Providers were concerned about the reactions of the parents of other children and also about lowering the quality of care available to these children if children with disabilities were included. In some cases other members of the family day care provider's family did not want disabled children in the household (Deiner & Whitehead, 1987; Fewell & Neisworth, 1987; Maryland Committee for Children, Inc., 1988).

An additional but related problem has to do with the cost of child care. Because of the increased work load, some caregivers felt that the rate charged for children with disabilities should be higher. Those in favor of a higher rate used the analogy that infant care is usually more costly. Others found higher rates discriminatory. There is little agreement about how much higher, if any, the rates should be and how this should be determined. It is also not clear who should be responsible for the difference in cost, the parents or a funding agency. Purchase of care rates in some states acknowledge the difference; in Maryland, providers receive $2 a day more for children with disabilities. However, according to Salkever and Connolly, "This rate is inadequate to cover day care services for a disabled child" (1988, p. 1).

BENEFITS OF INCLUDING CHILDREN
WITH DISABILITIES

The normalization aspect of integrated child care placements is important to parents of children with disabilities. They want their children to have the opportunity to play and socialize with children with disabilities (Karns & Kontos, 1987). Children with disabilities are disabled in only part of their development, and socializing with children without disabilities provides a way a focusing on the "abilities" of these children. Children need the opportunity to learn to cope with and accept limitations in a supportive environment, to experiment with and gain confidence in their strengths and abilities, and to be accepted by other children and adults (U.S. Department of Health, Education and Welfare, 1972).

Interestingly, family day care providers who decide to take children with disabilities often do it to expose their own children and those in care to a wider range of abilities:

> It has been the most rewarding work that I have ever done. It was hard for me to learn new things such as sign language, but when my two-year-old signed "drink" to me it was the best feeling. (Deiner & Whitehead, 1989, p. 29)

Although discussion of integrating children with disabilities into the mainstream often focuses on negatives, there can be many benefits as well. These include the provision of a positive background for teaching children about differences in people, gaining a greater understanding of children with disabilities and their families, understanding the problems of children with disabilities, and inspiration and hope for coping with their own problems (Bailey & Winton, 1987; Winton, Turnbull & Blacher, 1984; U.S. Department of Health, Education and Welfare, 1972).

The relationship between placement of a child with a disability in a family day care home and satisfaction of all the parents is an important issue. If the parents of children with disabilities do not see family day care as an appropriate placement, or other parents in integrated settings choose to move their children out of these settings, providers will be forced to go out of business or run segregated family day care homes. The success or failure of integrated programs will be partially determined by the satisfaction of parents and their willingness to use mainstreamed family day care on an ongoing basis.

Although situations are often highly individual for specific families, in general, parents seem to indicate that mainstreaming is effective for both children with disabilities and those without (Deiner & Whitehead, 1989; Bailey & Winton, 1987). Interestingly, of the 59 parents surveyed by Bailey and Winton (1987), parents of children who did not have disabilities were less concerned about the drawbacks of integration after their children had experienced nine months in an integrated child care setting.

FAMILY DAY CARE AND EARLY INTERVENTION

The role of family day care as an intervention setting is not clear. Can family day care providers function as primary interventionists with appropriate professional support and technical assistance, or is their role more appropriately focused on program adaptation and social integration? Are there specific factors in children and child care providers that influence this decision? We cannot answer these questions empirically. However, as more children with disabilities participate in family day care, the factors that facilitate positive outcomes may be determined.

Day care for children with disabilities is used in one of two ways: in addition to early intervention services or as a site for the delivery of early intervention services. In the latter case, related services may be provided in the child care setting or elsewhere. The New Mexico Developmental Disabilities Planning Council surveyed 17 early childhood intervention programs funded by the council to determine day care use. It found that 40 percent of the children were in other child care settings in addition to the early intervention service (Klein & Sheehan, 1987). These children spent an average of 26 hours a week in day care. Within this dual-service perspective, the day care provider was responsible for adapting activities to allow children with disabilities to participate and for supporting social integration. The provider was not responsible for the educational component of early intervention services.

Other programs that use consultation models, such as the Family Day Care Project in Michigan, Project Neighbor Care in Pennsylvania and Indiana, Special Care Outreach Project in California, and Delaware FIRST and DelCare in Delaware, train the day care provider to function also as an early childhood interventionist with the support of a family day care home visitor and other technical assistance. The provider is then a more active participant in the process. Regardless of the approach, the issue of quality in family day care must be addressed.

Quality in family day care is a relevant issue because it directly affects the welfare of all the children in care. Unfortunately, the quality of care provided in many family day care homes is low and does not provide a situation conducive to optimal growth and development of any young child regardless of need.

There are few objective measures of quality of care. The Family Day Care Rating Scale developed by Harms and Clifford (1989) is one of the most widely used. The Family Day Care Rating Scale requires that an outside observer rate 33 items in the family day care home on a Likert Scale of 1–7, with 1 being inadequate and 7 being excellent. The major issue concerns the amount and appropriateness of the planning the provider does.

In sixty-seven initial Family Day Care Rating Scales evaluated as part of the Delaware FIRST program (Deiner & Whitehead, 1988), caregivers received an average overall rating of 3.6, with a range of 2.5 to 4.9 (with 4 being the midpoint on the scale). Caregivers in general scored above average on items related to the overall running of the family day care home and below the minimal acceptable rating of 3.0 on items related to programming and activities offered. More specifically, the highest mean rating was 4.81 for "informal language with infants and toddlers," with "arriving and leaving" and "balancing personal and caregiving responsibilities" receiving the second highest scores at 4.77 each. The lowest mean score was 2.13 for "cultural awareness," with the second lowest score being 2.41 for "visual display" (Deiner & Whitehead, 1988). Other mean scores below 3 included "safety," "blocks," "dramatic play," diapering/toileting," "teaching language," "sand/water play," and "personal grooming." Many of these items are important in the learning processes of young children.

An overarching issue is whether the amount and quality of individual attention provided are enough to meet the needs of children with disabilities. This is actually part of the much broader issue addressing adequacy of care for all young children, particularly infants.

EARLY IDENTIFICATION IN FAMILY DAY CARE

Family day care providers have the potential to provide early identification of children with disabilities. The more severe the disability the more likely it will be identified before the child is placed in care. However, children with mild to moderate delays, especially in the area of language development, may not be identified. Family day care providers can be particularly helpful in identifying such delays. Training the providers dramatically increases the possibility that they will identify and refer children with possible developmental delays.

SPECIAL TRAINING FOR FAMILY
DAY CARE PROVIDERS

Training issues focus around the population to be trained, the content of the training, and whether the focus is on preservice or inservice training and technical assistance.

Family day care providers are child care professionals who have small businesses in their homes. They have diverse experiential and educational backgrounds. They are primarily adult women, most of whom are or have been married and who have had children. Many have participated in some type of inservice training, but the training may have varied greatly in content and duration, from the minimum requirements for a license to college degrees in early childhood education. Their characteristics as a group influence both the level and type of training.

Initially, most programs that train family day care providers to care for children with disabilities start with a needs assessment or value clarification as a way of helping providers understand their feelings about disabilities. Training typically includes information on normal child growth and development as well as delayed and atypical growth patterns and specific disabilities. Information on early identification, programming adaptation, and working with parents is usually included. Information on community resources is also part of the training agenda (Special Care Outreach Project, 1984; Kontos, Dunham, Litchfield, Murphy, Tiffany & Morey, 1987; Jones & Meisels, 1987; Maryland Committee for Children, Inc., 1988; Deiner & Whitehead, 1989; Deiner & Prudhoe, 1990).

Teaching adult learners requires different teaching strategies than teaching college students. Teaching techniques should use information about how adult learners best comprehend information (Kontos et al., 1987; Jones, 1986; Sakata, 1984). An active learning approach, which utilizes lecture as only one means of teaching, is most appropriate for experienced adult learners (Jones, 1986; Sakata, 1984). Trust and respect for the learners is a basic precondition that must be present before learning will occur (Jones, 1986). The reading level of materials used needs to be considered as well as the experiential background of the providers. The leader does not just lead the group but becomes a participant member in the group as well (Jones, 1986). Leaders require skill in respectfully reframing inaccurate statements.

It is important to recognize and include family day care providers' life experiences as an integral part of the training (Harms, Bourland, Lewis & Cryer, 1985; Jones, 1986; Sakata, 1984). The training should include both what the family day care provider wants to know as well as what the teacher wants to teach (Jones, 1986). A problem-centered approach works well. Family day care providers want to apply what they have learned directly to their current situations (Harms et al., 1985; Sakata, 1984). They are capable of self-directed learning (Harms et al., 1985).

It is important for family day care providers to spend time getting to know one another and to develop long-term supportive relationships. This is especially important because family day care providers are relatively isolated from one another during their working hours (Blum, 1983; Schiller, 1980). Building a support network among providers and teaching some basic listening and peer counseling skills are essential components of training, especially for providers caring for infants and toddlers with disabilities.

Overall, training for family day care providers needs to be practical and useful. Family day care providers will learn what they perceive to be relevant to their situations. Information should be problem focused. Family day care providers change because they perceive the benefits of changing; they do not absorb information just to pass tests (Special Care Outreach Project, 1984).

Training holds the potential for improving the quality of child care. Untrained family day care providers may not know norms well enough to identify children with developmental delays, and even when they suspect a problem they often lack the confidence to approach the parents. They also may not be knowledgeable about the resources available for early diagnosis and intervention. Training increases the likelihood that family day care providers will identify disabilities and then refer children as well as adapt programming for children with disabilities. Although child care providers need training in basic child development, an even greater need is in matching activities to the developmental levels of the children in their care (Deiner & Prudhoe, 1990). Developmental knowledge is a means to an end, but it cannot be assumed that just presenting the information will change behavior in family day care homes.

Training child care providers through group inservice training is more effective than group preservice training. Given the amount of turnover in the field, those participating in preservice training may no longer be active in family day care when a child needs to be placed. Providers seem to be more attentive when children are in their homes already. Based on staff turnover, it is expected that at least two family day care providers will need to be trained each year for each child with a disability (Deiner & Prudhoe, 1990).

Behavior changes in child care providers occur on a one-to-one basis as a result of continuing inservice training. The modeling and motivation necessary to modify techniques for supporting children with special needs occur gradually through inservice visits on a one-to-one basis (Deiner & Prudhoe, 1990). Child care providers need technical assistance to care for children with special needs in the following areas: reading materials about specific disabilities, activity ideas, day care visits (weekly,bimonthly, or monthly), and additional training and telephone support (Deiner & Prudhoe, 1990).

HEALTH AND SAFETY CONCERNS

Increasingly both parents and family day care providers are focusing on issues of health and safety. Surprisingly, we do not have incidence data to show whether children are safer in child care or in their own homes (Aronson, 1986). We do, however, know that children in group care are exposed to more infectious disease agents (Aronson, 1986). No accurate assessment can be made of the relative risk of children becoming ill, but some studies indicate that children who attend child care are ill more than those who do not (Goodman, 1984). Younger children seem more at risk than older ones. The number of susceptible children in care is an important variable. For some children with disabilities their susceptibility to illness rules out center-based care. Infants and young children are expected to get six to nine viral infections a year, each lasting some three to seven days (Pantell, Fries & Vickery, 1982). These estimates are probably low for children with disabilities. For children who are at high biological risk, their own frequent illnesses and the possible presence of ill children in the family day care home are concerns. For parents of children with disabilities, providers' routine hygiene practices for diapering, toileting, and food preparation and how conscientiously these are adhered to may be an important criterion in selecting a family day care home.

Acquired immune deficiency syndrome (AIDS) is of particular concern in child care in addition to the traditional concerns about respiratory and gastrointestinal tract infections, skin infections, and invasive bacterial diseases.

The AIDS virus spreads through body secretions as well as blood products and contaminated needles. Casual contact does not spread the disease. Despite the fact that they are generally considered unfounded, concerns persist that transmission could occur in family day care homes through such activities as kissing, biting, or the sharing of toys (Sells & Paeth, 1987).

INDIVIDUALIZED CARE PLANNING

The purpose of individualized care planning is to meet the usual developmental needs as well as the unique needs of infants and young children with disabilities and their families. For children aged two and younger, Public Law 99-457 requires an individualized family service plan (IFSP). "The purpose of the IFSP is to identify and organize formal and informal resources to facilitate families' goals for their children and themselves" (National Early Childhood Technical Assistance System & Association for the Care of Children's Health, 1989, p. 1). For children aged three years and older an individualized education program (IEP) must be developed. Although different in some respects, the IFSP and IEP are both written documents developed jointly by the parents and the service providers. They detail the child's current level of development, the goals or outcomes expected, and a procedure to determine whether or not these have been achieved. They also detail the services to be provided; the frequency, intensity, location, and duration of these services; and when services will begin and end. The IEP must be reviewed annually, the IFSP at least every six months. The IFSP is more family oriented and includes family strengths and needs; it names a case manager and requires that a transition plan be developed to support children with disabilities as they move through the service delivery system.

It is expected that family day care providers responsible for carrying out the IFSP or IEP will have technical assistance available. Some question the effectiveness of family day care providers in implementing an IFSP when a consultant is not present. Many family day care providers have limited access to toys, games, and other materials. They may need help generating ideas for activities that meet the goals and objectives of the IFSP or IEP. Including day care providers in the planning process is expected to develop skills more effectively than would just providing them with a list of activities to carry out (Deiner & Prudhoe, 1990).

A Case Example

Juan was referred to the Delaware FIRST Program by a physical therapist working for the Delaware Department of Public Health. He was seven months old and had a severe hearing impairment. His family lived in a rural area. His father was working full time and his mother cared for him at home. Both parents had immigrated to the United States and were not native English speakers. Juan's family wanted respite care so the mother could take lessons in English, learn to drive, and look for a part-time job.

An individualized family service plan was developed for Juan to address both child and family needs. A potential trained provider was selected. The overriding variable was geographic location. Following a trial visit, Juan was enrolled in family day care for a half day a week, with the possibility of increasing hours as needed.

The family day care provider was given approximately six hours of specific training that included reviewing the results of the Family Day Care Rating Scale (Harms & Clifford, 1989) and viewing videotapes on hearing impairments and explaining disabilities to nondisabled children. A training session was also held with Juan's mother, his itinerant teacher of the deaf, his physical therapist, and the Delaware FIRST staff to train the family day care provider in signing, to suggest and demonstrate activities to enhance his motor development, and to offer other pertinent information.

Juan was placed in the family day care home and supported by telephone contacts, bimonthly visits, access to a toy lending system, and a bimonthly newsletter. After two months the family day care provider informed the Delaware FIRST staff that she was leaving family day care for a more economically profitable job. Juan returned to his home for a month and a half until a new family day care provider could be located and receive training. Juan has made developmental gains. His mother did obtain her license and a part-time job (adapted from Deiner & Whitehead, 1988).

FAMILY DAY CARE PROVIDERS
AS TEAM MEMBERS

Families and children with disabilities have multiple and diverse needs that change over time. Even for very young children, family day care may be only one of several programs families use to meet their children's educational, health, and therapy needs, as well as the parents' need for child care or respite care.

Thus families need a resource team from a variety of disciplines that they can draw on for information. The team may be different for each child and should be composed of family members and service providers. The family day care provider should be one member of that team. Her role may vary, but she, along with the parents, has probably seen the child for a greater amount of time and in more diverse circumstances than other team members. Her input is essential for the team, and her participation increases the likelihood that recommendations of the team will be carried out.

SUMMARY

Family day care appears to be a viable option for many children with disabilities. The role of the provider may vary with the provider's skills, parental preferences, and severity of the child's disability. Family day care's potential for flexibility is a positive factor in meeting the diverse needs of families and children with disabilities. Training of family day care providers increases their ability to identify and meet the needs of children with disabilities.

REFERENCES

Aronson, S. (1986). Maintaining health in child care settings. In N. Gunzenhauser & B. M. Caldwell (Eds.), *Group care for young children* (pp. 137–46). Skillman, NJ: Johnson & Johnson.

Bagnato, S., Kontos, S., & Neisworth, J. (1987). Integrated day care as special education: Profiles of programs and children. *Topics in Early Childhood Special Education, 7*(1), 28–47.

Bailey, D. Jr., & Winton, P. (1987). Stability and change in parents' expectations about mainstreaming. *Topics in Early Childhood Special Education, 7*(1), 73–88.

Barnard, D. E. (1981). An ecological approach to parent-child relations. In C. C. Brown (Ed.), *Infants at risk: Assessment and intervention. An update for health-care professionals and parents* (pp. 89–96). Skillman, NJ: Johnson & Johnson.

Blum, M. (1983). *The day-care dilemma: Women and children first.* Lexington, MA: Lexington Books.

Brooks-Gunn, J., & Lewis, M. (1982). Affective exchanges between normal and handicapped infants and their mothers. In T. Field & A. Fogel (Eds.), *Emotions and early interaction* (pp. 161–88). Hillsdale, NJ: Erlbaum.

Bryant, D., Ramey, C., Sparling, J., & Wasik, B. (1987). The Carolina approach to responsive education: A model for day care. *Topics in Early Childhood Special Education, 7*(1), 48–60.

Children's Defense Fund. (1990). *Children 1990: A report card, briefing book and action primer.* Washington, DC: Children's Defense Fund.

Cohen, S., & Warren, R. (1985). *Respite care: Principles and policies.* Austin, TX: PRO-ED.

Deiner, P. L., & Prudhoe, C. (1990). *DelCare: Final Report.* Delaware Department of Public Instruction: P. L. 99-457.

Deiner, P. L., & Whitehead, L. (1987). *Training family day care providers to work with handicapped infants and toddlers and their families.* Paper presented at the annual conference of the National Association for the Education of Young Children (NAEYC), Chicago.

Deiner, P. L., & Whitehead, L. C. (1988). Levels of respite care as a family support system. *Topics in Early Childhood Special Education, 8,* 51–61.

Deiner, P. L., & Whitehead, L. (1989). *Delaware FIRST: Final Report.* Newark, DE: College of Human Resources, University of Delaware.

Emlen, A. (1991). Personal correspondence.

Fewell, R. R. (1986). Child care and the handicapped child. In N. Gunzenhauser & B. M. Caldwell (Eds.), *Group care for young children* (pp. 35–46). Skillman, NJ: Johnson & Johnson.

Fewell, R. R., & Neisworth, J. (1987). Foreword. *Topics in Early Childhood Special Education, 7*(1), ix–x.

Field, T. (1982). Affective display of high-risk infants during interaction. In T. Field & A. Fogel (Eds.), *Emotions and early interaction* (pp. 101–25). Hillsdale, NJ: Erlbaum.

Fredericks, B., et. al. (1986). *A little bit under the weather: A look at care for mildly ill children.* Boston: Work/Family Directions.

Friedman, D. (1986). Child care for employee's kids. *Harvard Business Review, March-April,* 28–34.

Goodman, R. (1984). Infectious diseases and child day care. *Pediatrics, 74*(1), 134–39.

Harms, T., Bourland, B., Lewis, I., & Cryer, D. (1985). *Family day care: Trainer's resource manual.* Chapel Hill, NC: Frank Porter Graham Child Development Center.

Harms, T., & Clifford, R. M. (1989). *The family day care rating scale.* New York: Teachers College Press.

Hartley, M., White, C., & Yogman, M. (1989). The challenge of providing quality group care for infants and young children with special needs. *Infants and*

Young Children: An Interdisciplinary Journal of Special Care Practices, 8(2), 1–10.

Healy, A., Keesee, P., & Smith, B. (1985). *Early services for children with special needs: Transactions for family support.* Iowa City: University of Iowa.

Hofferth, S. L., & Phillips, D. A. (1987). Child care in the United States, 1970 to 1995. *Journal of Marriage and the Family, 49,* 559–71.

Jones, E. (1986). *Teaching adults: An active learning approach.* Washington, DC: National Association for the Education of Young Children.

Jones, S., & Meisels, S. (1987). Training family day care providers to work with special needs children. *Topics in Early Childhood Special Education, 7*(1), 1–12.

Karns, J., & Kontos, S. (1987). Mainstreaming handicapped preschoolers into center care. *Child Care Center,* November, 4–6.

Klein, N., & Sheehan, R. (1987). Staff development: A key issue in meeting the needs of young handicapped children in day care settings. *Topics in Early Childhood Special Education, 7*(1), 13–27.

Kontos, S., Dunham, J., Litchfield, M., Murphy, D., Tiffany, K. (1987). *Neighbor care: Training manual for family day care.* West Lafayette, IN: Purdue University.

Levy, J. M., & Levy, P. H. (1986). Issues and models in the delivery of respite services. In C. Salisbury & J. Intagliata (Eds.), *Respite care: Support for persons with developmental disabilities and their families* (pp. 99–116). Baltimore: Paul H. Brooks.

Maier, H. (1985). First and second order change: Powerful concepts for child care practitioners. *Journal of Children in Contemporary Society, 17*(3), 37–45.

Meisels, S., & Shonkoff, J. (Eds.). (1990). *Handbook of early childhood intervention.* Cambridge: Cambridge University Press.

National Early Childhood Technical Assistance System (NEC*TAS) & Association for the Care of Children's Health (ACCH). (1989). *Guidelines and recommended practices of the individualized family service plan.* Washington, DC: ACCH.

National Information Center for Children and Youth with Disabilities (NICHCY). (1991). *News digest: The education of children and youth with special needs: What do the laws say? 1*(1), 1–15.

Pantell, R., Fries, J., & Bickery, D. (1982). *Taking care of your child: A parents' guide to medical care.* Reading, MA: Addison-Wesley.

Powell, T., & Hecimovic, A. (1981). *Respite care for the handicapped: Helping individuals and the families.* Springfield, IL: Charles C Thomas.

Sakata, R. T. (1984). *Adult education: Theory and practice* (Outreach Series Paper, No. 2). Chapel Hill, NC: Technical Assistance Development System.

Salkever, M., & Connolly, A. (1988). *Day care for disabled Children.* Baltimore: Maryland Committee for Children, Inc.

Schiller, J. D. (1980). *Child-care alternatives and emotional well-being.* New York: Praeger.

Schuler, R. (1980). Definition and conceptualization of stress in organizations. *Organizational Behavior and Human Performance, 25*(1), 184–215.

Seligman, M., & Darling, R. (1989). *Ordinary families, special children: A systems approach to childhood disability.* New York: Guilford Press.

Sells, C., & Paeth, S. (1987). Health and safety in day care. *Topics in Early Childhood Special Education, 7*(1), 61–72.

Special Care Outreach Project. (1984). *Techniques for trainers.* Los Angeles: Child, Youth, and Family Services.

U.S. Bureau of the Census. (1983, November). *Child care arrangements of working mothers: June 1982.* Special Studies, Series P-23, No. 129. Washington, DC: U.S. Department of Commerce.

U. S. Department of Health, Education and Welfare (1972). *Day care: Serving children with special needs.* DHEW Publication No. (OCD) 73-1063. Washington, DC: Office of Child Development.

Winton, P., Turnbull, A., & Blacher, J. (1984). *Selecting a preschool: A guide for parents of handicapped children.* Austin, TX: Pro-Ed, Inc.

Zigler, E. (1990). Foreword. In S. Meisels & J. Shonkoff (Eds.), *Handbook of early childhood intervention.* New York: Cambridge University Press.

CHAPTER 9

The Physical Setting

ECOLOGICAL FEATURES OF FAMILY DAY CARE AND THEIR IMPACT ON CHILD DEVELOPMENT

Susan L. Golbeck

Family day care, by definition, occurs within the context of the caregiver's home. This distinctive physical setting might well provide the context for an optimal nonparental child care situation. The family day care provider might function as an extended family member caring for children in a manner reflecting the values of the children's home environments within a setting that looks and feels like home. However, family day care can also represent a much less desirable child care scenario. Managing several small children in a space designed for other purposes presents special problems that many providers may not be prepared to handle (see Johnson, 1987). Since family day care occurs within private homes, it is extremely difficult to regulate and monitor. Do children in family day care experience the typical homelike setting envisioned by family day care advocates? Or is family day care much like other forms of group care, just in a different kind of space?

Undoubtedly, the response to this question will be: It depends on the individual child and the specific child care situation. However, the answer for any given situation requires that the linkages between the social and physical components of the environment be identified and that their impact on the child be understood. Perhaps of greater importance, the relationship between setting characteristics and children's well-being must be clarified. These questions are explored in the present chapter through a selective examination of research on family day care settings. Of primary interest is empirical work examining connections between the physical setting and child behavior. Three broad categories of research are considered. The first includes comparative studies of family and center-based child care. These studies have considered indicators of children's behavior and well-being both in the child care setting and beyond. A second group of studies addresses relationships between setting features and children's play and social interaction. A third and final category of studies examines caregiver behavior as it relates to the physical setting. It is certainly the case that caregiver behaviors are vital to the quality of children's experiences in child care. Of concern here are ways in which the caregiver's caregiving behavior is enhanced and supported by the physical environment. Although this work cannot provide us with a definitive picture of the ecology of family day care, it can help to identify relevant setting characteristics and suggest directions for future inquiry. The ecology of family day care is obviously much broader and complex than the physical setting alone (see Fosberg, 1981, for one overview of family day care in the United States). In this chapter, the physical setting has been employed as a stepping-stone into the dynamic family day care system and represents just one aspect of children's experience in child care.

SETTINGS AND CHILD DEVELOPMENT: GUIDEPOSTS FROM THEORY

The role of the physical setting, particularly as it intersects with social variables, presents intriguing and important questions for developmental psychologists. For example, how readily can developmental and educational outcomes be modified as a function of physical setting variables? What is the long-term effect of specific environmental deficits on children's development? How are variations in the physical and social setting actually experienced by children? Studying context variables as evidenced in child care settings may provide insights into possible ways of influencing developmental outcomes in children.

There is now sufficient theory and research in psychology to argue convincingly that the physical environment can have impact on developmental and educational outcomes (Wachs, 1987; Wohlwill, 1980; Wohlwill & Heft, 1987). Three theoretical orientations are especially noteworthy in relation to these issues. These are the cognitive-developmental view, Bronfenbrenner's ecological view, and Barker's approach to the environment as a behavior setting. Each of these helps to make sense of the empirical findings on family day care.

A Cognitive-Developmental View

The first approach is a cognitive-developmental view. From this perspective, the child is born with a predisposition to act upon the environment.

Given this, the function of the environment is to provide opportunities for challenging experience and interaction. As described here, this is an amalgam of two orientations described by Wohlwill and Heft (1987); the environment as source of stimulation and the environment as source of feedback to the child. Such a view of the environment is consistent with both Piaget's (Piaget, 1952) and Werner's (Werner, 1948; Wapner, Cohen & Kaplan, 1976) theories of cognitive development.

Several points can be made about the nature of child and environment interactions. First, there is an optimal level of stimulation beyond which further stimulation is not enriching but actually interferes with behavior and development (Wachs, 1987; Wachs & Gruen, 1982). Hunt describes this as an optimal match between organism and environment (Hunt, 1961, 1963). Second, by influencing the feedback or stimulation received from the environment, a child actually creates new stimulation. For example, an infant who is sitting on the kitchen floor accidentally opens the cupboard door, discovering (or creating) a wonderful array of new objects (pots and pans). These, in turn, present many new opportunities for exploration and learning. Third, Wohlwill and Heft (1987) note that beyond the simple active/passive view of children, the ability to regulate stimulation is an important feature of this approach to the environment. Children functioning at varying developmental levels differ in their ability to control and to adapt to environmental input. For example, a noisy environment may be more problematic for a younger child than an older child, since the younger child is less able to regulate attention. Along similar lines, interesting responsive toys within reach may be more important to an infant than to a preschooler, since the preschooler is capable of remembering that the toys can be found behind the closed doors of the toy cupboard. Although this approach to the physical environment seems at least partially implicit in many approaches to early childhood environments (e.g., Montessori, 1909/64; DeVries & Kohlberg, 1990), it has seldom been articulated in a careful or consistent manner.

Bronfenbrenner's Framework

A second orientation to the environment is Bronfenbrenner's ecological approach (Bronfenbrenner, 1977, 1979; Belsky, 1984). From this contextually oriented perspective, the setting for development is a multilayered set of systems with which children have varying degrees of direct and indirect interaction. Importantly, however, activities at all levels of the system can influence development, even those in which children have no direct involvement. Proximal systems for children include the family day care setting and the home setting. More distal systems might include the parent's workplace, the community at large, or interactions between the members of the caregiver's family. A child is both a source and a recipient of influence within all levels in the system. Bronfenbrenner argues that relationships between these systems become better articulated and the variety of settings in which children participate increases with development.

Within Bronfenbrenner's ecological framework, the system most immediately and most directly influencing individuals is the microsystem. Bronfenbrenner defines a microsystem as "a pattern of activities, roles, and interpersonal relations experienced by the developing person in a given setting with particular physical and material characteristics" (Bronfenbrenner, 1979, p. 22). The primary microsystem is the family. However, for young children in day care, the child care setting is a second microsystem (Belsky, Steinberg & Walker, 1982). The components of any microsystem include both people and things. Within the microsystem of family day care, the people include the caregiver, other children she cares for, her family members, and perhaps her neighbors and friends. Each of these individuals has a specific role in the functioning of the system. The physical dimensions of the family day care microsystem include the objects found in the home as well as their organization and arrangement. The overall functioning of the system is influenced by a variety of factors apparently unrelated to child care (e.g., the caregiver's family, the caregiver's participation in a resource and referral group for family day care providers, and the caregiver's social network). Bronfenbrenner (1979) also argues that children's development is strengthened by linkages between the various microsystems they experience. These linkages are called mesosystems.

The bulk of Bronfenbrenner's work has focused on the influence of social relationships beyond the microsystem on microsystem functioning. He has studied the impact of both exosystem variables, or events in systems in which children are not direct participants, and macrosystems, or the broad cultural context. Although acknowledging the importance of the physical setting, he is seldom specific about how such setting features have an impact on children. This approach has the advantage of being consistent with currently popular theories in social and cognitive development; it is widely used in child development research and is distinctly developmental. The explicit concern with linkages between the various microsystems experienced by children is especially welcome in the child care area. Unfortunately, this framework has not been widely used in environmental psychology or studies of the relationship between the physical environment and behavior.

Barker's Approach

A third conceptualization, also useful in understanding the relationships between the family day care setting and children's development, is Barker's ecological framework. Also a contextual orientation, this approach has been more widely used in the study of physical environments for children. There is an emphasis here on the context for behavior rather than the individual child. The study of nonobservable cognitive characteristics and personality predispositions is frowned upon.

The key notion for researchers working from the Barker framework has been the *behavior setting*. The behavior setting cuts across both the physical and the social dimensions of the environment. Wohlwill and Heft (1987) note that the behavior setting is often defined in molar terms with particular emphasis given to the *function* of the setting, (e.g., church or school) without much attention to the specific physical characteristics. However, physical arrangements provide important cues that control or guide the behavior of users. This has been describe as a "synomorphy" between physical setting and the program of behavior associated with the setting (Gump, 1987). Not surprisingly, researchers working from this orientation make little reference to abstract psychological constructs such as developmental level.

Barker's approach, although more widely used in studies of the physical setting than the other two approaches, is highly mechanistic and deterministic (Wohlwhill & Heft, 1987), and it is difficult to relate to theory in social and cognitive development. However, it has been useful for analyzing the impact of the physical environment of the school (Barker & Gump, 1964; Gump, 1987), and specifically early childhood settings (Weinstein, 1987), on children's learning and behavior.

Conclusion

Each of these orientations offers a different perspective on child-environment relationships within the context of family day care. From the cognitive-developmental view comes an emphasis on the close interaction between the individual child and the physical setting. Children at different developmental levels are recognized as capable of experiencing the same environment in very different ways, and it is insufficient to construe the environment as simply "out there" and apart from the individual. Furthermore, children play an active role in creating and regulating the feedback received from experience. In contrast, Bronfenbrenner underscores the influence of systems outside the immediate microsystem of family day care upon the functioning of the microsystem. These might include the parent's workplace, the characteristics of the provider's family, neighborhood, and community, and so forth. Additionally, Bronfenbrenner calls our attention to the differing contributions of each participant in the microsystem of family day care: child, caregiver, and family members of each. Finally, Barker provides an emphasis on a close analysis of the setting itself, with a special focus on its function. This perspective returns our focus to the characteristics of the setting itself rather than the individual.

EMPIRICAL STUDIES OF FAMILY DAY CARE ENVIRONMENTS

An early and influential study of early childhood environments was conducted by Elizabeth Prescott and her colleagues in the late 1960s. That work is important for purposes of this chapter because it serves as a reference point for much of the current work in child care environments. Prescott applied the Barker (1968) framework to a study of children's group experiences in family and center-based day care. The initial research focused on children in 50 day care centers (Prescott, 1987; Prescott, Jones, & Kritchevsky, 1972). In the Barker manner, the day was conceptualized as a series of behavior-activity settings. Each setting was described in terms of the physical setting itself and the program of behavior associated with the setting. Classrooms were rated on eight sets of features characterizing the physical setting (Prescott, Jones & Kritchevsky, 1972; see also Kritchevsky, Prescott & Walling, 1969). These features were: (1) organization of pathways; (2) variety of equipment and learning materials; (3) complexity of equipment and materials; (4) amount to do; (5) novelty, including variations in both schedule and equipment; (6) source and amount of intrusion from the world beyond the classroom; (7) seclusion potential (opportunities to get away from other people); and (8) softness. Prescott and her colleagues claim that in the centers with high-quality physical environments, children were more involved and teachers spent less time on management and enforcement of rules and more time responding to children and fostering social interaction (Prescott & Jones, 1967). Two forms of overall program organization within the centers were also identified: closed structure, or highly teacher directed; and open structure, resembling the traditional morning nursery school or presumably the traditional child development nursery school (Evans, 1975). Program structure and the physical characteristics of the setting proved to be closely related.

This work was extended to family day care in a study comparing children's experiences in four types of child care: open- and closed-structure center day care, family day care, and a combination of home and center care (Prescott, 1973). The sample included 112 children, aged two to five years, distributed across each of the four setting types. Apparently all the family day care homes participated in a demonstration community family day care project. Observations focused on identifying the opportunities provided by adults and the personal settings selected by the children from those available (Prescott, Jones & Kritchevsky, 1972, p. 3).

According to Prescott, family day care and nursery school/home care present markedly similar profiles in terms of child environment interactions:

> Adults in both home-based settings were more available to children than in group care; opportunities for the child to make choices and control the environment were higher than in group care. Supports for self esteem appeared high. Opportunities for cognitive engagement did not appear to be lower in family day care than in open structure group care, although adult input toward this goal may be somewhat less. (Prescott, 1973, p. 7)

Further differences between centers and family day care homes could be seen in the physical and spatial features of the two settings. The home environment was evaluated according to a set of criteria paralleling the classroom spatial inventory discussed above. Information regarding access to the outdoors, designated play space for children other than the family living room, children's choices about where to play, specific items and type of play equipment, presence of child-sized furniture, and use of regular household furnishings was included. Some of the more intriguing items included risk-taking opportunities, overlap between children's work and the adult work, and availability of "treasures" in the home. The home was also rated on a number of dimensions such as formal/informal, quiet/noisy, OK to be dirty/important to be clean, and loosely scheduled time/tightly scheduled time. Unfortunately, the scale used in the homes was not refined to the same degree as the classroom measure, and some important measurement problems were never resolved (see Prescott et al., 1972)

Despite these measurement issues, a number of differences between homes and centers are described by Prescott (1987). First, the objects in the homes were markedly different from those in day care centers. Homes have soft couches and easy chairs, books and magazines, and personal objects with special meaning. Such items contrast with the institutional, impersonal, standardized items often found in centers. Unlike many classrooms, the contents of the homes showed variety, softness, and novelty (Prescott & David, 1976).

Second, space and time boundaries are more flexible in homes. Most homes can provide some form of quiet space for children. This is less often true in centers. In homes, temporal structure is less rigid and more responsive to the needs of the children. Prescott notes that adult-pressured transitions were more frequent in closed-structure center care than in home care. In closed-structure centers, time spent in structured transitions such as lining up to go outside, using the toilet, or waiting for lunch averaged 24 percent of the children's time. In home-based care it dropped to less than 3 percent (Prescott, 1973). In homes, children were not bound by tight routines or schedules. For example, a book-reading activity between two children might evolve into a game of pretend, and such play could continue to a natural ending point. Lunch could wait for 20 minutes until children finished their play. This was less likely to happen in centers.

Third, social grouping and social relationships varied across homes and centers. Homes were often much more diversified social settings than day care centers. Frequently, children of varying ages were cared for by the same provider. Diverse social relationships were possible through contact with preschoolers of different ages as well as school-aged children later in the day; there were also visitors to family day care homes, such as neighbors, friends, and relatives. In contrast, children in centers were usually grouped by age with relatively little social contact outside the center.

A final feature of home environments noted by Prescott concerns the logic of everyday activities (Prescott, 1987). By this she seems to be referring to a quality of daily experience. In homes, children are integrally involved in meaningful everyday activity, whether it is helping to sort wash, greeting the UPS man at the front door, watching a fire truck race down the street, or discussing vegetables in the kitchen.

Prescott's work illustrates the rich array of experiences constituting the ecology of family day care. The physical and social settings are closely, if not inseparably, intertwined. How accurate is Prescott's characterization of homes and day care centers today, more than 20 years since her initial work? This remains unclear. Even if her characterization is correct, Prescott did not consider how these settings influence children's behavior or development beyond the actual child care experience. It is therefore not clear whether the differences she observed really matter in the long run. However, her analysis of children's experience in child care is insightful, and it reflects a sensitivity to the potential family day care provides for children.

In the remainder of this chapter, more recent research addressing these issues is considered. As already noted, special attention is given to the physical setting as a contributor to the ecology of the family day care environment. From the children's perspective, three broad areas of development are considered; social-affective development, cognitive development, and language development. However, complementing the children's perspective is that of caregivers. Therefore, relationships between the setting and caregiver behavior are also briefly examined.

SETTINGS AND SOCIAL-AFFECTIVE DEVELOPMENT

A great deal has been written about the influence of child care upon children's social and affective development (cf. Belsky, 1984, 1988; Lamb &

Sternberg, 1990). The focus here is on family day care, which has been much less studied than center care. In this section, several studies of children's social and affective well-being are discussed. The first concerns a comparative study of four types of child care arrangements in which developmental outcomes, the relationships between these outcomes, and specific features of the social and physical environments were considered. Complementing this comparative study are several smaller-scale studies examining setting variations and their effects on children's play behavior within the child care context. Taken together, these findings suggest that the picture is more complex than that described by Prescott and colleagues.

A Comparative Study

Clarke-Stewart and colleagues (Clarke-Stewart, 1981, 1987; Clarke-Stewart & Gruber, 1984) conducted a comparative study of four types of care in Chicago. A variety of setting measures were included. However, unlike the Prescott study, developmental outcomes in children were measured directly. Four forms of care for children were considered: full-day center-based care, traditional nursery school, family day care home, and a regular baby-sitter in the child's home. Setting features included caregiver characteristics (education and experience), the social context, (children, adults, and the types of interactions), the physical setting (types of toys, types of adult decorations, messiness, potential for danger), and program of activities (structure, opportunities for learning).

There are a number of interesting findings with relevance to comparative outcomes as well as the physical setting. Children's social and cognitive competence was followed over the course of a year. A variety of assessments were completed in the children's homes and in a laboratory playroom. These included measures of proximity and sociability with mother, social cognition, social competence with an adult stranger, negative behavior to a peer stranger, and social competence at home. The impact of child care experience on cognitive development was measured through standardized assessments of language comprehension, verbal fluency, object recognition, knowledge of concepts, and digit span. Although this section has been labeled social and affective development, for purposes of clarity all the findings relevant to the physical setting will be described.

In general, children attending nursery school programs scored the highest on developmental outcomes, and children cared for in their own homes by baby-sitters scored the lowest. Relative to the other three groups, the children in family day care homes scored highest on sociability with an unfamiliar peer but lowest on the measure of independence from mother. Hence, in terms of later developmental outcomes, family day care children fared less well than children in center-based programs, although there were some exceptions.

Of greater interest for present purposes are relationships between the home setting and development for those children not in the center and nursery school groups. How do features of the home setting for child care relate to these developmental outcomes? To answer this question, Clarke-Stewart collapsed the two home settings (combining family day care and baby-sitter care) and the two center settings (day care center and nursery school). Clarke-Stewart and Gruber (1984) report five measures of the physical setting: types of toys available, types of adult-oriented decorations, messiness, dangerous items, and structure. Toys alone were not related to any social or cognitive measure. However, structure within the physical setting was positively related to social and cognitive competence. The researchers summarized the relationships between the features of the home setting and measures of social-affective and cognitive development as follows:

> Children are most likely to benefit from a home day care setting where the physical environment is organized around and for them. When the setting and the schedule are structured so that there are areas and times set aside for play, when the environment is kept relatively neat and orderly, when there are fewer adult-oriented decorative items (and so less need for restriction) . . . children quite consistently score higher on measures of social and intellectual competence. On the other hand, just providing more toys and materials *per se,* within the limits observed in our home day care settings, does not make a difference in children's development. Children in homes where we observed more physical danger were more "fearless"—they were more aggressive toward an unfamiliar peer, less compliant with their parents, and more outgoing with an unfamiliar adult. (Clarke-Stewart & Gruber, 1984, p. 55)

These findings are consistent with a cognitive-developmental approach to the role of the environment. Organization of objects, space, and time appeared to be especially important for the two- and three-year-olds in this study. Presumably the mere presence of toys and materials was insufficient for children to benefit maximally. Rather, order and organization within the environment were needed.

Unfortunately, there are problems with this study. The role of social class in the correlations is ambiguous; attrition for the family day care group was quite high; and by combining the family day care and home care groups, it is not clear what the comparisons mean. However, in spite of these limitations, this study makes some important contributions. Clarke-Stewart considered many of the same variables discussed by Prescott and supplements them with developmental outcomes. Like Prescott, Clarke-Stewart and her colleagues also found that the types of materials and the structure provided in the setting are important for ongoing interactions. Importantly, Clarke-Stewart's work suggests that these variables are related to developmental outcomes beyond the child care setting. The findings also suggest that the quality of the child care experience is less positive than that reported by Prescott. Since Prescott's study has at least as many methodological problems as the Clarke-Stewart study, this is most unsettling. In short, the findings underscore the desperate need for further research on setting variables and child outcomes in family day care.

Settings and Their Influence on Peer Play

Children's play serves an important role in children's social, affective, and cognitive development during the preschool years. Furthermore, provision of developmentally appropriate play experiences is a long-standing aspect of early childhood programs (Klugman & Smilanoker, 1990; Kohlberg & Fein, 1987). Therefore, it is not surprising that play has been a target of study for researchers concerned with the effects of child care experience. In this section several studies exploring the influence of setting features and family day care are considered. Although play is an indicator of cognitive growth as well as social and emotional development, the work described here has a decidedly social bent.

Several studies have examined children's social play behavior in relation to the objects and materials in their play space. Howes and Rubenstein (1981) compared toddlers' social play behavior in center- and family-based care. Toddlers' interactions with peers were examined in relation to the size and age composition of the group as well as the physical space and play object availability. Forty toddlers, ranging in age from 18 to 22 months, were observed during free play. The frequency of socially directed behaviors toward peers was noted. These included vocalizations, positive approaches, and aggressive behaviors. In addition, the complexity of children's play was rated on a five-point scale. The results showed that there were no overall differences in socially directed behaviors across the two day care settings, although there was more vocalizing in family day care. However, physical setting characteristics were related to play in interesting ways. In day care centers, the highest level of interactive play was shown in the context of large nonportable objects. The family day care toddlers, who had less access to such equipment, also showed a high level of interactive play when they were able to use features of the home environment such as hallways, corners, and connecting rooms in play and when they were allowed freedom of movement across such areas. Children in family day care settings also showed more interactive play when they were *not* using smaller portable objects and toys.

Howes and Rubenstein (1981) note that both setting characteristics and setting contents influence social behavior and that the inanimate environment must be defined in terms of the available objects as well as the spatial arrangements of those objects.

Similar findings are also noted by Gump (1987) in a description of a study by Smith and Connolly (1980). Although this study was conducted within a preschool setting it seems worth noting in light of the Howes and Rubenstein (1981) findings. Several large, fixed playthings (a climbing apparatus) and a table and chairs were placed in a large playroom with or without a number of smaller toys. When the small toys were not present behavior changed, although not necessarily in a negative direction. Without small objects children became more physically active, more socially interactive, and made more creative use of furniture.

The research just described should not be taken to mean that small toys and objects need to be removed to facilitate social interaction. But as Howes and Unger (1989) argue, careful thought must be given to an appropriate arrangement of objects and space that serves to shape complementary actions and prevents children from intruding on one another's play space. For example, cooking material, a stove, and a small table with chairs set up under a climbing structure could provide a protected space and could focus peer encounters. The cooking materials and stove provide realistic props for pretend. Similarly, a large two-seater wooden car complete with steering wheel, ignition, and seat belts would support play. The two seats limit peer play to a dyad and focus the attention of partners on each other. The equipment suggests pretend activities.

In another study, Rothstein-Fisch and Howes (1988) examined several family day care setting features likely to influence peer group interaction. Setting features included aspects of the home environment and peer group configuration. The home environment included three types of variables: situational features (related to the type of child activity—arousal, motion, and noise), physical features (including location of activity and type of objects available), and caregiver features (referring primarily to the type of activity in which the caregiver was engaged). Significant differences in peer play appeared to occur as a function of the situational feature of arousal level. Children engaged in more complex play when they were in above-average or constant motion than when they were in below-average motion. However, children engaged in more solitary play under conditions of quiet alert arousal. There were also differences in play as a function of caregiver activity. Children engaged in more complex peer play when the caregiver was engaged in day care–related activity as opposed to when she was actively interacting with them. The physical features examined in this particular study were not related to peer play.

Additional research in preschool classrooms suggests that particular types of objects facilitate play and positive social interaction (see Gump, 1987; Weinstein, 1987 for excellent reviews). At least in preschool classrooms, children's affective and social experiences appear to be positively related to the presence of a sufficient number of play units. "Play unit" was defined in terms of Prescott's categorization described earlier (Getz & Brendt, 1982; Prescott, 1981). Hendrickson and her colleagues (1981) found that isolate behavior was predominate with puzzles, parquetry blocks, pegboards, Legos, Tinker Toys, and toy animals. Sharing behavior was associated with balls, puppet stages, dress-up materials, blocks, and housekeeping materials. Similar findings were reported by Shure (1963). Finally, Quilitch and Risley (1973) demonstrated experimentally that "social toys" such as games yield more social interaction than "isolate toys" such as Play-doh and Tinker Toys. Although social interaction is only one component of play, these findings suggest that the contents of the physical environment are related to ongoing interaction, which may well influence subsequent play activity. Although these studies were not conducted in family day care homes, they suggest directions for future work.

Finally, research using the Family Day Care Rating Scale (FDCRS) provides further evidence for likely relationships between setting characteristics and play. The FDCRS (Harms & Clifford, 1989) is an overall environmental rating scale presumably tapping the range of dimensions characterizing program quality. Importantly, a number of items measure aspects of the physical setting. Howes and Stewart (1987) found that after controlling for family characteristics, family day care quality, as measured by the total score on the FDCRS, did emerge as an important predictor of children's play with peers and with objects. Unfortunately, these relationships are discussed only in terms of a composite score on the FDCRS. The FDCRS defines setting very broadly, including diverse aspects of the physical and social environment. The scale is broken into seven subscales, but relationships between play and subscale scores were not presented. It is hoped that future researchers will focus more attention on teasing apart this composite measure into conceptually meaningful indicators of the environment and quality.

SETTINGS AND COGNITIVE AND LINGUISTIC DEVELOPMENT

As already noted, several researchers have examined the impact of family day care settings on children's cognitive and linguistic development. Clarke-Stewart (1981, 1987) focused on relationships between environmental characteristics and cognitive and language outcomes. She identified relationships between environmental characteristics and performance on standardized intelligence measures (e.g., WIPPSI). The work of Howes and her colleagues touches upon emerging representational capabilities as evidenced in social pretend (Howes & Unger, 1989). Prescott (1987) noted that family day care homes provided special opportunities for conversation between caregiver and child, an important source of input for cognitive and linguistic development. It is also worth noting that considerable attention has been devoted to enhancing children's play opportunities in center-based child care (see Moore, 1987; Moore, Lane, Hill, Cohen & McGinty, 1979). In this section, the extent to which the research supports the expectation that ecological features of the family day care setting can influence cognitive and linguistic functioning is more closely scrutinized.

An ongoing project addressing questions regarding cognitive and language development and family day care is being conducted by Goelman and Pence (1987a, 1987b, in press; Pence & Goelman, 1987a, 1987b) in Canada. In an early report on this project, the joint effects of family structure and characteristics of the child care setting on children's language development were considered (Goelman & Pence, 1987a; 1987b). This study spanned a two-year period and included a total of 105 child-parent-caregiver triads. The caregivers worked in three types of settings: licensed child care centers, licensed family day care homes, and unlicensed family day care homes. The children were two through four years of age. Several observational measures were used to determine the quality of the child care environment. These included the Early Childhood Environment Rating Scale (ECERS) (Harms & Clifford, 1980) or the FDCRS (Harms & Clifford, 1989) and a play observation measure.

Children's behavior in the three types of settings varied in several ways. Goelman and Pence (1987b) note that the center care children showed higher levels of cooperative play and lower levels of solitary and parallel play than the family day care groups. However, children in day care centers were actually a little older, so it is difficult to draw direct comparisons between centers and family day care homes on this developmental measure. The differences between licensed and unlicensed family day care homes, when they existed, tended to favor the licensed homes. Children in unlicensed homes viewed educational television more frequently than the children in either licensed homes or centers. Also, children in center programs were observed in informational exchanges, or informal, noninstructional conversations, with adults more often than children in either licensed or unlicensed homes (Goelman & Pence, 1987b). However, if such exchanges are more typical of older than younger children, a comparison between the family day care and center care groups is again problematic, since the children in center care were slightly older.

In an effort to relate dimensions of the early childhood setting to developmental outcomes, performance on two measures of receptive language—the Peabody Picture Vocabulary Test (PPVT) and the Early One-Word Picture Vocabulary Test (EOWPVT)—was related to the ECERS or the FDCRS. In general, the vocabulary scores seemed to be related to the environment in family day care but not center day care (both voluntary measures related to the social development subscale and the total scores on the FDCRS). In a subsequent analysis, Goelman and Pence (1987a) found that overall, although the centers showed some variation in quality, this variation was much less than that found in the homes. High- and low-quality centers had children with fairly comparable scores on the language and play measures. In contrast, day care homes varied much more widely in quality and the children showed comparable variations in language scores.

Recently, Goelman and Pence (in press) have looked more closely at the family day care environment and how the environment functions to support early language and literacy behaviors in children. The family day care environment was assessed directly with measures more sensitive than the FDCRS to the overall ecology of the setting. Specifically Caldwell and Bradley's HOME SCALE (Bradley & Caldwell, 1976; Elardo & Bradley, 1981) was used to measure the level of cognitive stimulation provided by the family day care setting. Of particular interest were relationships between cognitive stimulation as measured by the HOME scale and language development.

Twenty children between three and four years of age were studied in their family day care settings and their home settings. Children were observed interacting with their family day care providers and their mothers while playing with a standardized set of play materials. Adult and child talk was analyzed for the presence of features deemed likely to enhance later literacy behaviors. Separate measures of oral and receptive language were also administered. The authors report a number of relationships between various aspects of adult and child discourse and children's oral and receptive language. However, of special interest here is the finding that scores on the family day care HOME measure were related to children's expressive language but not receptive language. This is interesting, because HOME scores for the children's own homes were related to both expressive and receptive language. There were also strong relationships between children's home and family day care HOME scores. Goelman and Pence suggest that children's receptive language capabilities may have been well established before their entry into these family day care settings, but expressive languages skills may have been at a critical transition point and hence more receptive to environmental variations.

This study represents an important advance in understanding the relationships between the physical environment of the family day care setting and cognitive development. Although there is a literature on home environments and their impact on social and cognitive development (see Parke, 1978, for a review) prior work has focused on the role of the child's home, not the family day care home. Past work primarily considered the impact of social and physical stimulation and its effects on IQ (Gottfried, 1984). The most exclusive work has been done on IQ during infancy, although there is an increasing amount of data for the early childhood period (Elardo & Bradley, 1981; Wachs, 1987). There are many parallels between the dimensions considered for homes and other early childhood care settings, but none of the earlier work considered comparisons with family day care environments.

SETTINGS AND CAREGIVER BEHAVIOR

Up to this point, the family day care setting has been considered from the perspective of the child. However, just as the physical setting influences child behaviors, so can it influence caregiver behaviors. From this perspective, the physical setting can be seen as a facilitator of adult caregiving behaviors (Long, Peters & Garduque, 1985). Surprisingly, there is little research available in which features of the physical space were explicitly examined in relation to caregiving behavior.

One exception is a study by Howes (1983). She examined caregiver behavior in center and family day care as a function of setting characteristics. Not surprisingly, family day care children were less likely than center day care children to be cared for in a space specifically designed for child care. However, space specifically designated for child care proved to be an important variable influencing caregiving behavior within the family day care settings. Family day care providers caring for children in child-designated space were more likely to express positive affect and were less likely to express negative affect or to restrict toddler activity. A positive emotional climate in family day care was best predicted by a combination of child space, smaller groups of children, and caregiver training. Conversely, caregiver restrictiveness was best predicted by less child space. One might hypothesize that the design influenced both the behavior of the children and the stress experienced by the provider.

Taking a somewhat different approach, Johnson (1987) describes a study she completed of 300 family day homes in which providers were interviewed about the nature and location of children's activities in the home. She found that children spent relatively little time in active, creative, exploratory activity but that lots of time was spent watching television, reading books, and playing structured games. Johnson also describes the providers' concern about protecting the house from the children and the children from the house (Johnson & Dineen, 1981). She discusses this as one of the practical and symbolic problems of managing children in a multifunctional space (Johnson, 1987). Johnson concluded that overall, home environments were not well suited to the needs of young children.

In an effort to examine successful resolutions of the problem of integrating children's needs with the provider's family's needs, Johnson describes a study of 25 home environments reported to provide excellent physical environments for young children. Overall, children were given a great deal of freedom to travel through the house, and they were regularly allowed to use the furniture. She notes some distinctive features regarding allocations of rooms and space. For example, children were given visual and acoustic contact with adults. This was done by adapting a main living area, often a dining room, or by locating smaller activity areas throughout the house. Johnson argues that successfully adapting a home requires a distinctive set of attitudes about play and the home environment. Moore also has suggestions for modifying the home environment to better meet the needs of the family day care provider and the children she cares for (Moore et al., 1979).

Further information regarding caregiver behavior and setting variables is also available from the work described by Prescott (1987), Goelman and Pence (1987b; in press), and Clarke-Stewart and Gruber (1984). In general, the findings are consistent with the argument that caregiver behavior is related to the structure and organization of materials in the setting and that this, in turn, is related to constructive behaviors on the part of the children.

OVERALL CONCLUSIONS

In conclusion, a variety of ecological variables tied to the physical setting appear to be related to both children's ongoing behavior in the family day care setting and later developmental outcomes. Specifically, types of toys, amount of toys, temporal and spatial organization or structure, child-designated play space, and environments facilitating play all appear to be relevant here. However, the specifics are poorly understood. As noted at the outset, the ecology of family day care is obviously much broader than just physical setting. However, the physical setting is an entry point into this ecology. It plays an important role in structuring behavior and developmental outcomes.

In reaching conclusions about the impact of the family day care setting on children and caregivers, it is important to point out some shortcomings in the existing research. These problems concern limitations in three broad areas: theoretical conceptualization, the measures, and the research design.

Little thought has been given to the theoretical conceptualization of the environment of family day care and more specifically the connections between the environment and human development. An exception to such a focus was the work of Prescott and her colleagues, but this work is now quite old. It now seems time to reevaluate Prescott's approach to the physical setting in light of more contemporary theory in child development. Both a cognitive-developmental framework and a Bronfenbrenner systems approach could be consistent with her work. Both could be enriched by some of her ideas about the functions of physical arrangements in schools and homes.

Furthermore, greater attention needs to be given to characteristics of the individual child in interaction with setting characteristics. For example, the child's developmental level should be considered in interaction with the ecological features of the setting. Howes and Unger (1989) discuss this to some extent in terms of children's social interactions and structuring the environment for play. However, other questions concern how the child deals with and uses the environment differently as a function of advancing cognitive capabilities. For example, how might characteristics of environmental organization interact with the child's emerging logical and spatial abilities? Golbeck (1985; 1992) has discussed the impact of environmental organization on children's spatial representational capabilities and has explored ways in which such cognitive and organizational capabilities might be relevant to children's use of the environment (Golbeck & Liben, 1989). Another individual characteristic worth considering is temperament (Worobey & Blajda, 1989). Highly active as opposed to more passive children make quite different demands on the caregiver and the environment. Do specific types of arrangements follow from these demands? Although temperament has received some attention in the context of child care (e.g., Fein, 1991), relationships with the physical setting have not been considered.

A final comment about theoretical conceptualization concerns the need to flesh out and knit together existing theory in a way that will be useful to developmental and environmental psychologists along with early childhood design specialists. Wohlwill (Wohlwill & Heft, 1987; Wohlwill, 1980) has discussed two of the most widely used frameworks—those of Bronfenbrenner (1979) and those of Barker (1968). Both of these approaches are contextual and emphasize the inseparable interplay between organism and environment. A third approach that might be useful for understanding intellectual development in a social context is that of Vygotsky (see Rogoff, 1990). Vygotsky's approach is also contextual and may be useful for conceptualizing the temporal dimensions of the environment as well as the caregiving activities couched in the "logic of everyday routines" (Prescott, 1987).

A second area for concern is measurement. Many studies of family day care have employed measures of physical safety such as those used in the

National Home Day Care Study (Singer, Fosberg, Goodson & Smith, 1980). Although measures of physical safety are obviously important, when considered in isolation, they are not particularly useful in helping one understand the effect of the physical environment on children's cognitive, social, and emotional development. On the other hand, the ECERS and the FDCRS (Harms & Clifford, 1980, 1989) would appear at first glance to be quite useful for understanding the impact of the environment on child development. However, these scales may well approach the environment too broadly for certain purposes. Although all the items included seem to have surface validity, their generality makes it difficult to achieve a fine-tuned understanding of how the environment and the individual interact. Furthermore, the FDCRS may rely too extensively upon the ideal classroom as the model for appropriate child-environment interactions. Homes are not classrooms and may possess their own special attributes not accurately described in the FDCRS. Other types of measures derived in the context of the home (see Parke, 1978; Wachs, 1987) may be more appropriate. Obviously, no single measure of family day care home environments will ever fully capture the rich quality of these child care settings. A broader array of measures well matched to the purposes of the investigators must be developed.

The third area of concern with child care research is the research design. Several different types of problems can be discussed, the first of which is sampling. There is much to be said about problems in sampling family day care homes for research. However, at the very least, researchers need to carefully document the demographic characteristics of their samples. This is essential for making comparisons across studies. A second design problem concerns the long-term effects of experience in a family day care setting. It would be desirable to study the impact of varying child care environments over time. Presumably this could be done, as it was in the New York Infant Day Care Study (Golden, Rosenbluth, Grossi, Policare, Freeman & Brownlee, 1978), with a large enough investment of time and financial resources. A factor complicating such research is the high degree of turnover in family day care—initiated by both the providers and the parents. This was the problem encountered by Clarke-Stewart (1987). Whatever the cause of turnover, more longitudinal research is needed.

SUMMARY

In sum, there is now a growing research literature demonstrating that ecological features of the setting have an impact on developmental outcomes for children. Although there are problems with research designs and measures, it does seem that characteristics of the physical setting in the family day care home, especially such features as organization, amount of play materials, and daily routine, are related to developmental outcomes in children. Furthermore, setting features such as the availability and amount of child play space appear to be related to the occurrence of positive caregiving behaviors. Emphasized here has been the need to incorporate these setting variables into more systematic and comprehensive theories of development. It has also been suggested that more attention be given to individual variations such as developmental level and temperament as well as characteristics of the caregiver and her family. Emphasized throughout has been the need to piece together the overall ecology of the family day care environment in terms of both social and physical characteristics. Only then will it be possible to evaluate the impact of various ecological features on child development.

REFERENCES

Barker, R. G. (1968). *Ecological psychology*. Standord, CA: Stanford University Press.

Barker, R. G., & Gump, P. V. (1964). *Big school, small school*. Stanford, CA: Stanford University Press.

Belsky, J. (1984). Two waves of day care research: Developmental effects and conditions of quality. In R. Ainslie (Ed.), *The child and the day care setting* (pp. 1–34). New York: Praeger.

Belsky, J. (1988). The "effects" of infant day care reconsidered. *Early Childhood Research Quarterly, 3*, 235–72.

Belsky, J., Steinberg, L., & Walker, A. (1982). The ecology of day care. In M. E. Lamb (Ed.), *Nontraditional families: Parenting and child development* (pp. 71–116). Hillsdale, NJ: Erlbaum.

Bradley, R. H., & Caldwell, B. M. (1976). Early home environment and changes in mental test performance in children from 6 to 36 months. *Developmental Psychology, 12*(2), 93–97.

Bronfenbrenner, U. (1977). Toward an experimental ecology of human development. *American Psychologist, 32*, 513–32.

Bronfenbrenner, U. (1979). *The ecology of human development*. Cambridge, MA: Harvard University Press.

Clarke-Stewart, K. A. (1981). Observation and experiment: Complementary strategies for studying day care and social development. In S. Kilmer (Ed.), *Advances in early education and day care* (Vol. II). Greenwich, CT: JAI Press.

Clarke-Stewart, K. A. (1987). Predicting child development from child care forms and features: The Chicago study. In D. A. Phillips (Ed.), *Quality in child care: What does the research tell us?* Washington, DC: National Association for the Education of Young Children.

Clarke-Stewart, K. A., & Gruber, C. P. (1984). Day care forms and features. In R. C. Ainslie (Ed.), *The child and the day care setting: Qualitative variations and development* (pp. 35–62). New York: Praeger.

DeVries, R. (1987). *Programs of early education*. New York: Longman.

DeVries, R., & Kohlberg, L. (1990). *Constructivist early education: Overview and comparison with other programs.* Washington, DC: National Association for the Education of Young Children.

Elardo, R., & Bradley, R. (1981). The HOME observation measurement of the environment. *Developmental Review, 1,* 113–45.

Evans, E. (1975). *Contemporary influences in early childhood education.* New York: Holt, Rinehart & Winston.

Fein, G. (1991). *Infants and toddlers enter child care: The first week.* Paper presented at the American Educational Research Association, Chicago, April.

Fosberg, S. (1981). *Family day care in the U.S.: Summary findings and final report of the National Home Day Care Study* (Vol. 1). DHHS Pub. No. 80-30282. (ERIC Doc. No. ED 211218)

Getz, S., & Brendt, E. B. (1982). A test of a method for quantifying amount, complexity and arrangement of play resources in the preschool classroom. *Journal of Applied Developmental Psychology, 3,* 295–305.

Goelman, H., & Pence, A. (1987a). Effects of child care, family and individual on children's language development: The Victoria day care research project. In D. A. Phillips (Ed.), *Quality in child care: What does the research tell us?* (pp. 89–105). Washington, DC: National Association for the Education of Young Children.

Goelman, H., & Pence, A. (1987b). Some aspects of the relationships between family structure and child language development in three types of day care. In D. L. Peters & S. Kontos (Eds.), *Continuity and discontinuity of experience in child care: Advances in applied developmental psychology* (Vol. 1) (pp. 129–46). Norwood, NJ: Ablex.

Goelman, H., & Pence, A. (In press). Play, talk and literacy and the ecology of family day care. In H. Goelman (Ed.), *Children's play in day care settings.* Albany, NY: SUNY Press.

Golbeck, S. (1985). Spatial cognition as a function of environmental characteristics. In R. Cohen (Ed.), *The development of spatial cognition.* Hillsdale, NJ: Erlbaum.

Golbeck, S. (1992). Young children's memory for spatial locations in organized and unorganized rooms. *Journal of Applied Developmental Psychology, 13*(1), 75–95.

Golbeck, S., & Liben, L. (1989). A cognitive developmental approach to children's representations of the environment. *Children's Environments Quarterly, 5*(3), 46–53.

Golden, M., Rosenbluth, L., Grossi, M. T., Policare, H. J., Freeman, H., & Brownlee, E. M. (1978). *The New York infant day care study.* New York: Medical and Health Research Association of New York City.

Gottfried, A. W. (1984). *Home environment and early cognitive development: Longitudinal research.* New York: Academic Press.

Gump, P. V. (1987). School and classroom environments. In D. Stokols & I. Altman (Eds.), *Handbook of environmental psychology* (pp. 691–732). New York: John Wiley & Sons.

Harms, T., & Clifford, R. (1980). *Early childhood environment rating scale.* New York: Teachers College Press.

Harms, T., & Clifford, R. (1989). *Family day care rating scale.* New York: Teachers College Press.

Hendrickson, J. M., Strain, P. S., Tremblay, A., & Shores, R. E. (1981). Relationship between toy and material use and the occurrence of social interaction behaviors by normally developing preschool children. *Psychology in the Schools, 18*(4), 500–504.

Howes, C. (1983). Caregiver behavior in center and family day care. *Journal of Applied Developmental Psychology, 4*(1), 99–107.

Howes, C. (1987). Social competency with peers: Contributions from child care. *Early Childhood Research Quarterly, 2,* 155–67.

Howes, C., & Rubenstein, J. (1981). Toddler peer behavior in two types of day care. *Infant Behavior and Development, 4,* 387–93.

Howes, C., & Stewart, P. (1987). Child's play with adults, toys, and peers: An examination of family and child care influences. *Developmental Psychology, 23*(3), 423–30.

Howes, C., & Unger, O. (1989). Play with peers in child care settings. In M. N. Bloch & A. D. Pellegrini (Eds.), *The ecological context of children's play* (pp. 104–19). Norwood, NJ: Ablex.

Hunt, J. M. (1961). *Intelligence and experience.* New York: Ronald.

Hunt, J. M. (1963). Piaget's system as a source of hypotheses concerning motivation. *Merrill-Palmer Quarterly, 9,* 263–75.

Johnson, L. C. (1987). The developmental implications of home environments. In C. S. Weinstein & T. David (Eds.), *Spaces for children: The built environment and child development* (pp. 139–57). New York: Plenum.

Johnson, L., & Dineen, J. (1981). *The kin trade.* Toronto: McGraw-Hill, Ryerson.

Klugman, E., & Smilansky, S. (Eds.) (1990). *Children's play and learning.* New York: Teachers College Press.

Kohlberg, L., & Fein, G. (1987). Play and constructive work as contributors to development. In L. Kohlberg (Ed.), *Child psychology and childhood education: A cognitive developmental view* (pp. 392–440). New York: Longman.

Kritchevsky, S., Prescott, E., & Walling, L. (1969). *Planning environments for young children: Physical space.* Washington, DC: National Association for the Education of Young Children.

Lamb, M. E., & Sternberg, K. (1990). Do we really know how day care affects children? *Journal of Applied Developmental Psychology, 11,* 351–79.

Long, F., Peters, D. L., & Garduque, L. (1985). Continuity between home and day care. In I. Sigel (Ed.), *Advances in applied developmental psychology* (pp. 131–70). Norwood, NJ: Ablex.

Montessori, M. (1909/1964). *The Montessori method.* New York: Schocken Books.

Moore, G. T. (1987). The physical environment and cognitive development in child care centers. In C. S. Weinstein & T. R. David (Eds.), *Spaces for children: The built environment and child development* (pp. 41–72). New York: Plenum.

Moore, G. T., Lane, C. G., Hill, A. B., Cohen, U., & McGinty, J. (1979). *Recom-

mendations for child care centers. Milwaukee: School of Architecture and Urban Planning.

Parke, R. D. (1978). Children's home environments: Social and cognitive effects. In I. Altman & J. F. Wohlwill (Eds.), *Children and the environment* (pp. 33–82). New York: Plenum.

Pence, A., & Goelman, H. (1987a) Silent partners: Parents of children in three types of day care. *Early Childhood Research Quarterly, 2*(2), 103–18.

Pence, A., & Goelman, H. (1987b). Who cares for the child in day care? An examination of caregivers from three types of care. *Early Childhood Research Quarterly, 2*(4), 315–34.

Piaget, J. (1952). *The origins of intelligence in children.* New York: International Universities Press.

Prescott, E. (1973). *A comparison of three types of day care and nursery-school home care.* Paper presented at the Biennial Meeting of the Society for Research in Child Development, Philadelphia.

Prescott, E. (1981). Relationship between physical setting and adult/child behavior in day care. In S. Kilmer (Ed.), *Advances in early education and day care* (Vol. III). Greenwich, CT: JAI Press.

Prescott, E. (1987). The environment as organizer of intent in child care settings. In C. S. Weinstein & T. David (Eds.), *Spaces for children: The built environment and child development* (pp. 73–88). New York: Plenum.

Prescott, E. (n.d.). *The relationships of spatial characteristics to children's experience in group day care.* Mimeograph paper, Pacific Oaks College.

Prescott, E., & David, T. (1976). *The effects of the physical environment on day care.* Concept paper prepared for the U.S. Department of Health, Education and Welfare, Office of Child Development.

Prescott, E., Jones, E., & Kritchevsky, S. (1972). *Day care as a child rearing environment* (Vol. II). Washington, DC: National Association for the Education of Young Children.

Prescott, E., Kritchevsky, S., & Jones, E. (1972). *Day care environmental inventory assessment of child rearing environments: An ecological approach.* Part 1 of Final Report. (ERIC Doc. No. ED 076 228)

Quilitch, H. R., & Risley, T. R. (1973). The effects of play materials on social play. *Journal of Applied Behavioral Analysis, 6*(4), 573–78.

Rogoff, B. (1990). *Apprenticeship in thinking.* New York: Oxford University Press.

Rothstein-Fisch, C., & Howes, C. (1988). Toddler peer interaction in mixed-age groups. *Journal of Applied Developmental Psychology, 9*(2), 211–18.

Shure, M. B. (1963). The psychological ecology of the nursery school. *Child Development, 34,* 979–92.

Singer, J. D., Fosberg, S., Goodson, B. D., Smith, J. M. (1980). *Family day care in the U.S.: Research report.* Final report of the National Day Care Home Study (Vol. 2). Washington, DC: U.S. Department of Health and Human Services, ACYF. (ERIC Doc. No. ED 211 219)

Smith, P. K., & Connolly, K. J. (1980). *The ecology of preschool behavior.* Cambridge, England: Cambridge University Press.

Wachs, T. (1987). Developmental perspectives on designing for development. In C. S. Weinstein & T. R. David (Eds.), *Spaces for children: The built environment and child development* (pp. 291–308). New York: Plenum.

Wachs, T., & Gruen, G. (1982). *Early experience and human development.* New York: Plenum.

Wapner, S., Cohen, S. B., & Kaplan, B. (Eds.). (1976). *Experiencing the environment.* New York: Plenum.

Weinstein, C. S. (1987). Designing preschool classrooms to support development: Research and reflection. In C. S. Weinstein & T. G. David (Eds.), *Spaces for children: The built environment and child development* (pp. 159–86). New York: Plenum.

Werner, H. (1948). *Comparative psychology of mental development.* New York: International Universities Press.

Wohlwill, J. (1980). The confluence of environmental and developmental psychology: Signpost to an ecology of development? *Human Development, 23,* 354–58.

Wohlwill, J. (1983). The physical and the social environment as factors in development. In D. Magnusson & V. P. Allen (Eds.). *Human development: An interactional perspective* (pp. 111–129). New York: Academic.

Wohlwill, J., & Heft, J. (1987). The physical environment and the development of the child. In D. Stokols & I. Altman (Eds.), *Handbook of environmental psychology* (Vol. 1, pp. 281–328). New York: Wiley.

Worobey, J., & Blajda, V. M. (1989). Temperament ratings at 2 weeks, 2 months, and 1 year. Differential stability of activity and emotionality. *Developmental Psychology, 25,* 171–84.

CHAPTER 10

Dimensions of Parent-Provider Relationships in Family Day Care

Douglas R. Powell
Gail Bollin

The professional early childhood community historically has looked upon relationships between parents and family day care providers with a sense of idealism as well as suspicion. The arrangement has many actual and potential attributes conducive to the formation of strong bonds between parent, child, and provider: a continuity of child-rearing values and practices, a single provider with whom to establish ties, flexibility to accommodate special circumstances, and integration into a neighborhood setting that builds upon the support of informal social networks. The skepticism stems from the absence of reliable mechanisms for exerting professional influence on family day care providers. Can unsupervised and presumably untrained providers be trusted to develop and maintain productive relationships with parents and children without professional guidance? How might a provider talk intelligently with a parent about child development, for instance, without formal preparation in the subject matter?

These perceptions of family day care occur within the context of the early childhood field's long-standing interest in strengthening relations between parents and program staff. Generations of early childhood professionals have argued that close coordination and communication between parents and other significant caregivers improve children's socialization experiences (see Powell, 1989). Since the nursery school movement of the 1920s, numerous efforts have been pursued to foster supportive connections between home and nonfamilial child-rearing settings.

This chapter examines existing research on parent-provider relationships in family day care. The aim is to describe the ways in which parents and family day care providers interact and to identify factors associated with differences in parent-provider relationships. Attention is given to the frequency and content of parent-provider exchanges, sources of satisfaction and frustration from both parent and provider perspectives, images of family day care as an extended family or business arrangement, and work-family boundaries in the provider's home. The chapter begins with a brief consideration of the theoretical and empirical base of interest in parent-provider relationships in child care and ends with suggestions for future directions in research and program practice.

THEORETICAL AND RESEARCH BASES

Rationales for Supportive Parent-Provider Ties

There is a robust theoretical framework but a weak empirical base for the argument that close interpersonal ties between parent and child care provider contribute to positive child outcomes (for a recent review, see Powell, 1989). The continuity of children's experiences is the springboard for most discussions of strategies for strengthening relations between parents and child care providers. In brief, existing theoretical work encompasses the following propositions:

1. Discontinuities between families and other nonfamilial child-rearing settings are inevitable (Lightfoot, 1978; Litwak & Meyer, 1974; Katz, 1980) and probably of greatest magnitude for children from low-income and ethnic minority populations (Laosa, 1982; Getzels, 1974).
2. Appropriate levels and types of discontinuity enhance a child's cognitive competence and adaptive skills (Bronfenbrenner, 1979; Lightfoot, 1978), but major discontinuities between socialization agencies can lead to maladaptive behavior (Lippitt, 1968) and poor academic performance (Laosa, 1982).
3. Supportive linkages between socialization agents such as parent and child care provider are thought to contribute to a child's ease of adjustment to a new setting and to overall child competence (Bronfenbrenner, 1979; Lippitt, 1968).

Existing research indicates that there are discontinuities between families and nonfamilial child-rearing settings. These come in the form of differences between parents and caregivers in values, expectations of child behavior, and styles of adult-child interaction (Hess, Dickson, Price & Long, 1979; Hess, Price, Dickson & Conroy, 1981; Long & Garduque, 1987). The differences appear to be greatest for children whose parents are non-Anglo and not middle class (Winetsky, 1978). From an empirical perspective, we know little about the effects on children of discontinuities between families and early childhood settings and the effects of most practices aimed at strengthening linkages between families and child care programs (see Powell, 1989).

A limited research base has not kept leaders in the early childhood field from advocating supportive linkages between parents and child care providers. The themes of child care–family connectedness are found, for example, in an early set of practice guidelines for child care issued by the Study Group on Mental Health Aspects of Day Care of the American Orthopsychiatric Association (Heinicke, Friedman, Prescott, Puncel & Sale, 1973). It was recommended that day care providers have "an intimate and continuing relationship to both family and child" and that "members of this 'extended family' share their experience in order to instill a sense of working together" (p. 14). The group stressed that day care services should supplement and complement the family and avoid arrangements and practices that imply a replacement or denigration of family child rearing by communicating "we can do it better." Family day care was identified as a child care form especially amenable to close matches in cultural and ethnic value systems between child care users and providers.

More recently, the National Association for the Education of Young Children (NAEYC) has issued standards for professional practice in early childhood care and education that includes staff-parent interaction as a component of a high-quality program. The practice guidelines call for information about program philosophy and operations to be given to prospective parents, parent-staff communication regarding home and program child-rearing practices, parental involvement in programs as observers and participants, and a system of communication for sharing day-to-day happenings that may affect children (National Academy of Early Childhood Programs, 1984). Heinicke et al. (1973) emphasize that a parent must know, for example, "that a child has perhaps that day been struggling with his angry feelings toward a peer. Similarly, the day care staff must be made aware by the parents of the critical events occurring in the home" (p. 17).

The Existing Research Base

As suggested above, research on parent-provider relationships in child care is a fledgling area of inquiry. A small number of studies have been pursued in family day care settings, generally aimed at describing the nature of relationships between parents and providers. These studies provide a global portrayal of parent-provider connections and point to needed research directions that utilize a finer lens.

The research base on parent-provider relationships in family day care has serious methodological limitations. Primarily the existing studies have utilized cross-sectional designs and survey methods. Especially needed are observational studies of parent-provider interaction that employ a longitudinal design. Like research on family day care in general (see Chapter 6, this volume), studies of parent-provider relations use nonprobability sampling procedures that hamper the external validity of these studies because there are no empirical assurances the providers and parents who agree to participate in research are representative of their respective cohorts.

Relatively more research has been done on parent-provider relationships in center-based arrangements, but setting differences make it difficult to generalize the findings of center studies to family day care. Setting characteristics such as number of children and providers and relative emphasis on early childhood education presumably contribute to findings suggesting that parent-provider ties are stronger in family day care than in center care. Additionally, parents who choose family day care may differ from parents who choose center care on a variety of characteristics that might influence the nature of the parent-provider relationship. For example, in the Victoria Day Care Research Project, Pence and Goelman (1985) noted that parents of children in licensed family day care were more likely to prefer not to work full time than were parents of children in center day care. They also worried more about their children's emotional well-being than did the parents of children in center care.

In an interview study with 73 providers representing 35 homes and 38 centers, Hughes (1985) found that center providers spent an average of 13.7 minutes a week and home providers an average of 54.7 minutes a week with each parent. There were also differences between home and center providers regarding the frequency with which concerns were discussed with parents, but not the type of concerns. Compared to family day care providers, center providers reported more frequent discussions with parents about the child's learning, social development, behavior problems, peer relationships, and program policies. Family day care providers discussed relationships with parents' relatives more frequently than center providers. Hughes interprets these differences in relation to setting characteristics. For example, the higher child-staff ratio in centers translates into less available time for interaction with parents. Also, the greater number of children in centers may contribute to the frequent discussion of behavior problems, social development, and peer relations with center parents. The higher frequency of center providers discussing learning or educational progress with parents may be a function of the probable formal education component in center programs.

Parent reports also point to a stronger parent-provider relationship in family day care compared to center care. In a study of 126 parents in British

Columbia, Pence and Goelman (1987) found that parents using family day care reported closer personal relationships with caregivers than parents using child care centers. Compared with parents using center care, parents using family day care reported speaking with providers more often and were more likely to anticipate continued contact with the family day care provider after the child left the family day care home. Perhaps the constancy of one provider in family day care, versus a number of personnel who work different hours in center care, facilitates the development of stronger adult interpersonal ties in family day care.

Parent-provider relationships in family day care, then, function within a unique set of circumstances and appear to be qualitatively different from their counterparts in center care. The relationship, at first glance, appears to be of a more personal and enduring nature than that between center providers and parents. However, this may be a lopsided perspective, since only the parent is reporting expectations of continuing the relationship after the child has left care, and it is the parent, again, who is reported as sharing nonchild-related information with the provider.

UNTANGLING THE PARENT-PROVIDER RELATIONSHIP

Frequency and Type of Exchanges

Parent-provider relationships come in various forms. The frequency and content of interaction are basic indices of interpersonal relationship quality, and it appears that on these variables there is considerable variation in parent-provider interaction across and within child care settings (Powell, 1989). Hence, it is difficult to describe a typical set of exchanges. The existing literature points to some modal patterns as well as dimensions along which parent-provider interactions vary. Research indicates that contact between parents and family day care providers generally occurs during transitional times, when parents drop off and pick up their children. An observational study of family day care homes found that parents tended to express interest in and interact with other children in the family day care home during these transitions, perhaps contributing to parental feelings of having a family-type relationship with the day care home (Leavitt, 1987). Parents have been found to discuss a range of topics with providers (Hughes, 1985), but the extent of focused attention to child topics is unclear. In Leavitt's ten-month observational study of six providers and their interactions with parents, there was little support for parents' claims that there was considerable communication occurring regarding the children in care. She concluded that "very little information may actually be exchanged about the children" (p. 12).

In an interview study by Hughes (1985), providers described the typical ways in which they responded to parents' concerns. The most common responses included asking questions, offering sympathy, presenting alternatives, and just listening. Home providers were more likely than center providers to tell parents to count their blessings, but center providers were more likely to suggest that parents talk to someone else. The provider's age was positively correlated with discussion of parental issues (parent's job, marital problems, feelings of depression) in the Hughes study. This suggests that parents may be more comfortable talking about themselves with older individuals. Older providers used less active helping responses (e.g., just listening, telling parents to count their blessings). Providers with higher levels of education reported a higher frequency of discussions related to social development and child learning, and providers with more years of experience reported a higher frequency of discussions related to child discipline and physical growth.

Sources of Satisfaction and Frustration

Findings from available research on family day care offer a mirror image of the evidence from a larger set of studies on parent-provider relations in child care generally: The parent-provider relationship is more of a problem for providers than for parents (Powell, 1989). Typically, parents express satisfaction with their relationships with providers, but such satisfaction is not necessarily mutual. For example, in a small qualitative study of 31 providers and their clients, Leavitt (1987) found that parents were much more likely than providers to describe their relationships as "friendly" and to consider the provider as "family." Although providers characterized their relationships with parents as generally "good," they had many complaints on a specific level about parental responses to such matters as fees and policies and pointed to unrealistic parental expectations of providers.

A perception of helpfulness on the part of the day care families was identified in a Delaware survey as the most important predictor of provider job satisfaction (Bollin, 1989b). Helpfulness on the part of parents was a nonspecific term against which providers measured their parent clientele on a Likert-type scale from "extremely helpful" to "not at all helpful." Exactly how individual providers defined helpful, though, is not known. A sizable minority of providers in this study (27 percent) indicated dissatisfaction, specifically with the level of parental appreciation for their work.

Different levels of satisfaction with family day care have been reported in a variety of studies. Leavitt (1987) reported that all the parents in her qualitative study of parent-provider relationships felt that their child care was good, although the parents rarely spent time observing the actual care. In a larger study focusing on maternal satisfaction with family day care, White-head (1989) found that most parents did not offer suggestions for changes in their family day care arrangements when given the opportunity to do so. Pence and Goelman (1987), however, found that parental satisfaction with specific caregiver characteristics such as creativity and organization was lower for family day care parents than for center care parents. The dissatisfaction was more pronounced for parents using unlicensed family day care than for those using licensed family day care (Pence & Goelman, 1987).

Provider Perspectives.   Family day care providers point to satisfactions from working with children and problems from working with parents. In an interview study with 32 registered family day care providers in Iowa, Atkinson (1988) uncovered a number of parent-related problems, including late or partial payments, failure to pick up children on time, violation of policies about not bringing sick children to the family day care home, and parents not demonstrating concern about their children's problems.

In a study of 22 sponsored family day care providers in Massachusetts, Rubin (1974) found that providers did not put as much emphasis on getting along with parents as they did in caring for the children. "As one provider summarized, 'We don't concentrate on the parent-provider relationships because our first responsibility is to the child instead. If the mother cooperates, fine, but we tread on thin ice with most parents' " (Rubin, 1974, p. 54). The Rubin (1974) data also indicated that time exploitation was providers' most common complaint, followed by differences of opinion about discipline. Rubin (1974) further reported that providers were concerned that some parents were jealous of the relationship that develops between the child and the provider and that this occasionally became a source of conflict.

The actual prevalence of parent-related problems is unclear. Several instances of negligence may come to dominate some providers' overall assessment of parent support of the family day care arrangement. Data from a small six-month longitudinal sample within the Delaware survey offers some insight on this issue. Before opening day care homes, nearly half of the prospective providers thought that work with parents would be the most difficult aspect of the job. Although 43 percent anticipated late fee payments and 50 percent expected late pick-ups, these problems were encountered by only a handful of providers during the first six months of operation, and several of these instances were minor and easily corrected (Bollin, 1989b).

For some providers, tensions surrounding the relationship with parents are connected to feelings of being undervalued by society in general and by parents in particular. More than 100 of 392 respondents to a Delaware survey (Bollin, 1989a) took advantage of the option to write comments about their concerns regarding family day care. A common theme was the need to educate parents of day care children. As one provider stated, "We need to train parents that we are an important resource—not to be used and abused. . . . How can we remain feeling valuable when society and our clients disrespect our service?" A retired provider was more militant:

> Educating the public (parents), i.e. we are NOT "babysitters"—several children at one time necessitates routines, boundaries, contracts AND compensation as contracted. They seem to think $50.00/week × 4 kids = tons of money. They don't multiply "needs" by 4 . . . they just think you're "making good money" just for babysitting!! . . . I felt the service offered was more important than the parents felt it was.

Money appears to play at least two other roles in the parent-provider relationship. Bollin (1989b) found that one of the keys to women continuing their work as family day care providers was attaining a financial comfort level and the ability to deal with reduced income from less than full enrollment. This enabled the provider to either refuse an incompatible client initially or to later request that a disruptive child be removed from the family day care home.

Parent Perspectives. What contributes to a high level of parental satisfaction with family day care arrangements? In a study of 115 mothers and their 46 family day care providers, the mother's perception of similarity between her own and her provider's child-rearing beliefs and values was the sole predictor of the mother's child care satisfaction (Whitehead, 1989). Also, 79 percent of the parents in Atkinson's (1988) study rated having values similar to the provider's values as very important, second only to provider reliability and stability. Among the variables found not to be predictive of satisfaction in the Whitehead (1989) study were overall quality of care, training of the caregiver, group size, age of the child in care, distance traveled to the day care home, and cost of care.

In another study, the following parental perceptions were found to be the best predictors of parental satisfaction with family day care: provider awareness of the child's strengths and weaknesses; supply of material in the home; active provider engagement with children, including affectionate and play behaviors; provider acknowledgment and support of children's feelings; and provider cooperation in teaching parental values to the children (Winget, Winget & Popplewell, 1982).

Parents reporting dissatisfaction with a family day care arrangement have been found to desire a stronger educational component (Endsley & Bradbard, 1987). Information on this point is contradictory, however. In a sample of dissatisfied parents, Fosburg (1981) found that given a choice of fictitious family day care homes, parents chose unstructured over structured settings 3 to 2, but preferred a learning environment over a play environment 3 to 1. Presumably, the age of the child may be a factor here, since parents seem to prefer family day care for toddlers and infants (Stevens, 1982; Ginsberg, Galinsky & Perryman, 1988).

There appears to be a tendency for parents to lean heavily on their assessments of provider's personal characteristics in selecting a family day care home. For example, Stevens (1982) reports that parents seek a family day care provider on the basis of personality and experience with children. Reliance on referrals from other parents is heavy. Data from a national sample, now nearly two decades old, point to five factors considered by parents in selecting family day care (in order of importance): (1) provider reliability; (2) warm, loving nature of the provider; (3) safety and cleanliness; (4) the child's happiness with the setting; and (5) provider use of discipline when necessary (National Child Care Consumer Study, 1975). It is not clear whether these selection criteria used by parents continue to be important when parents assess satisfaction with an ongoing family day care arrangement.

Parental satisfaction with a family day care arrangement has not always been found to be an accurate reflection of the overall quality of care. Similarly, Whitehead (1989) found that independent ratings of the quality of family day care settings did not predict parental satisfaction with child care. In this study, quality of care was measured with two observational instruments administered by researchers, the Family Day Care Rating Scale (Harms & Clifford, 1989) and the infant/toddler and preschool versions of the HOME scale (Caldwell & Bradley, 1984). However, in the Victoria Day Care Research Project, parents' assessment of the quality of their day care arrangements did accurately reflect the judgments made by external assessments, particularly in the Vancouver area (Pence & Goelman, 1985).

Perhaps parents have limited information on which to judge quality or are unable or unwilling to admit that they have placed their children in less-than-optimal child care arrangements. Empirical information on this latter possibility is lacking, but data from a small observational study indicate that although all parents believed that their children were receiving good care, parents rarely spent time observing in the family day care home (Leavitt, 1987). It was not obvious, then, how parents arrived at their judgments about the quality of the setting. It is also possible that parents use criteria of quality that differ from the criteria established by professionals, although many of the criteria parents reportedly use in selecting and assessing a family day care arrangement (described above) are consistent with items found in observational rating scales for determining quality of care.

An Extended Family or Business Relationship?

A major dimension on which parent-provider relationships in family day care can be described is whether the arrangement is viewed as an extension of the family or as an independent business arrangement. This dimension is connected to a larger tension in society regarding images of how child care providers should relate to families: Is child care to be a service industry, with parents seen as customers to be pleased, or are providers to be viewed as a modern-day version of the extended family (Powell, 1989)?

In a survey study of 317 registered providers in Delaware, 48 percent claimed that they considered the children's parents as extended family, but another 48 percent did not. Although 85 percent considered themselves child care professionals, only 51 percent preferred a professional relationship with parents. Ninety percent considered themselves small-business owners, but only 65 percent actually had written contracts with all the families they served, and 77 percent considered the parents as customers. Eighty-five percent of the respondents felt close to both the day care parents and children; 74 percent encouraged families to share problems so they could better help the children; 44 percent shared their own problems with the day care parents; 40 percent wanted more time to talk to the parents; and only 37 percent indicated that their only contact with the families was about day care (Bollin, 1989b). In 149 responses to a national nonrandom survey, Manfredi (1988) found that the majority of family day care providers identified with a home-like image (92 percent), but of those only 64 percent considered their family day care homes as an extended family plus planned activities.

The family day care providers in the Delaware study seemed even more committed to an extended family model with regard to their relationships with the day care children. Ninety-one percent said that they treated the day care children as their own; 82 percent believed that the day care children used the providers' homes as their own; 87 percent did not mind caring for the children on weekends; and 83 percent had the same rules for the day care children as their own children. However, only 43 percent expected their own children to treat the day care children as siblings (Bollin, 1989b).

In the National Day Care Home Study, some providers believed that a close personal relationship was advantageous in dealing with issues between parent and provider, such as child-rearing attitudes or behaviors. Other providers submitted that such closeness often complicated discussions of problems or parental dissatisfactions (Divine-Hawkins, 1981).

In a study of 90 subsidized family day care providers in Pennsylvania,

Bollin (1989c) found that African-American providers were significantly more likely than white providers to consider their parent clientele as members of their extended families, to expect their own children to treat the day care children as siblings, and to expect the day care children to use the providers' homes as their own. In contrast, the white providers were more likely to plan separate activities for their own families and to ask parents to remove a disruptive child from their care.

Less is known about the extended family versus business model distinction from a parental perspective. In the Victoria Day Care Study in Canada, Pence and Goelman (1985) found that parents using family day care seemed to have stronger feelings of guilt about working than parents using center care. This appeared to translate into a desire for a homelike, caring atmosphere for their children that would more closely approximate what the children might have experienced had they been at home with their own parents. It would appear that parents using family day care preferred to think of their children as being in the care of a quasi-relative rather than a trained stranger and to regard the provider-child relationship as warm and enduring. Pence and Goelman also found that parents using family day care often selected a particular provider because of specific attributes of the caregiver instead of more conventional standards of quality. This emphasis on caregiver characteristics might translate into an assumption of friendship on no greater basis than an assumption of common values.

Differences were found by Pence and Goelman in the types of relationships that existed between parents and licensed or unlicensed providers. Licensed providers had more professional attitudes toward parents, which Pence and Goelman suggested might reflect the training required for licensing. Parents were more likely to perceive an unlicensed provider as a good friend, but at the same time to judge the unlicensed provider less positively on characteristics of the caregiving environment (Pence & Goelman, 1985).

Open-ended responses from parents in a questionnaire study by Whitehead (1989) suggested that parents differ in their expectations of what providers offer. Elements of an extended family mode seem evident in this parent's observation: "I do look to my provider for advice and use her as a role model when disciplining my son. I also appreciate all the special things she does—the trips to the library, the birthday parties, the holiday treats" (p. 99). A professional mode is emphasized in another parent's comments: "I couldn't be happier with my FDC—she has the perfect mix of a family atmosphere plus stimulating and interesting activities. (Plenty of time for free play and also structured time.) She takes her job seriously—she's professional—not just a 'stay-at-home mom' who wants to make a little money—she is also warm and loving" (p. 99). An extreme example of viewing the provider as a business entrepreneur is offered in the following parent comment: "At times I feel the provider is thinking of herself only. She is *extremely* concerned in making money and worries me at times that this is her only objective. I pray every day that she is interested in my child's well-being and happiness over any kind of money she makes" (p. 100).

Findings from one of the earliest studies of parent-provider relationships in family day care suggest that the nature of the family day care arrangement depends partly on whether the parent and provider were friends or strangers at the outset of the relationship (Emlen, Donoghue & LaForge, 1971). In a study of primarily white women in Portland, Oregon, it was found that friendship itself was the bond or social glue that held the family day care arrangement together in situations in which women had known each other before the arrangement began. Dissatisfactions threatened the arrangement as well as the friendship. Strains and drains of a day care arrangement involving friends seemed to involve "problems of status, dominance, definition of expectations, and renegotiation of the interpersonal relationship" (p. 172). Such status discrepancies are incompatible with the equality and freedom that characterize friendship. The findings serve as a reminder of an old maxim: Avoid doing business with friends. In arrangements in which mother and provider were strangers, mutual satisfactions in the relationship were not associated with the degree of friendship. Arrangements between strangers often developed elements of friendship that contributed to the stability of the arrangement.

Interface with Provider's Family

A salient yet sometimes overlooked characteristics of family day care is the presence of the provider's own family. Family day care is, in fact, the interaction of a multitude of systems, which include the provider's nuclear family, the children in care and their families, agencies of regulation and licensure, and various support systems ranging from extended family to professional services. The provider's family, being closest to the center of the system—the provider herself—is in a very influential position. How the provider chooses to incorporate her family into the system cannot help but have an impact on relationships with parents.

Systems theory indicates the need for clarity of roles for all system members for effective functioning (Boss & Greenberg, 1984). It also maintains the need for clear but flexible boundaries among system members (Kantor & Lehr, 1975). The family day care system must deal with frequently changing membership and must constantly maintain lines of open communication among members to meet all members' needs. It becomes the provider's responsibility, particularly when young children are present, to clarify the roles of family members so they do not feel threatened by the intrusion of other family day care system members into the home. The nature of the boundaries must also be communicated to parents so that they too know their appropriate roles.

In a predominantly white sample of 392 currently and formerly registered family day care providers in Delaware who responded to a mail survey, a weak connection was found between clearly defined boundaries and maintenance of the family day care system (Bollin, 1989b). The impact of the provider's family was apparent. Although 70 percent of the respondents were also caring for their own young children, job satisfaction was significantly lower for this group. This poses a curious paradox, since 67 percent of the Delaware sample said that their primary motivation for being a family day care provider was being able to stay home with their own children. The lower job satisfaction suggests that boundary clarity may be problematic when the provider's young children are present.

Bollin and Whitehead (1991) found that parental satisfaction with child care was also significantly lower when the provider's own children were present in the family day care home, suggesting that both providers and parents see the presence of the provider's own young children as a liability rather than an asset. In a sample of 32 registered family day care providers in Iowa, providers described both positive and negative impacts on family day care on their own children (Atkinson, 1988). Providers indicated that their own children had learned some socialization skills and had more to do, but the children also experienced adjustment problems such as jealousy and attention seeking. Some providers, though, did report that being a family day care provider allowed them to spend more time with their own children and made them more sensitive to their own children's needs. In a small six-month longitudinal study, Bollin (1989b) found that most aspiring providers had not anticipated behavior problems in their own children. However, after beginning to provide care, those with young children (under five years of age) reported experiencing exactly that. One provider in this study described her two-year-old son's initial reaction to the presence of nonfamilial children in his home as "horrible," including biting. She quoted herself as telling her mother that she was going to send her own son to another day care and keep the family day care open for the other children.

Bollin also found that satisfied providers differed in how they established boundaries around their day care services. Those providers who had their own young children tended to set more limits on the invasion of personal territory and time than did the older providers without their own children at home. For example, providers with young children often made the children's bedrooms off-limits and allowed their own children to keep favorite toys out of the communal toy area. A grandmother in the sample, on the other hand, had opened her entire home to the day care children. Similarly, Atkinson

(1988) found that providers with young children at home controlled the intrusion of family day care into the home through selective recruitment of new families, physical arrangement of the house, and policies regarding hours of operation.

The least studied member of the family day care system is probably the provider's husband. How does he define his role? There were marked differences in the actual amount of help given by husbands of providers who planned to continue giving care in the Bollin study. Some husbands participated in the day care to the extent that they would watch the children in order to provide their wives with a respite period; others involved themselves by remodeling and building special equipment; others simply did not complain. For this small group of providers, the support given by husbands matched the provider's original expectations, and they were satisfied. It would appear that it was the provider's perception or definition of adequate support from her spouse that was the critical factor rather than a minimum number of clock hours of actual labor.

NEEDED RESEARCH DIRECTIONS

Longitudinal research is needed regarding two issues: how individual parent-provider relations change over time, and how family day care systems change over time. Longitudinal research might uncover a pattern of development common to many family day care systems. Two scenarios are plausible. Providers may begin relationships with new families on a business basis but dispense with the formalities over time as trust develops between the provider and the parent. Perhaps, initially, the protection of business-type relationships is necessary until the provider has an established clientele and no longer has to rely on advertising and impersonal referral services to keep her full complement of clients. On the other hand, it might also be true that providers begin their day cares idealistically with few businesslike practices to intrude on what they perceive to be an intimate relationship based on common interest in the welfare of small children. Over time, with experience, they might see the necessity for more businesslike practices. As one provider in the Bollin (1989a) study commented: "I believe that over the years, as I have become much more businesslike, I have been able to decrease the amount of stress I feel in my job."

An assumption that either the extended family model or the professional business model is better suited to family day care needs to be examined carefully. The suitability of either model may depend on the expectations of both parties. These expectations may be influenced by socioeconomic status; geographic, cultural, and personality factors; and the structure of the provider's nuclear family. Future studies of parent-provider relationships need to include these variables and examine their interaction with both parental and provider satisfaction and with the quality of care provided.

Empirical research also needs to be done on the impact of discontinuities in child care values and practices on the relationship between parents and providers, with attention to the choices available to parents and providers when discontinuities surface. Dissolution of the relationship may be the most obvious choice in a free market, but the child care market has definite limitations, especially when affordability is an issue and child care subsidies are involved. Moreover, dissolution of the relationship might not be in the best interest of the child.

Finally, longitudinal research might unravel some of the complexities of the boundary issues with the provider's nuclear family in the family day care system. Many family day care systems are begun by women wishing to stay home with their own children. As the provider's children get older and less vulnerable, boundary definitions may also change.

The issues of change and stability in parent-provider relations and family day care systems are intertwined with the passage of time and the idiosyncratic nature of each family day care system. Only longitudinal research employing qualitative and quantitative methods can provide valid illumination.

Even though existing research on parent-provider relations is seriously limited, there is sufficient information to indicate that programmatic efforts should be pursued to improve relationships between parents and providers. Doing so within the context of a disparate and loosely regulated system of family child care is not easy. Yet available data underscore the contradictions and misunderstandings in both parents' and providers' perceptions of their mutual relationship. There is an obvious need for better education and training of both parties on how to manage the relationship in the best interests of each other and especially in the best interests of the child in care.

REFERENCES

Atkinson, A. M. (1988). Providers' evaluations of the effect of family day care on own family relationships. *Family Relations, 37,* 399–404.

Bollin, G. G. (1989a). [Family day care provider job satisfaction.] Unpublished raw data.

Bollin, G. G. (1989b). To be or not to be . . . a family day care provider: An investigation of turnover among family day care providers (doctoral dissertation, University of Delaware). *Dissertation Abstracts International, 49,* 9007A. (University Microfilms No. ADG90-10393)

Bollin, G. G. (1989c). Diversity of attitudes about family day care among sponsored family day care providers. Paper presented at the annual meeting of the American Educational Research Association, San Francisco.

Bollin, G. G., & Whitehead, L. C. (1991). *Family day care quality and parental satisfaction.* Paper presented at American Educational Research Association, Chicago.

Boss, P. G., & Greenberg, J. (1984). Family boundary ambiguity: A new variable in family stress theory. *Family Process, 23,* 535–46.

Bronfenbrenner, U. (1979). *The ecology of human development: Experiments by nature and design.* Cambridge, MA: Harvard University Press.

Caldwell, B. M., & Bradley, R. H. (1984). *Home observation for measurement of the environment* (Rev. Ed). Little Rock: University of Arkansas.

Divine-Hawkins, P. (1981). *Final report of the National Day Care Home Study: Executive summary* (DHHS Pub. No. 80-30287). Washington, DC: U.S. Government Printing Office.

Emlen, A. C., Donoghue, B. A., & LaForge, F. (1971). *Child care by kith: A study of the family day care relationships of working mothers and neighborhood caregivers. A report to Extramural Research and Demonstration Grants Branch, Children's Bureau, U.S. Department of Health, Education & Welfare.* Portland, OR: Portland State University.

Endsley, R. C., & Bradbard, M. R. (1987). Dissatisfaction with previous child care among current users of proprietary center care. *Child and Youth Care Quarterly, 16,* 249–62.

Fosburg, S. (1981). *Final report of the National Day Care Home Study: Vol. I* (DHHS Publication No. OHDS 80-30282). Washington, DC: U.S. Department of Health and Human Services.

Galinsky, E. (1988). Parents and teacher-caregivers: Sources of tension, sources of support. *Young Children, 43,* 4–12.

Getzels, J. W. (1974). Socialization and education: A note on discontinuities. *Teachers College Record, 76,* 218–25.

Ginsberg, S., Galinsky, E., & Perryman, A. (1988, April). Children and families are a national issue. *Work and Family Life,* 1–3.

Harms, I., & Clifford, R. M. (1980). *Early childhood environment rating scale.* New York: Teachers College Press.

Harms, T., & Clifford, R. M. (1989). *Family day care rating scale.* New York: Teachers College Press.

Heinicke, C. M., Friedman, D., Prescott, E., Puncell, C. & Sale, J. S. (1973). The organization of day care: Considerations relating to mental health of child and family. *American Journal of Orthopsychiatry, 43*(1), 8–22.

Hess, R. D., Dickson, W. P., Price, G. G., & Long, D. J. (1979). Some contrasts between mothers and preschool teachers in interaction with four-year-old children. *American Educational Research Journal, 16,* 307–16.

Hess, R. D., Price, G. G., Dickson, W. P., & Conroy, M. (1981). Different roles for mothers and teachers: Contrasting styles of child care. In S. Kilmer (Ed.), *Advances in early education and day care* (Vol. 2) (pp. 1–28). Greenwich, CT: JAI Press.

Hughes, R. (1985). The informal help-giving of home and center childcare providers. *Family Relations, 34,* 359–66.

Kantor, D., & Lehr, W. (1975). *Inside the family: Toward a theory of family process.* San Francisco: Jossey-Bass.

Katz, L. G. (1980). Mothering and teaching: Some significant distinctions. In L. G. Katz (Ed.), *Current topics in early childhood education* (Vol. 3) (pp. 47–63). Norwood, NJ: Ablex.

Laosa, L. (1982). School, occupation, culture, and family: The impact of parental schooling on the parent-child relationship. *Journal of Educational Psychology, 74,* 791–827.

Leavitt, R. L. (1987). *Invisible boundaries: An interpretive study of parent-provider relationships.* (ERIC Doc. No. ED 299 035).

Lightfoot, S. L. (1978). *Worlds apart: Relationships between families and schools.* New York: Basic.

Lippitt, R. (1968). Improving the socialization process. In J. A. Clausen (Ed.), *Socialization and society* (pp. 321–74). Boston: Little, Brown.

Litwak, E., & Meyer, H. (1974). *School, family and neighborhood: The theory and practice of school-community relations.* New York: Columbia University Press.

Long, F., & Garduque, L. (1987). Continuity between home and family day caregivers' and mothers' perceptions of children's social experiences. In D. L. Peters & S. Kontos (Eds.), *Continuity and discontinuity of experience in child care* (pp. 69–90). Norwood, NJ: Ablex.

Manfredi, L. A. (1988). *Results: 1988 survey of curriculum styles of family day care providers.* Manuscript submitted for publication.

National Academy of Early Childhood Programs. (1984). *Accreditation criteria and procedures of the National Academy of Early Childhood Programs.* Washington, DC: National Association for the Education of Young Children.

Pence, A. R., & Goelman, H. (1985). *Parents of children in three types of day care: The Victoria day care research project* (Report No. P9019209). Ottawa: Social Sciences and Humanities Research Council of Canada. (ERIC Doc. No. ED 278 524)

Pence, A. R., & Goelman, H. (1987). Silent partners: Parents of children in three types of day care. *Early Childhood Research Quarterly, 2,* 103–18.

Powell, D. R. (1989). *Families and early childhood programs.* Washington, DC: National Association for the Education of Young Children.

Rubin, S. (1974). *Home visiting with family day care providers: A report of research conducted with seven Massachusetts family day care systems* (Report No. P9011091). (ERIC Doc. No. ED 182 010)

Stevens, J. H. Jr. (1982). The National Day Care Home Study: Family day care in the United States. *Young Children, 37,* 59–66.

U.S. Department of Health, Education and Welfare. (1975). *Statistical highlights from the National Child Care Consumer Study* (DHEW Publication No. (OHDS) 78-31096). Washington, DC: Office of Human Development Services, Administration for Children, Youth and Families.

Whitehead, L. C. (1989). Predictors of maternal satisfaction with family day care (doctoral dissertation, University of Delaware). *Dissertation Abstracts International, 49,* 9011A. (University Microfilms No. ADG90-19295)

Winetsky, C. S. (1978). Comparisons of the expectations of parents and teachers for the behavior of preschool children. *Child Development, 49,* 1146–54.

Winget, M., Winget, W. G., & Popplewell, J. F. (1982). Including parents in evaluating family day care homes. *Child Welfare, 61,* 195–205.

CHAPTER 11

Training and Professionalism in Family Day Care

Susan Kontos
Sandra Machida
Sandra Griffin
Malcolm Read

Efforts to professionalize family day care are growing. Still we continue to struggle with the question of whether or not family day care providers can be considered professionals. To many, the word *professional* connotes credentials, business suits, briefcases, and offices. Can that word describe women caring for others' young children in their homes? The purpose of this chapter is to assess the status of family day care as a profession and to examine the relationship between specialized child care training and professional caregiving practices, assuming, of course, that the two are associated.

The chapter is divided into four parts. First, we provide background information about the regulatory climate regarding provider training as well as other contextual factors that may help or hinder professionalization of family day care. Second, we examine whether or not family day care providers have certain characteristics that are commonly associated with being a professional. Third, typical sources of training, training models, and desired outcomes are presented. Finally, research findings are presented that examine the role of training in professionalizing caregiving. Implications for future training and regulations are drawn from what we know to this point.

Consistent with the scope of this volume, this chapter focuses on the North American perspective, both U.S. and Canadian. For each topic with a separate Canadian and U.S. perspective, there are separate sections for each country. When a topic is covered by a single section, there is a unity of perspectives across North America.

CONTEXTUAL FACTORS

Before becoming immersed in the literature on professionalism and training in family day care, it is important to consider the context in which these issues exist. The context of family day care services in the United States and Canada appears to be one that is unlikely to nurture training and professionalism among caregivers. The regulatory climate, educational background of caregivers, and their view of the type of preparation they need, as well as turnover and job commitment, all result in the placement of a low value on training for family day care providers.

Regulations for Training in the United States

Twenty-nine states have a training requirement of some type (Children's Foundation, 1990). These requirements range from CPR or first-aid courses to courses in child development. Typically, however, states indicate the required number of inservice training hours per year without specifying the content. Twenty-two states have no training requirements for family day care providers. Aspiring family day care providers are required to participate in an orientation process in 11 states. Six states require both orientation and training of all regulated family day care providers. Even though more than half the states require some type of training or orientation, or both, it is important to remember that these requirements affect only the caregivers who choose to become regulated. It has been estimated that only 10 to 40 percent of all family day care providers become licensed (Kahn & Kamerman, 1987). Also, training content varies in the extent to which it is likely to address the critical aspects of creating nurturing environments for young children (e.g., CPR versus child development).

Regulations for Training in Canada

All standards and regulations for family day care in Canada are enacted through provincial legislation and administered at the provincial level. At present there are no specific requirements for formal training. However, a number of provinces require first-aid certificates as a condition of licensing, and at least one province requires the provider to be a member of an accredited agency, which in turn may require participation in a training program. In another province, where licensing is undertaken at the local level through local health units, some health units require participation in a 20-hour orientation program as a condition of licensing.

Education and Training in the United States

Most of the family day care research that has focused on education and training variables is based on samples of regulated caregivers. With that limitation in mind, a recent review by Kontos (in press) characterized family day care providers' typical education and training background. In general, family day care providers are most likely to be high school graduates and unlikely to hold college degrees. The child care training that family day care providers do receive tends to be informal (conferences and workshops) rather than formal.

A potentially important reason for minimal amounts of training is the perception held by caregivers of what appropriate training for family day care is. Several studies have shown that family day care providers tend to think that raising a family is the best preparation for their work (Divine-Hawkins, 1981; Fischer, 1989). To the extent that caregivers perceive their work as mothering, requiring natural dispositions and intuitions more than formal training, motivations for training are likely to be low (Fischer, 1989; Kontos, in press).

Education and Training in Canada

A national survey of 65 regulated family day care providers indicated that about 40 percent had completed high school and one-third had not (Schom-Moffatt, 1985). Similar figures have been reported in recent regional studies (Norpark Computer Design, Inc., 1989; Read & LaGrange, 1990; Pence & Goelman, 1987; Stuart & Pepper, 1985). Although few caregivers enter the field with training in early childhood, many engage in inservice professional development activities. A survey conducted in Ontario reported that within the previous year, 77 percent of caregivers had attended workshops, 32 percent had been a delegate at a conference, and 50 percent had received professional development assistance from a contracting agency (Norpark Computer Design, Inc., 1989). Similar to U.S. family day care providers, Canadian caregivers are likely to perceive their previous experiences as mothers or baby-sitters to be their primary qualification for their work (Alberta Social Services, 1988).

Other Work-Force Characteristics in the United States

One characteristic of the child care work force as a whole that affects training and professionalism is the high rate of turnover (National Association for the Education of Young Children, 1985). Turnover rates for family day care providers have been estimated to equal or exceed those for center-based staff, ranging from 37 percent to 59 percent annually (Nelson, 1990; National Commission on Working Women, 1985; National Association for the Education of Young Children, 1985). It is probably safe to say that training is less likely to be sought out by or to have an enduring impact on a rapidly fluctuating work force. Two factors potentially fueling the high turnover rate are job commitment and motivation for entering family day care. Once again, these data are based exclusively on regulated caregivers, who are likely to differ from unregulated caregivers on these dimensions.

Several studies have shown that work in family day care was chosen or is seen as a permanent occupation by the majority of caregivers (Fosburg, 1982; Aguirre, 1987; Bollin, 1989). In one study in which job commitment was assessed by two components—whether family day care was the chosen occupation and whether there was an indefinite commitment to it—only 23 percent of the caregivers stated both that family day care was their chosen occupation and that they planned to stay in it indefinitely (Kontos & Riessen, under review). Interestingly, in that study, the more committed caregivers were those with the least education and training but with the most experience.

Job commitment for family day care providers may be related to their reasons for choosing this kind of work. A literature review by Kontos (in press) found that the three most common reasons for entering family day care work were the love of children, a desire to stay home with one's own children, and economics. One could speculate that family day care providers whose primary motivation is to stay home with their own children may be likely to move on to other work when their children enter school full time. The salience of the economic motivation is likely to vary with the availability of financially lucrative employment alternatives for women with a high school education.

Another important family day care work-force characteristic affecting access to and motivation for training is the number of regulated caregivers. Since best estimates suggest that a minority of family day care providers are regulated (Kahn & Kamerman, 1987), the majority of caregivers are either legally or illegally unregulated (many states exempt caregivers from regulation for various reasons, most related to the number of children served). In either case, unregulated caregivers are less likely to be connected to formal support networks (e.g., sponsoring organizations or resource and referral agencies) that could make training accessible to them (Fischer, 1989).

Other Work-Force Characteristics in Canada

Turnover is high and long-term job commitment is low among caregivers in Canada. There is consistent evidence that the turnover rate is 50 percent annually (Schom-Moffatt, 1985; Norpark Computer Design, Inc., 1989; Alberta Social Services, 1988). Consistent with these data, the majority of caregivers intend to do family day care temporarily (Schom-Moffatt, 1985; Read & LaGrange, 1990). Their primary motivation for entering the field is financial and to provide company for their own young children (Schom-Moffatt, 1985; Read & LaGrange, 1990). Under these circumstances, there is little motivation or incentive to seek training.

Summary

There is little evidence to suggest that training for family day care providers is a priority in the United States or Canada for regulators or for the caregivers themselves. On the positive side, 11 states in the United States passed or improved training requirements between mid-1988 and early 1990 (Adams, 1990). As a counterbalance, however, many states are doing little or nothing to support training for child care providers (Adams, 1990). Contextual factors provide little motivation or incentives to caregivers for valuing or seeking training. Given what we know about family day care providers, questions about their professionalism and training are timely ones.

WHERE IS FAMILY DAY CARE AS A PROFESSION?

Several characteristics are typically associated with professionalism: (1) reliance on a knowledge base not normally possessed by others that guides judgment and practice, (2) standards for entry into the profession that are set by members of the profession who have a strong commitment to competence, and (3) required training that confers authority and status (Katz, 1984, 1988). Family day care, like child care in general, falls short of professionalism on each of these characteristics.

Reliance on a Knowledge Base

All available evidence suggests that society views child care work, particularly home-based child care, as paid mothering, a job for which any woman is qualified by virtue of her gender, not by a specialized knowledge base (Phillips, Lande & Goldberg, 1990; Phillips & Whitebook, in press). To the extent that many caregivers mirror society in their views regarding the nature of their work (Gramley, 1990), it is probably safe to say that reliance on a knowledge base is not characteristic of family day care work.

Standards for Entry into the Profession

In both the United States and Canada there is nothing to prevent potential family day care providers from simply advertising the availability of their services without first meeting certain standards. Many do just that, ignoring mandatory compliance with state licensing or registration policies. Even for those family day care providers (the minority) who choose to comply with their state or provincial child care regulations, licensing or registration represents something less than a professional commitment to standards and competence for several reasons. One reason is that child care regulations define minimal standards designed to protect children's health and safety rather than optimal standards to promote high-quality child care. The other reason is that the regulations are imposed by the state or the provincial government, not by the profession itself, implying the need for coercion to obtain compliance. Thus, a license is something less than a certificate of merit for performance as a family day care provider, and licensing does not function as a gatekeeping process.

Professional status for family day care providers will remain in doubt without a credentialing system that is both uniform and enforceable (Krause-Eheart, 1987). Currently, there are two ways that a family day care provider in the United States can be credentialed by a professional organization. Each is optional. Although these two credentialing systems are neither uniform nor enforceable, they represent the closest available approximation to professionalization in family day care.

Recently the National Association of Family Day Care (NAFDC) implemented an accreditation program based on assessments made of observable criteria in family day care homes. The assessment process involves a self-report from the provider, a completed survey by parents, and an observational assessment conducted by an NAFDC validator. During the assessment, information is collected and caregiving practices are observed in terms of the physical characteristics of the home, child care procedures and policies, and caregiver-child interactions. These characteristics are assessed across seven dimensions: indoor safety, health, nutrition, indoor play environment, interaction, outdoor play environment, and professional responsibility (Sibley & Abbot-Shim, 1989). Assessments are made in the seven dimensions based on direct observation. The provider must score at least 85 percent overall and not less than 75 percent in any one category.

The requirements for being accredited are minimal. The candidate must have cared for children for at least 18 months and meet voluntary and mandatory state requirements (Modigliani, n.d.). Providers can be recognized for the quality care they are providing without receiving training. They may be confident in and comfortable with the assessment procedures and criteria because the NAFDC validators are family day care providers themselves and know the constraints of the job. Moreover, the fees for accreditation are relatively low–$250 for the whole process. At present, 122 providers from across the country have been accredited (NAFDC, personal communication, January 1991).

A Child Development Associate (CDA) credential is another way to recognize competence in individuals working in the field of early childhood education, including family day care providers. The CDA credential is sponsored by the Council for Early Childhood Professional Recognition, an independent organization that administers the CDA National Credentialing Program.

The CDA credential is awarded to practitioners working directly with children (Spodek & Saracho, 1988). Initially, the credential was awarded if the practitioner demonstrated certain competencies regardless of previous child care training. In 1992, the credentialing process changed, with practitioners being credentialed through one of two options. Practitioners can become credentialed either based on previous experience and training (the direct assessment option) or through a year-long training program (the professional preparation option). Both options require formal early childhood education training and experience with children. Regardless of option, CDA candidates are expected to demonstrate competence in the following eight areas: observing and recording children's behavior, principles of child growth and development, health and safety, promoting socioemotional development, promoting physical and intellectual development, relationships with families, individual and group management, and professionalism (Lombardi, 1989).

Practitioners seeking CDA credentials must meet certain criteria before applying. The new 1992 eligibility requirements are more rigorous than previous requirements. The provider must:

- Be at least 18 years of age,
- Have a high school or general education diploma,
- Meet minimum state or local regulations,
- Care for at least two unrelated children under age five,
- Have at least 480 hours of work experience with children five years old and younger, and
- Have 120 hours of formal training with at least 10 hours in each of the above eight competency areas.

The applicant need not have completed a formal program of study at a college or university, but still must have some formal training from approved institutions including colleges, resource and referral agencies, and vocational schools.

Several problems, however, loom in the background. First, neither NAFDC accreditation nor the CDA credential is recognized by most child care licensing agencies. Second, the CDA assessment fees have increased to $1,500 per candidate, making it unaffordable for many family day care providers. Third, it will take time for the caregiver preparation programs at universities and colleges to accommodate the new CDA training requirements and to shorten course times to meet the time constraints of providers.

Required Training That Confers Authority

Few states or provinces require training of any kind, and family day care providers are typically not formally trained (Kontos, in press). The perception that child care work is unskilled and requires little or no training affords family day care little authority or status. Caregivers themselves perceive family day care work as low status (Read & LaGrange, 1990).

Summary

There is no reliance on a knowledge base, no standards for entry into the profession, and no required training for family day care providers. Thus, professional status (as it is traditionally defined) has successfully eluded family day care providers even more than it has eluded caregivers working in centers. Increased attention to licensing and registration issues, accreditation and credentialing programs, and inservice training may help alter this situation.

SOURCES OF TRAINING

One way to promote professionalism is through specialized training. Training can occur through several mechanisms. For instance, providers themselves can organize periodic training. Local professional organizations often offer training as part of their membership meetings.

Alternatively or in addition, providers can become a part of a system or become affiliated with centers that conduct relevant training. In a family child care system, a group of providers (from 6 to 100) band together under one administrative umbrella. One administrative office helps consolidate services and reduce costs. One service that the hub model provides to its members is training (Lauritzen, 1988). Providers can also be linked with a child care center. This model is called satellite family child care homes (Lauritzen, 1988). The center provides training and support services to providers—similar to family child care systems. Affiliations in either model appear to increase a sense of professionalism among providers and provide needed training.

Also, child care resource and referral agencies may offer training with funding from state or provincial licensing departments. The training often covers topics necessary to meet state or provincial requirements and specific programmatic or business needs. In some states and provinces (e.g., British Columbia), community colleges offer formal training leading to a certificate.

Another source of training is private foundations or agencies. Several private, state or provincial, and national family day care initiatives include training components. For instance, child care advocates in California have designed innovative programs to increase the supply and quality of family day care providers. Over a three-year period, the California Child Care Initiative (CCCI) project has helped over 2,000 providers become licensed and has provided over 8,550 new day care spaces for children (Bellm, 1989).

The CCCI is innovative for a number of reasons. First, it has organized the resources of the private and public sectors to train and retain providers. Second, project staff designed a curriculum to meet the specific needs and interests of providers who are in the early years of the family day care business—the most critical time for determining retention in the field. For example, during the first year, providers were asked to evaluate themselves and their situations critically to see whether family day care was the best career for them. Through a process of self-evaluation, it was determined that some providers should seek other employment.

Training sessions were purposely short (i.e., two to four sessions per topic) and dealt with providers' special concerns. The topics included orientation to the profession, program planning, environment setup, child development, and business aspects of day care.

For providers in the second year of business, the training focused on courses in child development, business management, parent-provider communication, and avoiding burnout. With providers who were more experienced before joining the CCCI project, concrete support and feedback from peers seemed to be most effective in increasing professionalism.

Although there is no magic formula that helps predict which providers will remain open for business, approximately 77 percent of 157 licensed recruits had participated in training sessions with an emphasis on successful business management (Lawrence, Brown & Bellm, 1989). When providers could see financial success or at least stability, they were more likely to continue providing day care and obtain training to increase their professional image and income.

Project staff also went to great lengths to remove barriers to training (Lawrence et al., 1989). For example, training was scheduled during the day and substitutes were paid to supervise participants' children. The setting was relaxed and refreshments were served. Training was low key, focusing on concrete skills and projects (i.e., "make it and take it approach"). Trainers were flexible and sensitive to the learning styles, levels of experience, and abilities of providers. Multiple formats were used. Some training occurred in one-time workshops, and other training included home visits or mentor approaches.

Another large-scale training project, the National Family Day Care Project, is sponsored by the National Council of Jewish Women (NCJW) (Cohen, 1990). Funded by the NCJW and numerous foundations and agencies, it is a three-year project to pioneer effective roles for community groups in increasing the quality, supply, and visibility of family day care. Twenty-nine local volunteer groups in 20 states are implementing community service projects, education, and advocacy groups in family day care. Each volunteer group can determine what type of project would best suit its community. For example, training volunteers in Houston, Texas, are recruiting and orienting providers in health and safety, child development, guidance, nutrition, and business management. In Louisville, Kentucky, volunteers are identifying unregulated providers and inviting them to conferences on regulation and training. Advocates in Kentucky are also organizing a campaign to improve overall state licensing regulations.

The California Child Care Initiative and the National Family Day Care Project are excellent examples of how caregiving standards can be improved, training can be implemented, and family day care can be professionalized through the partnership of the private and public sectors. We can also learn lessons from our colleagues abroad.

In France, for instance, it is assumed that a skilled staff is the key to quality (Richardson & Marx, 1989). Teachers and other professionals who work with young children (among them family day care providers) are expected to have high levels of training in child development and early childhood education. To meet this end, training schools are subsidized by the government and on-site training and supervision is expected. In family day care network systems, infant and toddler educators have an equivalent of two years of college followed by a two-year professional degree in child development. Providers not only receive training but also salaries and benefits (e.g., social security and health insurance) comparable to professionals with equivalent levels of training. It is a model that assumes that government has a role in optimizing licensing standards and opportunities for child care training, especially for care of infants and toddlers. It also assumes that full-time child care workers should earn above the poverty threshold.

DOES TRAINING INFLUENCE FAMILY
DAY CARE PROVIDERS?

The research on family day care provider training is neither abundant nor methodologically pristine (for a more detailed review of this literature, see Kontos, in press). Only 3 of 20 quasi-experimental training studies included a control or comparison group of untrained caregivers. Pre-post designs were the most dominant form of program evaluation used. Because of this limitation, we cannot conclude that training per se improves provider caregiving practices or that one training model is more effective than another. There is, however, suggestive evidence from correlational studies that positively links specialized caregiving training to changes in provider behavior.

Another gap in methodology of family day care training studies is the lack of observations of caregiver behavior. Most of the studies focusing on changes in caregiver behavior as a function of training relied on caregiver self-reporting. Thus, objective accounts of what trained caregivers do (as opposed to what they think or say) differently after training are at a premium. In spite of these weaknesses, the research is useful for characterizing the typical format, content, and intensity of training.

Training Format, Content, and Intensity

The most common format for training family day care providers has been group meetings (e.g., workshops, "rap" groups) combined with home visits (e.g., Radin, 1970; Brout & Krabbenhout, 1977; Jones & Meisels, 1987; Kontos, 1988). A few programs have conducted just group meetings (Colbert & Enos, 1976; Greenspan, Silver & Allen, 1977; Poresky, 1977), and several others have included home visits but not group meetings (Howes, Keeling & Sale, 1988; Machida, 1990; Rubin, 1976). Only one program, a home study course, included neither (Marshall, 1987). Another common component of family day care training programs has been resource/toy lending libraries (e.g., Colbert & Enos, 1976; Jones & Meisels, 1987; Kontos, 1988).

The content of family day care training has been highly consistent across programs (Kontos, in press). The most commonly addressed topics are health/safety/nutrition, child development, guidance and discipline, working with parents, and business practices. Several programs include infant/toddler care, caring for atypical children, and selecting and planning activities for children. Format has not dictated content, since it appears that concepts were reinforced by covering the same material in several different formats.

Training intensity is related to both frequency and duration. Programs utilizing group meetings generally held four to six week sessions (the range was one to 13) lasting from 90 minutes to three hours (Kontos, in press). In most instances these sessions were scheduled once or twice a month on weekday evenings (a few met on Saturdays). Home visiting schedules ranged from once a week to once every six weeks. With two exceptions, however, home visiting was scheduled one or twice a month. Length of training programs varied from short term to ongoing (Kontos, in press). Neither short-term nor ongoing training programs were the norm, however. More typically training was spaced across six months to a year.

Training Outcomes

Problems with attributing changes in caregiver knowledge or behavior to training on the basis of available research have already been discussed. According to Kontos (in press), the most frequently documented result of training was caregiver reports of satisfaction with or helpfulness of the training, which have been overwhelmingly positive. Even if there had been comparison or control groups, evidence of positive change in caregiver knowledge, attitudes, and behavior would be weak if not nonexistent. In other words, changes, if they were detected at all, were usually modest. The results of several studies exemplify this generalization.

Howes, et al. (1988), for instance, found small but statistically significant changes (.6 point per item on a 7-point scale) in child care quality ratings (based on the Family Day Care Rating Scale, Harms & Clifford, 1989) of caregivers who received home visits, regardless of frequency, compared to ratings of caregivers who received no visits. In another study (Machida, 1990), family day care providers who received two home visits providing personalized health care information received barely minimal scores (M = 76 percent) on a test of health care knowledge following these visits. Two studies that included comparison groups of untrained caregivers found no differences in knowledge (Crowe, Pine & Titus, 1977) and behavior (Vartuli, 1989) between trained and untrained caregivers. The results of these studies are typical of findings from family day care training studies.

It might be tempting to infer that training family day care providers is an ineffective enterprise that is not worth the time and effort. There are two reasons why this reasoning is premature. First, the quality of most of the research is sufficiently poor that the merits of family day care training have yet to be truly tested. The question is, does training influence family day care providers? The answer is, we don't know yet. Only future research of high quality can change the answer to that question. Second, correlational studies suggest that there is a relationship between training and caregiver performance. A summary of these studies follows.

Correlational Studies in the United States

The National Day Care Home Study (Divine-Hawkins, 1981: Fosburg, 1982) was the first study to systematically examine relations between training and behavior in family day care providers. Regulatory status had to be taken into account, however, because training and regulatory status were confounded in this sample of urban caregivers (80 percent of the sponsored caregivers had some training, but only 30 percent of the regulated and 20 percent of the unregulated caregivers). Results revealed positive associations between training and behavior in all three groups of caregivers. For example, training was associated with more teaching, helping, and dramatic play and with less activity not involving interaction with children in sponsored and regulated homes.

Howes (1983) predicted caregiver behavior from training in a sample of 20 family day care providers. Results revealed that of eleven caregiver behaviors, there were three significant training-behavior associations. Caregivers with more training were more likely to play, mediate objects, and respond to positive toddler bids.

A study of family day care providers in California (Fischer, 1989) revealed that 70 percent of the variance in family day care quality was accounted for by caregiver training, support, and years of schooling. Training was the strongest predictor of the three, however, accounting for 50 percent of the variance. A similar relationship between training and family day care quality was found in a northeastern sample of caregivers ($r = .45$; Bollin, 1990).

Correlational studies such as these cannot support causal inferences concerning the impact of training on caregiver behavior. Their results do suggest, however, that future work on the efficacy of training family day care providers is warranted. We need studies that can tell us whether training family day care providers can change what they think and do, and also what training processes are mostly likely to effect certain types of changes.

Correlational Studies in Canada

Few Canadian studies have dealt with caregiver training or education. Pence and Goelman (in press) found that training specifically related to family day care and a commitment to family day care as professional employment were factors associated with quality for family day care providers in Vancouver. A recent study found that family day care providers with specific early childhood training were twice as likely as those without such training to remain caregivers for at least five years (Read & LaGrange, 1990).

Motivation and Recruitment Issues in the United States

The majority of caregivers participating in two separate studies (52 percent in Eheart & Leavitt, 1986; 60 percent in Peters, 1972) were uninterested in any type of training. If these data are at all representative, the issue of how best to involve family day care providers in training activities is a crucial one. Several studies have addressed that issue.

Based on a multifaceted two-year training program offered to over 900 family day care providers in Minnesota, Wattenberg (1977) identified four clusters of family day care providers with varying motivations and preferences for training. She found that caregivers in these four clusters varied in the amount and type of training in which they were willing to participate. The "traditional" family day care providers who considered training unimportant and intrusive were most likely to get involved in neighborhood peer groups where the stated focus was support rather than training. The "modernized" family day care provider had a career-development orientation and a concern about professionalization with a concomitant interest in all training opportunities. This group of caregivers was likely to be particularly interested in "accredited coursework" through a college or university, and they were not deterred by long-term training commitments or participating in training outside of the neighborhood. "Novice" family day care providers had a "shallow and unstable commitment" to their work and were thus more likely to respond to home-based training. A fourth category, the "transitional" family day care provider, was vaguely defined as "emerging into a developmental role for herself." This group responded best initially to short-term commitments and then, as their interest increased, more lengthy training commitments were obtained. Approximately 50 percent of the family day care providers were characterized as either traditional or novice. It is important to note that the typology of caregivers was based on the 58 percent of the family day care providers who involved themselves in some sort of training; 42 percent of the eligible caregivers chose not to become involved in any way.

Of those caregivers who participated in some aspect of training, those who participated in the most training were likely to have a driver's license, be more experienced, care for more children, be stable caregivers, have been previously employed outside the home, and use the toy resource center. Wattenberg (1977) concluded that initially, the top priority for a training program has to be overcoming initial resistance to training. This can be accomplished through strategies such as using a buddy system, neighborhood information parties, outreach by family day care associations and paraprofessionals, and so forth. Results of the training project suggested that resistance is lessened once a caregiver participates in any type of training, and that trainers can build on the initial entry into training. Wattenberg (1977) also recommended that a continuum of training options be developed that require varying amounts of initiative, commitment, and travel.

Snow (1982) reported that achieving maximum participation in inservice training depended on accessibility and on the recognition achieved by caregivers for their participation. In a qualitative study of a training and credentialing/accreditation program for family day care providers, Cohen and Modigliani (1990) found that the major obstacles to training were access (cost and location), time and energy, and fear of failure in a school-like program. They found that caregivers' motivations for getting involved in the program were intrinsic (e.g., professionalism, pride, socializing, and networking with peers). None of the respondents in their interviews could identify an extrinsic motivator for caregivers (the exception might be caregivers who entered training because state regulations required it). Since the caregivers who were in the program were described as among the best and most self-motivated in the community, Cohen and Modigliani questioned whether intrinsic motivation alone is likely to attract other providers for whom the effort to become credentialed/accredited does not seem worth it. One extrinsic motivator they suggested is increased earning power for caregivers who are involved in training and credentialing/accreditation through higher rates, fewer empty spaces, and better business practices (e.g., late fees, paid vacations).

Motivation and Recruitment Issues in Canada

Surveys have shown that in spite of the lack of incentive to do so, Canadian family day care providers do take advantage of professional development activities and exhibit a more positive attitude toward training than may be assumed (Alberta Social Services, 1988). Read and LaGrange (1990) reported that 86 percent of the caregivers in their survey indicated a willingness to complete training requirements if they did not have to leave their present jobs and if they received financial support.

Summary

It is clear that motivation and recruitment of family day care providers must be a crucial component of any training program. Wattenberg's (1977) results revealed that half of the family day care providers involved in her training program (traditional and novice caregivers) did not consider themselves to be professionals; only one of her four types of caregivers (modernized family day care providers) had a professional orientation toward their work. Making training accessible, varying the format to suit the varying needs of a diverse caregiver population, and offering intrinsic and extrinsic rewards for successful completion of training have all been recommended as important aspects of program design. Thus, there seems to be a greater priority placed on "carrot" as opposed to "stick" (i.e., licensing) approaches to recruitment into training. Although it is premature to say that provider training increases professional practices, the research does suggest positive associations between caregiver training and behavior.

CONCLUSIONS

Family day care providers cannot claim professional status yet but could come closer to doing so through more rigorous licensing standards, linkage of training with licensing, and increasing community awareness of the complexities of child care work and the concomitant need for training. Before these factors can come into play, however, there needs to be a measure of consensus regarding the content of a core curriculum for family day care provider training. The need to specify the training and education required for all child care workers has been frequently articulated (e.g., Hayes, Palmer & Zaslow, 1990). There is not a consensus, however, regarding what this means for family day care. Some trainers have emphasized the need to focus on providing support and reducing isolation among family day care providers (Snow, 1982); others have emphasized the need for specific knowledge and skills in addition to network support for caregivers (Kontos, 1988). The CDA credentialing process with its specified core competencies may be a logical starting point for addressing the training needs of family day care providers.

Increasing the number of states and provinces requiring training for family day care providers as well as the amount of training required might provide an incentive for more family day care providers to seek out training. For several reasons, however, it cannot solve the problem. First, large numbers of caregivers choose to avoid licensing or registration, so a minority of caregivers would be affected by more rigorous licensing regulations. Moreover, many states and provinces exempt large numbers of caregivers from licensing on the basis of the number of children they care for. Second, due to the informality and low visibility of many family day care arrangements, licensing regulations are difficult to enforce. Enforcement difficulties are usually compounded by inadequate resources for monitoring compliance with regulations. Since licensing regulations may help but cannot eliminate the problem of training family day care providers, other strategies must be relied upon.

Accessibility of training for family day care providers must be maximized. Training must be low in cost and convenient in time and place. Timing is particularly important due to the long hours that family day care providers work. For day-time training during the week, substitute caregivers can be provided or individualized home visits can be made. Evening or weekend training may appeal to some and avoids the need for substitutes. However, infringements on personal time may lower the incentive to participate. These decisions must be made with a particular audience of family day care providers in mind.

More innovative training approaches appropriate for adult learners (such as the CCCI) must be developed. This means several things. First, it means that training must be based on the informal knowledge base that family day care providers bring to their work (the skills of mothering) rather than assuming that their knowledge base is nonexistent. One purpose of training practitioners who vary in knowledge and skill is to link their informal knowledge base to a more formal knowledge base to enhance their understanding and implementation of best practices in child care. Second, it means that the content of training must be uniquely suited to the audience. New versus experienced, urban versus suburban, educated versus uneducated caregivers will have different needs and interests that must be addressed in training if we expect them to be interested in taking part in it. "One-track" training that is condescending toward the skills caregivers bring with them is doomed to failure.

There is also some evidence that relying on intrinsic motivation to entice caregivers into training is not enough (Cohen & Modigliani, 1990). Family day care providers need to be made more aware of the concrete benefits of training to them and their programs (e.g., higher income due to better business practices, fewer empty spaces due to reputation for high-quality care).

At this time, it appears that training as the prime route to professionalism is a reality for a minority of intrinsically motivated family day care providers. Perhaps the major barrier to linking training and professionalism is the belief by some caregivers that family day care is simply an extension of mothering and that, as such, suggesting a need for training denigrates a woman's natural caregiving abilities (Wattenberg, 1977; Nelson, 1990; Gramley, 1990). Thus a key to increasing professionalism in family day care providers may be to expand the self-concept of caregivers to include the teacher role, helping them to understand that teaching can occur in the context of spontaneous, naturally occurring events embedded in the activities of everyday life and not just in formal and didactic circumstances. If family day care providers understand that mothering and teaching are complementary rather than mutually exclusive, they may be more likely to understand that an educational focus is not a devaluation of mothering (Gramley, 1990) and that training is a worthwhile endeavor.

REFERENCES

Adams, G. C. (1990). *Who knows how safe?* Washington, DC: Children's Defense Fund.

Aguirre, B. (1987). Educational activities and needs of family day care providers in Texas. *Child Welfare, 66*(5), 459–65.

Alberta Social Services. (1988). *Results of the survey of the Family Day Home Program.* Edmonton, Alberta: Author.

Bellm, D. (1989). *A guide to the California child care initiative.* San Francisco: California Child Care Resource and Referral Network.

Bollin, G. (1989, March). *Diversity in attitudes about family day care among sponsored family day care providers.* Paper presented at the American Educational Research Association annual meeting, San Francisco.

Bollin, G. (1990, April). *An investigation of turnover among family day care providers.* Paper presented at the American Educational Research Association annual meeting, Boston.

Brout, B., & Krabbenhout, K. (1977). The Red Hook family day care training program. *Young Children, 32*(5), 49–52.

Children's Foundation. (1990). *Family day care licensing study.* Washington, DC: Author.

Cohen, N. (1990). *Highlights of the national family day care project.* New York: National Council of Jewish Women.

Cohen, N., & Modigliani, K. (1990). *The evaluation report of the family to family project.* New York: Families and Work Institute.

Colbert, J., & Enos, M. (1976). *Educational services for home day caregivers. Final Report.* (ERIC Doc. No. 134–341)

Crowe, M, Pine, B., & Titus, J. (1977). An educational program for family day care mothers: A pilot project. *Children Today,* July–August, 6–10.

Divine-Hawkins, P. (1981). *Family day care in the United States: Executive summary.* Final Report of the National Day Care Home Study. (ERIC Doc. No. 211 244)

Eheart, B., & Leavitt, R. (1986). Training day care home providers: Implications for policy and research. *Early Childhood Research Quarterly, 1,* 119–32.

Fischer, J. (1989). *Family day care: Factors influencing the quality of caregiving practices.* Unpublished doctoral dissertation, University of Illinois, Champaign-Urbana.

Fosburg, S. (1982). Family day care: The role of the surrogate mother. In L. Laosa & I. Sigel (Eds.), *Families as learning environments* (pp. 223–60). New York: Plenum.

Gramley, M. C. (1990, April). *Providers' role perceptions and the design and delivery of family day care services.* Paper presented at the American Educational Research Association annual meeting, Boston.

Greenspan, S., Silver, B., & Allen, M. (1977). A psychodynamically oriented group training program for early childhood caregivers. *American Journal of Psychiatry, 134,* 1104–08.

Harms, T., & Clifford, R. (1989). *Family day care rating scale.* New York: Teachers College Press.

Hayes, C. D., Palmer, J. L., & Zaslow, M. J. (1990). *Who cares for America's children?* Washington, DC: National Academy Press.

Howes, C. (1983). Caregiver behavior in center and family day care. *Journal of Applied Developmental Psychology, 4,* 99–107.

Howes, C., Keeling, K., & Sale, J. (1988). *The home visitor: Improving quality in family day care homes.* Unpublished manuscript.

Jones, S., & Meisels, S. (1987). Training family day care providers to work with special needs children. *Topics in Early Childhood Special Education, 7*(1), 1–12.

Kahn, A., & Kamerman, S. (1987). *Child Care: Facing the hard choices.* Dover, MA: Auburn House.

Katz, L. G. (1984). The professional early childhood teacher. *Young Children, 40,* 3–10.

Katz, L. G. (1988). Where is early childhood education as a profession? In B. Spodek, O. Saracho & D. L. Peters (Eds.), *Professionalism and the early childhood practitioner* (pp. 75–83). New York: Teachers College Press.

Kontos, S. (1988). Family day care as an integrated early intervention setting. *Topics in Early Childhood Special Education, 8*(2), 1–14.

Kontos, S. (In press). *Family care: Out of the shadows and into the limelight.* Washington, DC: National Association for the Education of Young Children.

Kontos, S., & Riessen, J. (Under review). Predictors of job satisfaction, job stress, and job commitment in family day care providers.

Krause-Eheart, B. (1987). *Training day care providers.* (ERIC Doc. No. ED 261 608)

Lauritzen, P. (1988). Family child care systems and satellite family child care homes. In A. Goodwin & L. Schrag (Eds.), *Setting up for infant care* (pp. 62–64). Washington DC: National Association for the Education of Young Children.

Lawrence, M., Brown, J., & Bellm, D. (1989). *Helping family day care providers stay in business: Retention strategies from the California Child Care Initiative.* San Francisco: California Child Care Resource and Referral Network.

Lombardi, J. (1989). New directions for CDA: Deciding what it means for your program. *Child Care Information Exchange, 70,* 41–3.

Machida, S. (1990). In-home health education for family day care providers. *Child and Youth Care Quarterly, 19,* 271–88.

Marshall, M. (1987). *Family day home care provider program: Evaluation report.* College Station, TX: Texas Agricultural Extension Service.

Modigliani, K. (n.d.). *The quality of family child care: A comparison of five instruments.* New York: Bank Street College of Education.

National Association for the Education of Young Children (NAEYC). (1985). *In whose hands?* Washington, DC: Author.

National Commission on Working Women. (1985). *Child care fact sheet: Working mothers and children*. Washington, DC: Author.

Nelson, M. (1990). Mothering others' children: The experiences of family day care providers. *Signs: The Journal of Woman in Culture and Society, 15,* 586–605.

Norpark Computer Design, Inc. (1989). *A survey of private home day care services in Ontario*. Toronto: Child Care Branch, Ministry of Community and Social Services.

Pence, A., & Goelman, H. (1987). Who cares for the child in day care? An examination of caregivers from three types of care. *Early Childhood Research Quarterly, 2*(4), 315–34.

Pence, A.R., & Goelman, H. (In press). The relationship of regulation, training, and motivation to quality of care in family day care. *Child and Youth Care Forum*.

Peters, D. (1972). *Day care homes: A Pennsylvania profile*. (ERIC Doc. No. ED 647 097)

Phillips, D., & Whitebook, M. (In press). The child care providers: Pivotal player in the child's world. In Chehraz, S. S. (Ed.), *Day care: Psychological and developmental implications*. New York: American Psychiatric Press.

Phillips, G. C., Lande, J., & Goldberg, M. (1990). The state of child care regulations. *Early Childhood Research Quarterly, 5*(20), 151–79.

Poresky, R. (1977). *Evaluation report of the pilot project to evaluate effectiveness of utilizing licensed day care home providers as trainers of potential day care home providers. Phase 1*. (ERIC Doc. No. 154-938)

Radin, N. (1970). *Evaluation of the daycare consultation program*. (ERIC Doc. No. 047-331)

Read, M., & LaGrange, A. (1990). *Those who care: A report on approved family day home providers in Alberta*. Red Deer, Alberta: Child Care Matters.

Richardson, G., & Marx, E. (1989). *A welcome for every child. How France achieves quality child care: Practical ideas for the United States. The report of the child care study panel of the French-American Foundation*. New York: French-American Foundation.

Rubin, S. (1976). Home visiting with family day care providers. *Child Welfare, 54,* 645–57.

Schom-Moffatt, P. (1985). *The bottom line: Wages and working conditions of workers in the formal day care market*. Report prepared for the Federal Task Force on Child Care. Ottawa: Status of Women in Canada.

Sibley, A. S., & Abbot-Shim, M. A. (1989). *Study guide for the Assessment Profile for Family Day Care*. Atlanta: Quality Assist.

Snow, C. (1982). In-service day care training programs: A review and analysis. *Child Care Quarterly, 11*(2), 108–21.

Spodek, B., & Saracho, O. (1988). Professionalism in early childhood education. In B. Spodek, O. Saracho & D. L. Peters (Eds.), *Professionalism and the early childhood practitioner* (pp. 59–74). New York: Teachers College Press.

Stuart, B., & Pepper, S. (1985). The contribution of the caregivers' personality and vocational interests to quality in licensed family day care. *Canadian Journal of Research in Early Childhood Education, 2*(2), 99–109.

Vartuli, S. (1989, April). *Family day care provider training and assessment.* Paper presented at the biennial meeting of the Society for Research in Child Development, Kansas City, MO.

Wattenberg, E. (1977). Characteristics of family day care providers: Implications for training. *Child Welfare, 56,* 211–27.

CHAPTER 12

Models of Family Day Care and Support Services in Canada

Irene J. Kyle

The development of formally organized family day care services with responsibility for monitoring and supporting home-based child care is a relatively recent one in Canada. Although historical information about how these
services began has not been collected, it is believed that they were first
initiated in the late 1960s in response to the growing demand for public child
care as more and more mothers with young children entered the labor force.
Initially, family day care was based on the idea that mothers at home caring
for their own young children could always take in a few extra children to help
out their neighbors who worked and, at the same time, earn a few extra
dollars on the side. It was also thought to be a low-cost service, especially
suited to infants because of its family-like setting, and one with the potential
to be more flexible in meeting parents' needs by offering part-time care or
more flexible hours.

Perhaps because of the recent development of family day care as an
organized service, there has been no overall consensus about how it should
be operated, funded, and regulated, so that approaches to family day care
have varied considerably across Canada. Part of the problem in gaining
recognition for family day care has stemmed from the difficulties associated
with transforming an informal exchange (one historically operated in the
private domain) into a more formal and public service. Although parents
have placed children with unrelated caregivers or baby-sitters in the neighborhood for many years, it is only recently that suggestions have been made
that there should be a public role in determining the kind of care provided in
these formal arrangements. There are still many who view government involvement in this area as intrusive and inappropriate and as an infringement
on parents' rights to make their own child care arrangements and on providers' rights to offer care (Enarson, 1990).

Consistent with this view, family day care legislation was initially introduced in some provinces not out of a concern for the quality of care provided but as a way of providing subsidies to help families pay for home day care. By so doing, it was hoped to diffuse some of the pressure to expand the formal (group) day care system. In Ontario, for example, legislation to provide fee subsidies for private home day care was first introduced in 1971, and although many agencies readily adopted voluntary guidelines for practice, standards were not legislated until 1978 and fully implemented until 1984 (Kyle, in press).

As a further indication of the lack of consensus about how family day care services should be operated, other provinces have required that caregivers be licensed and meet minimal requirements, but, with few exceptions, have offered little by way of ongoing supervision or support. For example, the recent Task Force on Child Care in British Columbia (1991) noted: "Family day care support agencies and programs are in their infancy in British Columbia with only four such services in effect prior to 1990" (p. 30).

For the most part, provincial governments[1] have been reluctant to become involved in family day care because the monitoring of potentially large numbers of children cared for in private arrangements presents a formidable management and organizational problem (to say nothing of the related financial commitment). As well, family day care arrangements are more difficult to access and assess than center care and by their nature are less open to public scrutiny.

MODELS OF FAMILY DAY CARE
AND SUPPORT SERVICES

Because of the complexity of these issues and the difficulties inherent in resolving them, a variety of approaches to family day care have been developed. In a recent paper, Corsini, Wisensale, and Caruso (1988) proposed a framework for describing existing family day care services (or systems). They identified six regulatory and support models that are not mutually exclusive and can be operated in a complementary fashion and in the same community:

1. Registration (minimal standards, largely self-regulatory);
2. Licensing (generally higher standards than registration, with more thorough approval and monitoring);

3. Resource and referral model (consultation to business, with a broker or clearinghouse function for the community);
4. Supervisor model (similar to the Canadian agency model);
5. Provider accreditation model (providers' professional association sets and monitors standards); and
6. Independent advocacy model (the authors propose an ombudsman system to deal with complaints and issues related to family day care; Corsini et al., 1988, pp. 20–21).

These models are characterized by differing approaches to various aspects of service, such as what standards are adopted; how the initial approval, monitoring, and renewal processes are carried out; the amount of help provided to parents; the extent to which children's development is monitored; and the amount and kind of provision for financial and professional support to caregivers.

Although Corsini, Wisensale, and Caruso (1988) have referred to a number of the important elements of family day care, the models they propose do not appear to be clearly delineated. The first two models—registration and licensing—are variations of regulatory approaches; the resource and referral and provider accreditation models have to do with the provision of support and education; the supervisory model appears to combine regulation, support, and education; and the sixth model focuses almost entirely on consumer protection and is concerned with how to implement and monitor an existing regulatory approach. Instead of presenting six models of family day care, the authors have outlined various strategies (or combinations of strategies) developed to address the need for differing philosophies about regulation, support, and education.

As an alternative, it might be more useful to conceptualize family day care from a functional perspective. From this viewpoint, various approaches to family day care can be seen to develop based on how their regulatory, support, and educational functions have been defined. The definition of these functions is determined by such factors as local/regional social philosophy and policies (i.e., political positions), need, auspices, and availability of funding; these functions, in turn, tend to define the various service strategies or program components that are adopted.

The following lists outline some of the potential program components associated with family day care according to how they relate to various regulatory, support, and educational functions.

Approaches to Regulation. These approaches are based on a concern for the protection of children—a continuum from no or minimal regulation to licensing:

- *Unregulated:* Unrelated caregivers, often referred to as "informal" caregivers, remain in the private domain. The responsibility for supervision is assumed to rest with parents.
- *Self-Regulation:* Caregivers voluntarily adopt professionally defined standards (certification or accreditation) determined by agencies, provider associations, or unions.
- *Indirect regulation:* Legislated requirements are not specifically directed to family day care programs but may apply to them and may or may not be enforced—for example, employment standards and other labor legislation, income tax legislation, zoning and other local by-laws such as fire and health.
- *Direct regulation:* Legislated requirements are specifically directed to family day care and may include registration or licensing of providers and/or agencies and fiscal regulation (requirements apply only to funded caregivers and agencies). Standards are generally concerned with provider qualifications and characteristics; the physical environment; children's health, safety, and programming; and expectations regarding supervision.

Approaches to Support and Education.   These approaches provided various combinations of support and educational opportunities for caregivers, parents, and children. The range and kinds of support typically vary according to the regulatory approach and auspices, e.g., whether offered by agencies, provider associations, or family resource services. Caregivers' support programs can include:

- Pre- and/or inservice training, workshops, and courses;
- Drop-in programs, peer support, and child management;
- Relief services, such as backup for illness, emergencies, vacations, or to attend workshops;
- Group supports, such as collective insurance, group purchasing, equipment, and toy exchanges;
- Technical assistance for caregivers, covering income tax, business aspects of care, programming ideas, and other information; and
- Advocacy by, or on behalf of, caregivers.

Parents' support programs can include:

- Information and referral—assistance with locating care and information to help evaluate caregivers;
- Support with special needs and circumstances—with emergency situations, family problems, or children's special problems;

- Parent groups to discuss parenting and child management issues; and
- Advocacy concerning parents' needs, e.g., for subsidies, for more day care, for parental leaves.

Children's support can include:

- Play groups, drop-in programs, and toy libraries;
- Special events on professional development days and summer camps;
- Early identification of special needs and programs for children with special needs; and
- Advocacy concerning children's needs.

When governments view family day care as largely falling in the private domain, regulatory, support, and educational strategies tend to be fairly limited. Where family day care services have evolved, becoming more formalized and seen as part of a public child care system, there has tended to be more regulatory intervention as well as the development of a variety of support and educational provisions and the adoption of a more professional role by caregivers. The present proliferation of regulatory and support strategies across Canada, therefore, reflects differing views about family day care and its functions and the dilemmas associated with implementing them.

One of the other implications of adopting a functional approach is that services that appear to be quite different on the surface—e.g., agency-supervised family day care and family resource centers—can be seen to have a number of similarities. Although such services may take similar approaches to support and education, their differences often arise as a result of their regulatory functions.

DEMOGRAPHIC INFORMATION

The discussion of family day care and other support services that follows considers Canadian services from a functional perspective, examining them based on their approaches to regulation, support, and education. In Canada, supervised family day care services are generally seen to be one of the service alternatives that make up part of a more comprehensive and public child care system. The role of resource and support services, however, is not as clear. Sometimes resource centers are specifically focused on child care and seen as complementary to licensed child care services; in other instances, child care needs are only one of a number of family and community needs that are being addressed.

Licensed, supervised family day care services make up a very small proportion of the child care arrangements of Canadian families in which the parents are working or studying; they also serve a small proportion of children in formal child care programs. Based on information from the Canadian National Child Care Study (CNCCS), in 1988, approximately 31,000, or 1.2 percent of 2,633,100 Canadian children 0 to 12 years of age whose parents were working or studying, were cared for in licensed or supervised family day care programs (see Chapter 4 in this volume for a fuller description of the CNCCS findings). The care received by these 31,000 children in regulated family day care programs in 1988 constituted approximately 11 percent of care provided by a variety of formal child care programs (day care centers, kindergartens or nursery schools, and before- and after-school programs). The availability of care also varied with age, so that, for example, regulated family day care services provided approximately 18.4 percent of supervised care for children 0–2 years; 8.1 percent of supervised care for children 3–5 years; and 10.7 percent of supervised care for children 6–12 years whose parents were working or studying. The majority of children 0–12 years old whose parents were working or studying were cared for either by their own parents or relatives (approximately 1,296,700 children, or 49.2 percent) or by unrelated caregivers in unlicensed arrangements (607,100 children, or 23 percent).

The distribution of licensed, supervised family day care services also varies widely across Canada. Table 12.1 provides information about the number of family day care spaces reportedly available by province or territory and traces their development in the period from 1986 to 1990. Although there are some problems with the data (e.g., different definitions of what constitutes a "space" by different provinces and over time), they are the only national statistics that have been collected on any consistent basis. According to the *Status of Day Care in Canada* reports (Health & Welfare, Canada, 1987, 1988, 1989, 1990, 1991), in 1990 there were 38,159 licensed, supervised family day care spaces in Canada, with an increase of about 15,444 spaces, or 40 percent, since 1986, suggesting a steady development of service.

This development seems to have been concentrated in the central and western parts of the country and to a much lesser extent in the maritime provinces and northern territories. Ontario, Québec, British Columbia, and Alberta have all developed substantial family day care programs (approximately 7,000–12,000 spaces); Manitoba and Saskatchewan have somewhat smaller-sized programs (approximately 2,000–3,000 spaces); and the remaining provinces and territories have small programs (about 35–125 spaces). Over time there have also been provincial differences in the development of family day care programs, so in some provinces there appears to be a pattern of progressive growth, as, for example, in Québec, Ontario, and

TABLE 12.1. Licensed, Supervised Family Day Care Spaces in Canada, 1986/90

Province	1986	1987	1988	1989	1990
British Columbia	4,086	4,096	5,494	6,480	7,155
Alberta	5,349	5,588	6,157	6,029*	6,962
Saskatchewan	1,892	2,022	1,900	1,758	1,980
Manitoba	1,530	1,755	2,057	2,310	2,623
Ontario	6,412	9,182	10,115	10,000	11,792
Quebec	3,060	3,860	4,850	5,423	7,273
New Brunswick	72	33	33	114	96
Nova Scotia	82	115	145	123	123
Prince Edward Island	154	132	49	35	35
Newfoundland	0	0	0	0	0
Yukon	48	52	72	88	84
Northwest Territories	30	25	n/a	42	66
Total	22,715	26,860	30,872	32,402	38,159

Sources: Health and Welfare, Canada (1987/91).
* The Status of Day Care in Canada reports Alberta as having 11,819 family day care spaces in 1989. This figure does not make sense in terms of the number of spaces reported either in 1988 or 1990. The figure 6,029, which appears to be more realistic, was taken from the Child Care Information Sheets prepared by the Child Care Resource and Research Unit (1990). These information sheets also contain estimates of the number of family day care spaces in 1988/89 in each province; some of these numbers are consistent with the federal reports, some of them are not.

British Columbia. In other provinces the programs have remained relatively stable, e.g., in Saskatchewan and Nova Scotia, or appear to be in some decline, e.g., in Prince Edward Island. Unfortunately, research about the development of family day care in Canada has not been carried out, so to date, little information is available that would help explain these differences, apart from the obvious differences due to population size and density.

Information about the availability of family resource and support services is even more difficult to obtain and has not been consistently collected by either the federal or the provincial governments. There are a number of direct and indirect linkages between family resource services and family day care, including the provision by family resource services of such programs as information and referral services, caregiver registries, play groups, drop-ins, toy libraries, and educational workshops. Some resource centers also include licensed and supervised family day care services as one of their service components. Family resource services vary in size and program complexity, and over time may evolve into multiservice programs that become a focal point for organizing child care in their local communities. Initially, family resource programs may consist of a few programs such as a drop-in, a toy library, and a baby-sitting exchange; over time, and in response to local interest and need, they may add on a number of program components. Sometimes resource services may be "nested" in larger, more traditional child care or community services and be developed because the organization recognizes the need to provide families with child care support and is interested in exploring innovative ways to offer it.

To give some indication of their availability, in 1990, the Canadian Association of Toy Libraries and Parent Resource Centres (TLRC Canada) included in its data base 556 family resource programs, with 67 reported in British Columbia, 32 in Alberta, 11 in Saskatchewan, 26 in Manitoba, 341 in Ontario, 34 in Nova Scotia, 26 in Québec, 11 in New Brunswick, 6 in Newfoundland, and 2 in the Yukon; there were no family resource programs reported for the Northwest Territories and Prince Edward Island (TLRC Canada, 1991). This number increased from an earlier estimate of approximately 375 programs at the end of 1988 (Kyle, 1991).

REGULATORY APPROACHES

At present, nine of the ten Canadian provinces and the two northern territories, (the Yukon and Northwest Territories) have introduced legislation related to family day care (see Table 12.2). Most provinces license providers directly (with licensing being administered by provincial authorities); in Ontario, Québec, and Nova Scotia the agencies responsible for recruiting and supervising providers are licensed. Newfoundland does not have any legislation or supervised family day care.

There is considerable variation in how the licensing process is carried out, with provinces such as Manitoba requiring that provincial consultants visit homes at least four times a year and become involved in providing various supports to providers and parents. Other provinces, such as Saskatchewan and British Columbia (before 1990), have generally limited their involvement to an annual inspection (Deller, 1988).

Also indicative of some of the different approaches to family day care is the variety of terms used to refer to the service: family day care, private home day care, community day care homes, and family child day care homes. The Québec term for family day care, *service de garde en milieu familial,* is often translated as agency-coordinated home day care (Government of Québec, 1988). "Informal" care is the term often used to refer to care provided privately by unlicensed caregivers; it is not always clearly defined, so that in some instances it may include unrelated caregivers both in and outside the child's home as well as relatives who provide care.

Although both Ontario and Québec license agencies, the focus of the regulatory requirements has been quite different. In Ontario, agencies act as agents that are held accountable for ensuring that day care providers meet certain standards and observe certain practices that are set out in some detail in the regulation. Agencies can include family day care services operated directly by municipal governments, nonprofit agencies, and commercial operators. The regulations specify that an agency must employ one full-time home visitor for every 25 homes and that home visitors are required to visit all provider homes at least once every three months. Home visitors are required to have postsecondary training in child development or family studies as well as two years' experience working with children. Although the specific details of the regulation are different in Nova Scotia, the approach taken is similar to that of Ontario, although the agencies must be nonprofit.

In Québec, the legislation puts more emphasis on agency requirements and does not address the specific expectations of providers.[2] Agencies applying for a Québec license must submit a child care needs assessment for the local community as well as a proposal for how they plan to supervise and support their day care homes. They must be either nonprofit corporations or cooperative associations and must make provision for a parents' consultative committee, whose role is to "examine aspects related to the quality and educational role" of the service. Québec does not have any specific training requirements for family day care agency staff (Government of Québec, 1988).

Alberta combines two approaches by licensing providers directly and by contracting with agencies that in turn approve homes under what began as the "Satellite Family Day Home Project" (Read & LaGrange, 1990). Although the agencies are not formally licensed, their contracts with the provincial government set out certain standards that they are expected to meet (Alberta Family and Social Services, 1989).

A summary of regulations concerning the maximum number of children that can be cared for in a day care home is presented in Table 12.2. For regulated and supervised homes, the maximum number of children allowed varies from four to eight children (including the provider's own). Group sizes vary according to the children's ages, with the number of children allowed decreasing substantially when infants and toddlers are in care. Most provincial legislation also sets a limit on the number of children that can be cared for in an unregulated or unsupervised home (excluding the provider's own children), with the number ranging from no more than two children up to a maximum of seven.

Table 12.2 Summary of Family Day Care Regulation in Canada

Province	Terminology	Regulatory approach	Maximum # of children in regulated care[a]	Maximum # in unregulated care[b]
British Columbia	Family day care	Providers are licensed	Up to 7 children <12 yrs; max 5 preschoolers, 2 under 2 yrs, 1 under age 1	No more than 2
Alberta	Family day homes	Providers are licensed; agencies have contracts	Up to 6 children; max 3 under 3 yrs, 2 under 2 yrs	No more than 3
Saskatchewan	Family child care home	Providers are licensed	Up to 8 children; max 5 under 5 yrs, 2 under 3 mos	No limits
Manitoba	Family day care	Providers are licensed	Up to 8 children <12 yrs; max 5 children 3/6 yrs, 3 children under 2 yrs	No more than 4 under age 12; 2 under 2 yrs.
Ontario	Private home day care	Agencies are licensed	Up to 5 children <12 yrs; max 3 under 3 yrs, 2 under 2 yrs	No more than 5
Quebec	Service de garde en milieu familial	Agencies are licensed	Up to 6 children, no more than 2 under 18 mos	No more than 6
New Brunswick	Community day care homes	Providers are licensed	Up to 6 children, up to 3 infants	No more than 4; max 2 infants

Nova Scotia	Family day care	Agencies are licensed	Up to 5 children; max by age; e.g., 2 children under 2 yrs, 1 under 1 yr	No more than 3
Prince Edward Island	Family child day care homes	Providers are licensed	Up to 6 children <10 yrs; max 3 under 2 yrs; if 5 preschoolers no more than 2 under 2 yrs	No more than 7
Newfoundland	n/a	No legislation	Homes with >4 children are licensed as centres	No more than 4
Yukon	Family day homes	Providers are licensed	Max 8 preschoolers, no infants; 6 preschoolers if 3 infants; max 4 infants	No more than 3
Northwest Territories	Family day homes	Providers are licensed	Up to 8 children <12 yrs; no more than 6 under 5 yrs, 3 under 3, 2 under 2	No more than 4

Sources: Child Care Resource and Research Unit (1990); Nova Scotia Department of Community Services (1990); Pence & Griffin (1990).

[a] Including the provider's own children.
[b] Excluding the provider's own children.

Québec, Manitoba, and Prince Edward Island have, in addition, made provision for family group day care for a somewhat larger number of children and require the presence of two providers. Québec allows for six to nine children in family group care, with a maximum of four children under 18 months; Manitoba allows for eight to twelve children (under age 12), with a maximum of three children under two years of age; Prince Edward Island allows for the care of seven to twelve children (Child Care Resource and Research Unit, 1990). Ontario has done some limited experimenting with this approach, but for various reasons it has not proven to be successful.

To date, no formal standards or regulations concerning family resource services have been proposed by any provincial government, and in Ontario, where there are now a significant number of family resource programs in operation, there is a lively debate among service providers about whether the traditional child care regulatory approaches are appropriate.

APPROACHES TO SUPPORT

Some of the earliest family day care services in Canada were agency initiated and developed along lines similar to the Children's Aid Society model of foster home care, which was based conceptually on a casework approach to service delivery. This traditional casework model[3] assumed that a high standard of home care for children could be achieved through a thorough initial assessment of providers and families, careful placement of children, and ongoing individual contacts with providers and parents supplemented by various support and training opportunities. In this approach supervisory (monitoring), support, and education functions were closely interwoven, usually with some mandatory provider training. In practice, and as they became more professionalized and concerned with improving the quality of care provided, a number of these agencies voluntarily introduced additional opportunities for support and education in response to the particular needs of their providers and their families.

In provinces where governments opted to license providers directly and monitor their homes (usually on an occasional basis), recognition of the importance of giving support and training to family day care providers has also varied. Initially, when support was available, it was often offered separately from the licensing system and on a voluntary basis (Manitoba has been an exception to this). In some communities, where support was not legislated, community play groups, drop-ins, and parent/child and community resource centers have often broadened their mandates to include home-based caregivers, so there are now a number of links between unlicensed family day care and family resource centers.

With time and experience, the importance of providing support for family day care has been increasingly recognized. For example, British Columbia recently expanded the Day Care Support Program from the four original projects to 30 services that operate like an agency model. Their four basic functions are "to recruit, train, support family and home-based caregivers, and provide information and referral services to parents" (Task Force on Child Care, 1991, p. 30).

The range of support and educational components that are and can be offered by family day care agencies and family resource services is considerable and, as outlined above, they are variously addressed to meet the needs of providers, parents, and children. As both groups evolve it is becoming apparent that they share many commonalities.

In Ontario, private home day care agencies and resource centers, for example, can both be involved in provider screening, training, and support; in providing toys and equipment to caregivers; and in providing information and referral and a variety of other support services to parents. The major differences between them have to do with the fact that private home day care agencies direct their support to a more limited group of approved providers and to the children and families they serve. Based on the regulations and through the contracting process, private home day care agencies also have the authority to enforce provider participation in training and other activities and have the mandate to close down homes that prove to be unsatisfactory.

Resource centers, on the whole, have tended to view a specific community as their target group so that parents as well as providers can be equally involved in their programs. Participation in various resource center programs is entirely voluntary, and where child care registries are in operation they are largely dependent on the veracity of provider self-reports. Dealing with unsatisfactory homes is much more difficult for resource centers, and the question of how to handle this problem has been the subject of much discussion among those who operate registries. Also associated with the voluntary nature of resource services is a service philosophy based on the principles of community development, social support, self-determination, and self-help; in contrast, private home day care agencies tend to operate from a more traditional social service philosophy, which puts agency staff in the role of experts and providers, and families and children served into the role of clients.

In some areas, a more complex service seems to be emerging that can best be described as a multiservice child care/family support agency. In some instances, this service has evolved from a traditional, well-established family day care agency; in others, from a developing family resource center. In the case of family day care agencies, which often began by offering traditional group and family day care services, the family day care component is combined (or collaborates) with a variety of other child care and family services. This development can be illustrated by giving some examples of Ontario agencies that fall into this category.[4] Family Day Care Services in Toronto was the first Ontario agency to offer private home day care, beginning in 1966. It presently offers a number of child care services in metropolitan Toronto and in the nearby York and Peel regions, including:

- Subsidized private home day care with support and training programs for providers.
- Care for developmentally and physically handicapped children.
- Day care finders programs for families ineligible for government subsidies.
- School-aged group programs—before-school, lunch, and after-school programs tailored to the needs of children aged 6–12.
- School-based group centers serving children aged 2½–12.
- Temporary child care programs that provide short-term child care for family emergencies and for sick children in their own homes.
- The Working Parents Day Care Assurance Plan, which provides 14 corporations with work-site consultation, information, and referral about parents' child care arrangements. Work is in progress to extend this service to include information and referral services regarding elder care—The Elder Life Plan.
- Consulting services to employers interested in developing workplace day care centers; the agency also conducts a number of professional workshops and seminars related to various aspects of child care (Family Day Care Services, 1989).

Similar to Family Day Care Services, Andrew Fleck Child Centre in Ottawa operates a number of traditional group, private home day care, and school-aged programs. It also offers information and referral services to parents and caregivers; provides consultation services to employers about workplace child care; and sponsors seminars for local agencies on board training, development, and other management issues. With two other Ottawa groups it cosponsors a short-term service providing child care during family emergencies and for sick children in their own homes. The agency is also active on a community and interagency committee planning a primary prevention and early intervention project to meet the needs of high-risk families and young children (Andrew Fleck Child Centre, 1989).

In addition to providing a similar variety of private home, group care, and consultation services, the MacCaulay Child Development Centre in Toronto offers consultation to assist staff from other child care programs in integrating children with a variety of special needs into regular child care settings. The MacCaulay Centre has also developed a pilot project bringing together agency-approved and unsupervised providers from the local area for a variety of workshop and discussion groups.

The Westcoast Child Care Resource Centre in Vancouver, British Columbia, provides an example of the evolution of a child care resource and referral center into a broader umbrella organization offering a variety of services to its member organizations and the Vancouver community. In operation since 1989, its services include:

- Early Childhood Multicultural Services: consultation to child care programs; professional development and resource library services.
- Information Day Care: resource and referral services.
- Vancouver Child Care Support Services: financial management and administrative support services to child care programs.
- Vancouver Family Day Care Support Program: a caregiver registry, caregiver assessment, training and support programs, information and support to parents.
- Westcoast Resource Library: a wide range of materials—books, reports, videotapes—related to child care.

Its member organizations include the B.C. Daycare Action Coalition, the Children's Services Employees' Union, the Association of Early Childhood Educators of B.C., the School Age Child Care Association, and the Western Canada Family Daycare Association, B.C. (Westcoast Child Care Resource Centre, 1991).

All of these multiservice child care/family support organizations are nonprofit corporations controlled by community boards; their funding comes from a variety of sources including government grants and fee subsidies, supplementary funding from the United Ways, special project grants from foundations, and other community sources. In addition to the formal services these organizations offer, both staff and board members are active in a variety of planning and advocacy efforts to further the development of child care services at local and provincial levels.

Another important source of support and education has come about through the formation of provider associations in some areas. At this stage in their development, many are springing up at the local level, so that not much is known about how many there are and where they are located. In Ontario, the Ottawa/Carleton Child Care Providers Association, focusing on informal caregivers, was started in 1981. Provider associations have also been formed in the Toronto and Kitchener-Waterloo areas. Deller (1988) also reports a Family Day Care Providers Association in Saskatchewan and a provider support group operating in conjunction with the Prince Edward Island Association for Early Childhood Education (p. 118).

Perhaps one of the best known Canadian provider associations is the Family Day Care Association of Manitoba. Incorporated in 1983, it currently represents over 375 providers across the province. Its objectives include:

> the promotion of high quality family day care through the development of support, information, services and training for providers and parents; advocacy on behalf of family day care; efforts to eliminate the isolation of providers through mutual support and provider networking groups, and a desire to work towards the greater public recognition of family day care as a valued child care alternative throughout Manitoba and Canada. (Family Day Care Association of Manitoba, n.d.)

The association, governed by an elected board of family day care providers, offers a variety of resources and services, including a bimonthly newsletter, a record-keeping system and calendar for providers, a variety of workshops and training programs, provincewide conferences, advocacy, and support for monthly networking groups that meet in various locations throughout the province. The association also offers its members comprehensive liability insurance; a group life, disability, medical, and dental insurance plan; and opportunities to participate in group purchasing of certain supplies and equipment.

In addition to provider associations, both Ontario and Québec have provincial associations that primarily represent agencies and staff working in family day care, although they include a few parent and provider members. British Columbia's Western Canada Family Daycare Association also seems to combine provider, agency, and association memberships (Westcoast Child Care Resource Centre, 1991). Recently the Canadian Child Day Care Federation published a *National Statement on Quality Child Care* (1991), which includes a major statement on family-based child care or family day care. With the support of the federation, efforts are also being made to form a National Family Day Care Network to begin to link members of the family day care community across the country.

OUTSTANDING ISSUES

Although family day care and support programs have evolved considerably from their origins in the 1960s, there are a number of outstanding issues that must be addressed if these programs are to continue to operate successfully in the future. Among the most critical of these issues is the question of how the provider role is to be defined; closely related to this issue is the problem of how to attract and retain a sufficient number of providers to allow home-based care to continue to be a viable service option.

In Canada the labor force participation rate of women with young children has increased dramatically in recent years; for example, for married women with children under age six, it increased from 27.1 percent in 1971 to 59.5 percent in 1986 (Ram, 1990). Further, it has been estimated that women's participation rates will continue to increase so that by the year 2000, their rates of participation will approach that of men (Jones, Marsden & Tepperman, 1990). To the extent that this trend continues, it is unclear who will be at home to provide care for young children, and some researchers have suggested that it will tend to be those who are less fit or capable of providing good care for children (Johnson & Dineen, 1981, pp. 57ff.).

The high rates of provider turnover in some areas also contribute to this problem. In Ontario, a recent study found that the average annual rate of provider turnover in supervised private home day care was approximately 45 percent (Norpark Computer Design, 1989, p. 32). Low fees; the absence of benefits such as pensions, vacation, and sick leaves; burnout; and the lack of recognition of family day care as "real work" all contribute toward the loss of providers, a number of whom view their caregiving experience as a transitional stage in their return to work outside the home.

The low status of providers is in part related to their unresolved role definition: Are they homemakers or home care professionals? independent caregivers or agency employees? There are a number of contradictions apparent in our current expectations and treatment of providers. With agency involvement in family day care has come a thrust for providers to become more professional and thereby gain recognition for their work. At the same time, the more traditional view of family day care—as an informal, "homey" service that values providers for their homemaking and caring characteristics as opposed to seeing them as offering a miniature day care center program—continues to be perpetuated. Although most agency-supervised providers must conform to a number of government and agency requirements and participate in training efforts geared toward improving their caregiving skills, they continue to be paid poorly and as though they were independent "business" people.

The contradictions inherent in the provider role were clearly highlighted in the Ontario Labour Board hearings related to the efforts of two groups of agency-supervised providers to become unionized and acquire employee status. Although one group of providers did succeed in forming a union, they were not able to obtain official recognition as employees under the relevant legislation and thus were ineligible for the statutory rights and benefits such as minimum wage and vacation pay.

However the provider's role is defined, it seems essential to find more ways to recognize the importance and social value of good caregiving if family day care is to continue as a service option involving competent and caring providers. It is also necessary to make it more worthwhile for women to stay at home to offer care, to stop exploiting them financially, and to provide sufficient income so that family day care can begin to compete with "real jobs" outside the home.

Finally, the question of how best to ensure the provision of quality in family day care remains. As noted earlier, there is considerable variation in approaches to regulation; this diversity reflects, in part, the lack of agreement about who should be regulated, which standards should be adopted, and how they should be enforced. To date, no province appears to have found a totally satisfactory answer to these questions. For example, British Columbia and Québec have both recently revised the provider-child ratios with a view to allowing greater flexibility in the numbers and ages of children in day care homes. They found that the previous ratios limited the number of children cared for and thereby undermined the economic viability of the homes (Task Force on Child Care, 1991, p. 16; Government of Québec, 1988, p. 33). To what extent such changes may ultimately affect the quality of care provided, however, has not been thoroughly investigated.

Although there appears to be a trend across the country toward the development of a variety of family and child care support services, some of which are provided by family day care agencies, there is still considerable confusion about their role. The complementary linkages between child care, other social services, and resource centers need to be recognized and much better articulated. At present, most social and human services are organized on a categorical basis, but family resource services generally cut across a number of traditional categories. As a result, they do not easily fit into existing program and funding policies; as preventive services, they are often viewed as less important and therefore more expendable in times of budget restraint. Their funding is often extremely precarious, resulting in extraordinary efforts (that could be better directed to providing service) having to be made just to raise basic operating costs. The growing understanding of the value of family support programs now needs to be translated into specific program and funding policies that support their operation and future development.

Alongside these efforts is a continuing need for research about program and policy development in relation to family day care and family resource programs. The natural diversity of Canadian approaches offers many interesting possibilities for comparative analyses that could contribute to a greater understanding and evolution of these important child care and family services. There is much to be learned from one another.

NOTES

1. In Canada, responsibility for development of child care services rests with provincial governments; however, cost sharing for fee subsidies is divided between the federal and provincial governments—and in some provinces, with local municipalities.

2. At the time of writing, the Québec government had introduced proposals and set up a consultation process to develop standards for family day care providers that would be administered by the agencies. Personal communication from Jocelyne Tougas, Régroupement des Agences de Services de Garde en Milieu Familial du Québec.

3. The adoption of this approach was not surprising. Many of the agency directors who began these early family day care programs had been trained in social work, not early childhood education.

4. The focus on Ontario examples is not meant to imply that these agencies do not exist in other parts of the country; rather, it has not been possible to obtain information about them.

REFERENCES

Alberta Family and Social Services. (1989, November). *Family day home program manual*. Edmonton, Alberta: Author.

Andrew Fleck Child Centre. (1989). *Annual report: 1989*. Ottawa: Author.

Canadian Child Day Care Federation. (1991, August). *National statement on quality child care*. Ottawa: Author.

Child Care Resource and Research Unit. (1990). *Child care information sheets*. Toronto: Centre for Urban and Community Studies, University of Toronto.

Corsini, D. A., Wisensale, S., & Caruso, G. (1988). Family day care: System issues and regulatory models. *Young Children, 43*(6), 17–23.

Deller (Pollard), J. (1988, July). *Family day care internationally: A literature review*. Toronto: Ministry of Community and Social Services.

Enarson, E. (1990). Experts and caregivers: Perspectives on underground day care. In E. K. Abel & M. K. Nelson (Eds.), *Circles of care: Work and identity in women's lives* (pp. 233–45). Albany, NY: State University of New York Press.

Family Day Care Association of Manitoba. (n.d.). *Background information about the association*. Winnipeg, Manitoba: Author.

Family Day Care Services. (1989). *Annual report: 1989*. Toronto: Author.

Goelman, H., Pence, A., Lero, D. S., & Brockman, L. (In preparation). *Where are the children? An analysis of child care arrangements used while parents work or study*. Ottawa: Minister of Supply and Services.

Government of Québec. (1988). *A better balance: Orientation paper*. A policy statement on day care services (Ministre déléguée à la condition féminine). Quebec: Bibliothècque nationale du Québec.

Health and Welfare, Canada. (1987). *Status of day care in Canada–1986.* Ottawa: National Child Care Information Centre, Social Services Programs Branch.

Health and Welfare, Canada. (1988). *Status of day care in Canada–1987.* Ottawa: National Child Care Information Centre, Social Service Programs Branch.

Health and Welfare, Canada. (1989). *Status of day care in Canada–1988.* Ottawa: National Child Care Information Centre, Social Service Programs Branch.

Health and Welfare, Canada. (1990). *Status of day care in Canada–1989.* Ottawa: National Child Care Information Centre, Social Service Programs Branch.

Health and Welfare, Canada. (1991). *Status of day care in Canada–1990.* Ottawa: National Child Care Information Centre, Social Service Programs Branch.

Johnson, L., & Dineen, J. (1981). *The kin trade: The day care crisis in Canada.* Toronto: McGraw-Hill Ryerson.

Jones, C., Marsden, L., & Tepperman, L. (1990). *Lives of their own: The individualization of women's lives.* Toronto: Oxford University Press.

Kyle, I. (1991). The role of family resource services as a child care support. In Statistics Canada, Family and Community Supports Division (Eds.), *Caring communities: Proceedings of the symposium on social supports.* Ottawa: Supply and Services, Cat. No. 89-514E.

Kyle, I. (In press). *Canadian child care in context: Ontario report of the National Child Care Study,* ch. 2. Ottawa: Minister of Supply and Services.

Norpark Computer Design. (1989). *A survey of private home day care in Ontario, 1988.* Toronto: Queen's Printer.

Nova Scotia Department of Community Services. (1990, March). *Guidelines for operating a family day care program in Nova Scotia.* Halifax: Day Care Services, Department of Community Services.

Pence, A., & Griffin, S. (1990). A window of opportunity. In *Interaction* (pp. 12–17). Ottawa: Canadian Day Care Federation.

Ram, B. (1990). *Current demographic analysis: New trends in the family.* Ottawa: Supply and Services, Cat. No. 91-535E.

Read, M., & LaGrange, A. (1990, August). *Those who care: A report on approved family day care home providers in Alberta.* Red Deer, Alta: Child Care Matters, P.O. Box 2, RR4, Site 2, Red Deer, Alta, T4N 5E2.

Task Force on Child Care. (1991). *Showing we care: A child care strategy for the '90s.* Victoria, BC: Minister of Government Management Services and Minister Responsible for Women's Programs.

TLRC Canada. (1991, January). *Regional development project.* Ottawa: Author.

Westcoast Child Care Resource Centre. (1991). *Annual report.* Vancouver: Author.

CHAPTER 13

Models of Family Day Care and Support Services in the United States

Joe Perreault

It is difficult to determine exactly how many women (or men) offer family day care in the United States. Kahn and Kamerman estimate that there are one and a half to two million providers (Kahn & Kamerman, 1987, pp. 8–10). Their figure includes all forms of relative care. On the other hand, there are only about 200,000 regulated family day care homes (Children's Foundation, 1989, p. 6). Despite the variation in estimates, family day care is believed to be the most widely used form of child care in the United States (O'Connell, 1989). Given this reality, it would seem logical that society as a whole and the early childhood profession in particular would want to help family day care providers. Instead it has been a long slow process of gaining public recognition and support for family day care. Fortunately many obstacles have been overcome. As this chapter will show, there are now support projects for family day care providers in every major city as well as in most smaller communities and rural areas. These projects do not serve all providers, particularly the unregulated providers. But the number of projects and the range of providers served place the United States ahead of most countries in the effort to ensure high-quality care through strengthening the family day care profession.

The rationale for supporting family day care in the United States seems similar to the rationale developed in Canada. Initially support arose as a result of attempts to regulate providers. At a later date, attempts to help working parents by improving specific aspects of the supply or quality of care led many groups to discover and value family day care.

APPROACHES TO REGULATION

Many states began regulating family day care as early as the late 1940s or early 1950s. At the time, however, family day care was viewed as a protective service. That is, a caseworker might use a specially trained and supervised family day care provider rather than remove a child from the parents' custody and place the child in foster care. By the mid-1960s, however, regulatory authorities began to realize that they had a tiger by the tail.

They had established legislative authority to license family day care homes for a narrow social-service purpose, but the legislation often called for the licensing of all providers. Some licensing agencies were happy to have such broad authority, since they viewed family day care as an appropriate form of child care and one that needed to be regulated. Other licensing agencies recognized that the number of providers who ought to be licensed was enormous and that legislatures were unwilling to authorize enough workers to meet this responsibility adequately. The basic dilemma of whether and how to regulate family day care continues today.

Currently all states regulate family day care to some degree. According to the Children's Foundation, 21 states regulate by means of a licensing approach, and 16 states use a registration approach. Other states use a combination of these approaches or at least certify certain kinds of providers, such as those receiving public funds or providers participating in the Child Care Food Program (Children's Foundation, 1990, p. 15–24).

There is considerable agreement in the legislation and accompanying regulations about aspects of family day care that are regulated, such as the use of space, approaches to discipline, and accident-prevention practices. However, there are great differences in the definitions of who must be regulated based on exemptions given to providers who serve fewer than a designated number of children. Four states exempt providers who care for one or two children, three states exempt providers with up to three children, three with up to four children, and four with up to five children. Similarly the maximum number of children a provider can care for varies dramatically. Eight states have a five-child limit, 28 states have a six-child limit, and ten states exceed these limitations (Children's Foundation, 1989, pp. 20–37). The result of these widely varying definitions is that many caregivers are legally unregulated and others care for many more children than is traditionally thought of as a family day care home.

Despite inconsistencies in the definition of family day care and weaknesses in the enforcement process, the regulation of family day care has influenced the amount and nature of the supports available to providers in the United States. Inherent in regulatory philosophy is the belief that people who are regulated are entitled to consultation on how to meet the required standards. Thus in many communities, licensing agencies were the first organizations to offer any kind of support to family day care. Usually the support was in the form of a training session on how to meet the regulations or on how to start a family day care home.

In addition to protecting children, advocates of regulation have always felt that regulation would serve family day care by making it "visible." Any step to call attention to the existence of family day care and identify who is involved in this form of work would lead to favorable community interest in family day care.

By and large, the theory has proven correct. A number of the earliest training projects were developed by organizations working in close cooperation with the licensing agency. These projects focused on the process of starting a family day care home but also developed content and approaches for continuing education and training as well as the first efforts to encourage support groups and associations of providers. Vocational schools, community colleges, colleges and universities, the U.S. Department of Agriculture Cooperative Extension, and some early childhood associations were all pioneers in developing such programs (Travis & Perreault, 1983, pp. 2–3).

APPROACHES TO SUPPORT AND EDUCATION

There are a number of supply and quality issues that influenced community and professional groups to become involved with family day care. One of the most helpful efforts has come from the concern that children who are in child care be well fed. This resulted in the Child Care Food Program, which has been an enormous benefit to providers and to children in their care. Attempts to help parents find child care, attempts by employers to improve the supply of care available to their employees, and attempts by civic and voluntary groups to improve the quality of care and working conditions of providers have all contributed to a steady level of forward progress.

The Child Care Food Program

The Child Care Food Program (CCFP) was established by Congress and is administered by the United States Department of Agriculture (USDA). The primary purpose of the CCFP is to ensure that children being cared for in family day care homes (and in nonprofit day care centers) receive nutritionally balanced meals. The CCFP does this by reimbursing the provider a fixed amount of money for the meals served to children.

From the family day care provider's point of view, the CCFP offers immediate assistance. Providers who are not participating in the program usually use parent fees to cover the costs of serving food to the children. Because the CCFP pays for the food, the provider can keep more of the parent fee and her standard of living is improved.

Providers discover that the program offers additional benefits they did not anticipate. The reimbursement helps them increase the amount of food they serve children, and they receive nutrition training, which ensures that the foods served are nutritionally sound. The nutrition training program also brings the provider in contact with other providers. As soon as a group of family day care providers meet face to face, they begin exchanging ideas, and an informal process of self-help emerges.

The CCFP acts as an incentive for a women to comply with child care licensing regulations. Because the CCFP requires providers to meet state licensing regulations or registration requirements, it is a powerful economic incentive for providers to go through the licensing process.

The community group that administers the CCFP must be a nonprofit organization and is called a "sponsor." Currently there are about 1,100 sponsoring organizations—some serving only ten to twenty providers, but others serving a thousand or more. Altogether there are about 130,000 family day care providers who participate in the CCFP in the United States (Glantz, 1988).

As CCFP sponsors got to know providers better, they began to realize that providers had many needs in addition to the need to provide nutritious meals. In many communities, CCFP has become the jumping-off place for broader efforts to support providers.

Family Day Care Agencies

A family day care agency (sometimes called a family day care system) is an organization that assumes responsibility for administering and operating several family day care homes. Generally the agency is responsible for establishing policy, recruiting and screening homes, providing orientation and ongoing training, and supervising homes through regular home visits. In most cases, the agency is responsible for the recruitment of children, payment of caregivers, and provision of social services to parents. In addition to training and home visits, most agencies place supplies and equipment in the home, offer help securing or paying for liability insurance, help providers secure substitutes, and in some cases offer fringe benefits such as health insurance. Providers may be attracted to affiliation with an agency for a variety of reasons. They may like the ease of attracting clients and the assurance of being paid. They may like the support and assistance offered by the agency.

The first family day care agency in the United States began in 1927, and one or two others date from the 1930s. The majority of agencies began in the mid-1960s and early 1970s (Travis & Perreault, 1983, p. 4). Most agencies were started in order to provide child care for low-income parents. It was an era of expanding social-services money. There was growing interest in the use of family day care in child protective cases, and there was a desire to help welfare recipients get off welfare by providing support services such as child care.

An essential characteristic of a family day care agency is that it is a supervised form of family day care. It satisfies the need of some professionals to be sure that children are protected when placed in a family day care home. Yet the supervision aspect may have undermined the long-term prospects for family day care agencies. At its height, there were 200 family day care agencies in the United States. Currently there are probably fewer than 100. A decrease in social-services money is the principal explanation for the decline in numbers. However, it should be noted that many state agencies responsible for administering social-services funds concluded that a family day care agency was an unnecessary element of the system. They chose to contract directly with providers, assuming that the only thing that should be required of providers was that they meet licensing standards or a slightly higher set of certification standards.

Family Day Care in the Military

Although interest in family day care agencies has declined somewhat, some of the basic concepts have been adopted by the U.S. military in what has become a large and unique movement. All branches of the military provide child care as a support to military personnel who are parents. In 1983, the U.S. Army began considering the potential of family day care. It was a time when the army was rapidly expanding the number of centers it operated but also realizing how expensive it would be to build centers for all eligible children. Simultaneously the army saw the need to provide family day care for those parents who preferred that form of care.

The plan that was developed closely approximates the role agencies play with other providers. The army has established strict regulations for offering family day care on a military installation. The provider receives regular training, is visited often, and receives help with securing supplies and equipment.

The use of family day care in the military grew rapidly. As of 1988, the army had 8,000 family day care homes in its program, the air force had 3,100 homes, the navy had 1,300 homes, and programs were being established by the marines and Coast Guard too.

Child Care Resource and Referral

The development of child care resource and referral (CCR&R) programs has also produced wide-scale support for family day care. The purpose of a CCR&R program is to help parents find child care and to provide advice and information about selecting a child care arrangement. CCR&R programs emphasize the importance of parental choice in selecting care and, to that end, try to maintain a complete listing of all available care, including family day care. The CCR&R movement has grown rapidly since its inception in the mid-1970s. Currently there are over 300 CCR&R agencies in the United States, serving every major city. Efforts to develop multicounty and statewide networks of CCR&R agencies may soon mean that every parent in the country has access to a CCR&R program.

When CCR&R programs were started, the founders had some sense that they would need to work with family day care. At the very least they would need to enroll providers in the system. However, they quickly discovered that a high percentage of parents requested family day care. In some cases, 70 percent of the parents who called requested family day care or requested information about centers and family day care (Foote, 1990, p. 3).

CCR&Rs were important in documenting the fact that so many parents prefer family day care. At the same time, CCR&R agencies began to realize that their fate and the fate of the family day care profession were inevitably connected. The CCR&R must have as much information as possible about the family day care available in each neighborhood. It must also work to increase the supply of family day care in neighborhoods where few family day care homes exist. Through these actions, the CCR&R can be responsive to the high percentage of parents who call seeking family day care.

The Influence of Employers. CCR&Rs were further influenced to help family day care when they started developing an "enhanced" form of referral for employers that contracted for the service. These contracts are customized to meet the needs of a special work force and include additional consumer education experiences for employees as well as efforts to increase the supply of care in neighborhoods where the employees live or work.

Similar to referral to the general public, employer referral contracts demonstrated a marked preference for family day care. A number of employers were quite intrigued by this phenomenon. As they learned more about family day care, they discovered that high turnover was prevalent and that little training or other help was available to providers. As a result, employers began urging CCR&Rs to recruit more providers and to find ways to retain existing providers.

The first employer to provide CCR&R services to its employees nationwide was International Business Machines Inc. (IBM). Work/Family Directions, a work- and family-life consulting organization, administers the CCR&R service for IBM and in turn uses local CCR&R agencies in a number of communities to carry out the work.

The IBM program began in 1984, and Work/Family Directions has subsequently initiated contracts with many other national companies. Work/Family Directions maintains a data base on all the efforts that local CCR&Rs have made to help new child care centers and family day care homes get started. Since 1984, Work/Family Directions has identified over 30,000 family day care homes that have been started through the contributions of employer funds as well as local government and charitable funds.

Another large effort involving employer leadership is the California Child Care Initiative. The initiative was created in 1985 to address the shortage of child care, particularly family day care, in California. The initiative was developed by the BankAmerica Foundation and is funded by a partnership of 10 public and 23 private funders. The initiative is managed by the California Child Care Resource and Referral Network, which in turn works with 16 local CCR&R agencies to recruit, train, and provide ongoing support and technical assistance to new family day care providers. As of 1989, the California Child Care Initiative had recruited over 2,000 new licensed family day care providers, making 8,100 spaces available for children. Over 8,800 potential, new, and existing providers received training in child development and business management (Belam, Darrah & Lawrence, 1989). Because the initiative has been so successful, the Ford Foundation has provided funds to replicate the project in other states.

Civic and Voluntary Efforts

Civic and voluntary groups have also been important to the development of family day care. Their efforts are aimed at what Nancy Cohen and Barbara Taylor have termed "infrastructure development" (Cohen & Taylor, in press). Such efforts are designed to created systemic changes in attitudes, establish new organizational leadership for family day care, remove barriers, and increase incentives for providers to participate in services.

Several long-standing efforts fit this description. The Children's Foundation has supported family day care, and particularly the development of the National Association for Family Day Care, for many years. Save the Children sponsors an annual Family Day Care Technical Assistance Conference. The conference, in its fifteenth year, facilitates a national exchange of information about family day care, commissions position papers on national issues, and has been the launching pad for a number of joint projects by advocates of family day care.

In recent years, there have been some impressive additions toward creating strong societal backup for family day care. Mervyn's Department Stores, Target Stores, and the Dayton Hudson Foundation have teamed up to sponsor the Family to Family Project. This project operates in 30 communities. It offers training to over 8,000 family day care providers and assists providers who want to meet accreditation standards. Most recently, the Family to Family Project joined with the National Association on Child Care Resource and Referral and the Child Care Action Campaign to launch a consumer education campaign to help parents choose high quality in family day care.

Another important initiative is the National Family Day Care Project of the National Council of Jewish Women (NCJW). In 31 communities in 20 states, local NCJW sections have assessed family day care needs and developed appropriate community service and advocacy projects to respond to these needs. Each of the projects has been implemented by a section in partnership with key local and private-sector leaders and organizations. Partners have included CCR&R agencies, family day care associations, government licensing agencies, mayors' offices, statewide Associations for the Education of Young Children, and local affiliates of the Association of Junior Leagues, the League of Women Voters, the National Black Child Development Institute, Alpha Kappa Alpha Sororities, and Kiwanis International. The projects developed by participating sections reflect four strategies for improving the quality and supply of family day care: recruiting and orienting providers, creating resources for providers, zoning advocacy, and organizing community education campaigns. The project has been successful at the local level and has also issued a number of important publications. The culmination of the project will be an effort to encourage other national volunteer groups to become similarly involved in family day care.

THE PROFESSION AND ASSOCIATION MOVEMENT

In the United States, there has always been a strong desire for professionalization in the family day care movement that has been led by providers themselves. The first provider association was established in the state of Washington in 1966. By 1973, associations were operating in California, New York, Minnesota, and Tennessee. These initial groups as well as most subsequent associations received encouragement and help from licensing workers, trainers, and other nonproviders, but their real strength came from the fact that providers saw the need to meet and work together as a group.

In the beginning, providers met one another by participating in workshops. Group experiences help providers overcome their sense of isolation, the feeling that no one else does this kind of work or understands what it involves. Eventually the training and group meetings lead to an improved self-image and a sense of empowerment that family day care work is worth-while.

Once providers are in touch with one another, a professionalization movement is likely to occur. The evolution of the movement takes on a different pace and form in different communities. However, some of the common characteristics are:

- A desire to socialize with people who have common problems and interests.
- The discovery that providers have some common values related to the work.
- The discovery that providers have some common problems that cannot be solved without the benefit of a collective effort.
- A feeling that family day care work is not fully understood or appreciated by people who do not do this work. In its extreme sense, it is a realization that providers have common enemies—parents, licensing workers, CCR&R staff, the general public, other providers who offer poor-quality programs.
- A desire to improve the quality of the profession by setting standards for those who do this type of work, defining the kind of preservice and inservice training required, or otherwise controlling quality by some method of accreditation or certification.
- A desire to see that members of the profession are adequately compensated for their expertise and hard work.
- A need to ensure the good standing of the profession in relation to other professions or to societal trends that might affect the status and economic well-being of members.

Today there are about 500 local and state family day care associations in the United States. Undoubtedly leaders of the association movement would like to see more associations and a better linkage among local, state, and national levels, but even the current stage of development is impressive. The National Association for Family Day Care (NAFDC) was established in 1982. In 1988, NAFDC established a program for accreditation of family day care homes. So far, 294 providers from 33 states and the District of Columbia have completed the accreditation process.

Family day care providers have also learned to speak out articulately about their own special views of the profession. In 1990, a group of four family day care providers saw the need to write a position paper about the relationship between family day care providers, CCR&R agencies, and other agencies that relate to providers. The paper is entitled *The Provider Connec-*

tion; it was subsequently endorsed by NAFDC and has been widely circulated among providers and agencies working with providers. Although the paper covers many themes, this excerpt illustrates the kind of issues that are being raised by providers themselves:

> Herein lies the problem . . . existing programs and services appear to espouse "doing for" providers, rather than "working with" providers.
>
> In the development of many programs and services, assumptions are often made about who providers are or should be, leading to sometimes arbitrary decisions based on inaccurate or incomplete input.
>
> The result is a tendency toward pigeonholing providers with singularities—one answer, one way, one path. This manner of thinking denies the inherent diversity of children and families which is the cornerstone of family child care homes and of the unique services each provider offers. To be successful, programs developed in the interest of family child care must not only maintain this diversity, but validate it and celebrate it as a very effective method of child care delivery.
>
> The cycle of "doing for" providers must be broken. The resources already existing within the ranks of experienced current or former providers are generally being overlooked. Only when child care agencies begin to "work with" providers can they expect to increase provider involvement, thus creating *appropriate* resources and support for the profession.
>
> In an unspoken, and sometimes unwitting way, R&R's and project funders have assumed, or are *perceived* to have assumed, ownership of family day care. It is true that in many instances this ownership has been seemingly thrust upon them. The unfortunate result is that many projects involving family child care have been conceived, designed, developed, implemented and evaluated without THE PROVIDER CONNECTION. That is not to say that provider input was not obtained. However, too often that input was lost or discarded somewhere between development and implementation, or was gleaned from only one or two carefully chosen providers. (Windflower Enterprises Inc., 1990, pp. 7–8)

CURRENT ISSUES

Although the momentum has clearly shifted to the side of the advocates, there continue to be advocates for and skeptics of family day care in the United States. The skeptics of family day care usually make comments like, "if we only get enough good centers, family day care will go away" or "the problem with family day care is that you never really know what they do when no one else is present." The skeptics worry that there is potential for child abuse in family day care homes because there is no way to monitor the actions of providers in their own homes. Advocates of family day care have focused on the many characteristics of family day care that make it adaptable to a variety of parent and child needs.

Until recently, the mainstream early childhood profession did not look favorably on family day care. Today that picture has changed dramatically. Symbolic proof of that change occurred in 1990, when for the first time a family day care provider was elected to the board of the National Association for the Education of Young Children (NAEYC). NAEYC, with 77,000 members, is the largest and most widely representative early childhood education group in the United States.

Today it is almost conventional wisdom to say that family day care is a part of the early childhood profession. Providers are actively recruited to join local early childhood associations, and most of the people who are considered leaders in the early childhood field have some degree of involvement with family day care.

Family day care has reached the point of achieving interest and respect from community leaders and the early childhood profession. The future looks bright, but family day care still faces challenges. These challenges are likely to be more subtle and complex than in the past.

Improving the Image of Family Day Care

Family day care has achieved recognition within the profession and among certain parents, but it is often overlooked or treated negatively by the media and the public. Family day care advocates have begun to address this issue. Attempts have been made to define root causes of the problem (Adams, 1990). NCJW has gone so far as to provide a marketing consultant to NAFDC. NCJW has also issued a helpful publication showing providers how to work at the local level to improve the image of family day care (National Council of Jewish Women, 1991).

Preparing for the Impact of Research

Although there have been many small studies of family day care and one large study (the National Day Care Home Study), the family day care profession has not been researched extensively, nor has a study ever stirred up controversy about the profession. These circumstances may change in the near future. Two major studies of family day care were initiated in 1991.

A study on quality in family day care is being conducted by Ellen Galinsky of Families and Work Institute, Carollee Howes of UCLA, and Susan Kontos of Purdue University. An equally important study on the economics of family day care is being conducted by Kathy Modigliani of Wheelock College and Suzanna Helburn of the University of Colorado, Denver. The results of these studies, whether positive or negative, friendly or hostile, are likely to affect the family day care profession profoundly.

In addition, two new volumes on family day care were released in 1992: (1) This volume, with its unique U.S. and Canadian research and policy perspective, and (2) a major overview published by NAEYC (Kontos, 1992). Family day care providers are much more likely to read these studies and publications than they were in the past. Providers have association newsletters and other means of communications that they did not have previously. These studies will be announced ahead of time, preliminary results will be well publicized, and final conclusions will be scrutinized closely by providers as well as by a large audience of other interested people. For the most part, providers do not have firsthand experience with the public policy consequences of a research study. It is hoped that this first experience will be a satisfactory one. But one way or another, the research community is a force that family day care providers will have to contend with in the near future.

Defining What Is Unique about Family Day Care

The final frontier for family day care is to define quality and achieve it on a large scale. In a field where only 200,000 of the estimated 1.5 million providers have met licensing standards, there is much work to do. However, in the drive to achieve quality, there is a danger of extinguishing some of the behaviors and characteristics of providers that make this form of care somehow unique. Kathy Modigliani, for example, points out the uniqueness of family day care when discussing differences in provider styles. She writes:

> I would say that there are two basic styles of good family day care providers. One type is the provider who is like a good preschool teacher. She is warm, loving, and responsive to children. Her house, at least during the week, looks like a mini-preschool. There are shelves displaying an interesting array of toys and materials. The planned activities may include a circle time with songs and group discussions.
>
> The other type of good provider is like a good parent. She too is warm, loving, and responsive to the children. But that is where the resemblance ends. Her home may look like any large family's home: quite a few toys, perhaps not well displayed, a couple of high chairs, more than one riding toy. But the materials and equipment are not distinguishing. What is exceptional is "her way with children." All the children are playing together like one big happy family. The 3-year-old is playing peek-a-boo with the baby, and it's hard to tell which one is enjoying it more. Two children are busy peeling the carrots for lunch. The morning outing always includes checking in on an infirm neighbor, and usually

produces an addition to the science collection. The children are seldom bored. The provider finds opportunities in everyday routines to help meet each child's needs. For some children her style is ideal. (Modigliani, 1991, p. 18)

Modigliani goes on to point out that it is easier for assessment instruments to identify and evaluate the good preschool teacher style than the good parent style, and that a bias toward the latter style seems to be built into programs for training, research, and accreditation.

In general, advocates of family day care are concerned that all the attention to family day care may change the nature of the profession. There is a need for providers to articulate a vision of family day care, why and how it works, what makes it unique, and how their field can achieve unity while respecting the wonderful diversity that currently exists.

REFERENCES

Adams, D. (1990). *Understanding the image of family day care.* Atlanta: Save the Children/Child Care Support Center.

Belam, D., Darrah, R., & Lawrence, M. (1989). *A guide to California child care initiative.* San Francisco: California Child Care Resource and Referral Network.

Children's Foundation. (1989). *1989 family day care licensing study.* Washington, DC: Author.

Children's Foundation. (1990). *1990 family day care licensing study.* Washington, DC: Author.

Cohen, N., & Taylor, B. (in press). Increasing the quality of family day care: Combining infrastructure development, basic services, and intensive services. *Child and Youth Care Forum.*

Foote, R. A. (1990). *Finding childcare in metropolitan Atlanta 1990.* Atlanta: Save the Children/Child Care Support Center.

Glantz, F. (1988). *Study of the child care food program. Final report.* Cambridge, MA: Abt Associates.

Kahn, A. J., & Kamerman, S. B. (1987). *Child care: Facing the hard choices.* Dover, MA: Auburn House.

Kontos, S. (1992). *Family day care: Out of the shadows and into the limelight.* Washington, DC: National Association for the Education of Young Children.

Modigliani, K. (1991). *Assessing the quality of family child care: A comparison of five instruments.* New York: Bank Street College of Education.

National Council of Jewish Women. (1991). *Marketing kit for family day care providers.* New York: Author.

O'Connell, M. (1989). Child care cost estimated at $14 billion in 1986, Census Bureau survey shows (Press Release, CB 89-119). Washington, DC: U.S. Department of Commerce.

Travis, N., & Perreault, J. (1983). *A history of family day care*. Atlanta: Save the Children/Child Care Support Center.

Windflower Enterprises Inc. (1990). *The provider connection: A close look at the relationship between family day care providers, resource and referral and other day care agencies*. Colorado Springs, CO: Author.

CHAPTER 14

Assessing Quality in Family Day Care

Richard M. Clifford
Thelma Harms
Susan Pepper
Barbara Stuart

Assessing quality in family care depends on four important considerations: what is being assessed, who is performing the assessment, why it is being undertaken, and how the assessment is being conducted. Parents who seek care, caregivers who provide it, teachers who train caregivers, governmental workers who regulate care, and researchers who study care all use assessment in some form. Since they do so from their own unique points of view, they hold different pictures of what quality family day care looks like. More often than not, these perceptions of quality are informal, still in the minds of the person, and not written down. The result is that we try to communicate about quality from a large number of perspectives that are poorly understood and impossible to share.

Most parents seeking care use personal standards to assess quality. Therefore, the components of their definitions of quality may not be easily identifiable. Parents typically compare family day care with what is available in their own homes and, to a lesser degree, with other family day care homes they may have seen. Generally, parents may have little information about the wide range of indices of quality and may be at a loss as to what to look for.

As much of a problem as this situation is for individual families, it is of even more concern to the profession that we have no generally accepted standard against which to judge the quality of family day care. State regulatory standards vary widely from one state to another (Morgan, 1987). Although we discuss the existing array of instruments developed to measure quality, there is little consensus among professionals or evaluators about the basic standards and approaches that are most appropriate for assessment of family day care.

Since the middle of this century there have been several significant shifts in the definition and evaluation of the quality of child care (Stallings & Wilcox, 1978). Influenced by Bowlby's studies of institutionalized children (1951), high-quality child care was first defined in terms closely resembling the warm, nurturing care parents were thought to provide to their own children. High-quality child care was redefined in the 1960s and 1970s to focus on factors that brought about cognitive gains for children. This definition was broadened during the 1980s to focus on the whole child. Measurement of quality is currently based on a more liberal definition that includes factors seen as related to children's progress across the range of developmental outcomes. These changes in the definition of quality family day care reflect, to some degree, the changing values of the society at large and, more specifically, the reflection of those values through the eyes of professionals.

THEORETICAL FRAMEWORK

It is fundamental to the whole issue of concern about the quality of family day care homes that the behavior of children be seen as evolving from the interaction between the child and the environment, including the people in the environment, in which that child develops (Lewin, 1935; Bronfenbrenner, 1979). We consider the evaluation of such settings important because we see the quality of the care environments as critical for the optimal developmental progress of the next generation.

The theoretical framework that underlies this chapter relates any particular family day care home to the larger contextual influences. The importance of contextual influences on child care and other educational environments is recognized in the formulations of Bronfenbrenner (1977, 1979); Moos (1980); Whitebook, Howes, and Phillips (1989); and Doherty (1991a). In particular, the work of Bronfenbrenner, conceptualizing the environment as a nested set of spheres of influence on children, initiated a rethinking of the way in which early childhood professionals view learning settings for young children (Bronfenbrenner, 1979).

At the heart of Bronfenbrenner's model is the immediate setting containing the developing individual—the microsystem. For our purposes, the family day care home and the children in the home make up the microsystem. Factors outside that setting may also have a significant, direct impact on the individual. This set of factors is referred to as the mesosystem. A third level of influence on the development of the individual includes events occurring where the individual is not even present, but that have an indirect influence on what is happening to the individual and thus on that individual's development. This third level is referred to as the exosystem. Bronfenbrenner argues that there is also a fourth level of influence on the development of individuals. This fourth level includes influences of the culture and subculture within which the individual develops and is referred to as the macrosystem (Bronfenbrenner, 1979).

As we consider assessment of family day care homes, we are concerned primarily with the immediate influences on the children in the home itself and, to a lesser extent, on the direct and indirect influences on that setting from the outside. That is, we are concerned with the microsystem and somewhat with the mesosystem and exosystem. The impact of the larger culture is typically through the features of the exo- and mesosystems.

It is in the context of these systems and other influences that family day care is provided to young children. Although our assessment procedures ordinarily do not address these meso- and exosystem factors directly, it is imperative that the measurement of quality in family day care take these external factors into account when decisions are made about what should be assessed and how the assessment should be conducted. For example, family day care homes are often not subject to regulation by public health authorities. Thus, assessment instruments for family day care must be more specific about the health and safety concerns of children than instruments for day care centers, which are typically inspected by health inspectors as part of the licensing procedure.

The primary focus of measurement of family day care homes is on the children and caregivers in the setting. Figure 14.1 gives a more detailed view of key aspects at the individual home level. The most striking feature of the model is the set of overlapping responsibilities of the family-based caregiver for the child care group and for the caregiver's personal family. These two spheres of the caregiver's life are each further divided into two dimensions. Goelman and Pence (1987a, 1987b) have pointed to the importance of considering both structural and process dimensions of home-based care and center-based care for young children. As our model shows, both dimensions are important in determining the ultimate quality of the family child care experience for children in that setting. The structural or frame conditions in both the child care and personal family spheres include components related to the people, space or materials, and recurring patterns. The particulars of each of these components of the structure and process dimensions are specific to the child care and personal family domains.

In addition to the child care group and personal family responsibility spheres, there is a management function not directly involving the children, but that has a significant impact on them. The personnel, program, and

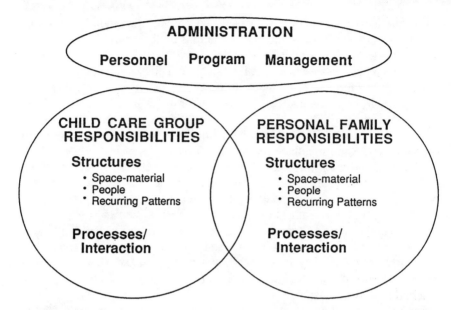

FIGURE 14.1.   Family day care home.

operations features of management are shown in Figure 14.1 only for the child care portion of the total operation of the home. It is important to recognize that family caregivers have management concerns paralleling those of other forms of nonparental care and education in our society. Family child care home management includes personnel concerns such as hiring and training of substitute providers, program concerns such as providing appropriate toys, books, and other resources for play, and operational concerns such as meeting regulatory requirements.

The family child care home is a complex microsystem constantly being influenced by the external environments in which it exists and, in turn, exerting influence on those environments. Assessment systems must be designed to deal with the complexity and fluidity of the setting. A particular difficulty from a measurement point of view is that these various aspects of the family child care setting are not independent of one another.

INSTRUMENTS FOR ASSESSING FAMILY
DAY CARE QUALITY

Description of Measurement Instruments

Our search revealed six instruments designed to provide global evaluations of family day care quality. Several other measures that have appeared in the family day care literature were not included in this review for one of three reasons. Some, like the Carew/SRI Observation System (Stallings & Wilcox, 1978) developed for the National Day Care Home Study (Fosburg, 1981), and the observation instrument used by Golden et al. (1979) in the New York City Infant Day Care Study, were behavioral coding schemes for recording caregiver and child behaviors rather than global assessments of the quality of the family day care environment. Other measures of day care quality, such as Howes's (1990) composite of adult to child ratio, caregiver training, and stability of caregivers, or Winget, Winget, and Popplewell's (1982) parental questionnaire, were designed for a particular study or research program and not, to our knowledge, intended to be used as global indicators of quality in applied settings. Still others, such as the HOME scale (Caldwell & Bradley, 1984) and the Infant/Toddler Environment Rating Scale (Harms, Cryer & Clifford, 1990), were not directed specifically toward assessing family day care. Brief descriptions of the six instruments selected for review follow.

1. *CDA Advisor's Report Form* (Council for Early Childhood Professional Recognition, 1991). This observation instrument is used in the Child Development Associate (CDA) credentialing process for either child care center staff or family child care providers. The CDA credential, administered through the Council for Early Childhood Professional Recognition, is recognized throughout the United States. To be awarded the CDA credential, a family day care provider must demonstrate competence in each of 13 functional areas, including safety, health, learning environment, physical development, cognitive development, communication, creativity, self-esteem and independence, social relationships, guidance (or discipline), family relations, program management, and professionalism. Evaluation of the provider is based on five sources of information: the CDA observation instrument or advisor's report form, a parent opinion questionnaire, a professional resource file, a formal interview, and a written examination (C. Phillips, personal communication, July 8, 1991). The provider's competence is evaluated by a local assessment team comprising an advisor who works with the provider, a parent, and a CDA representative. Their positive recommendation and extensive supporting materials documenting provider training and competence are reviewed by the national CDA office before the credential is awarded. It should be noted that the CDA program approves the caregiver, rather than the day care setting, for a credential, although these are generally equivalent in family day care.

Of the 13 functional areas covered by the CDA observation instrument, two areas, program management and professionalism, are assessed through interviews or the advisor's personal knowledge. Assessment of the other functional areas is based on direct observation by the advisor during visits at least three weeks apart and during one visit by a local CDA representative. The CDA observation instrument provides broadly stated goals for each functional area and three to five subgoals, organized as numbered items, each accompanied by behavioral exemplars illustrating how the provider might achieve these subgoals. The advisor summarizes the provider's performance, as observed over three visits, by rating whether the subgoal expressed in each numbered item was achieved "rarely," "sometimes," or "mostly." Although not required for the accreditation process, these numerical scores could be averaged to reflect the provider's degree of competence in each functional area.

2. *Assessment Profile for Family Day Care* (Abbott-Shimm & Sibley, 1987a, 1987b, 1987c). This measure was developed for the National Association for Family Day Care (NAFDC) and is used exclusively for NAFDC accreditation. The NAFDC assessment profile is a structured observation, supplemented by documents and providers' reports of unobservable items. The 194 items employ a yes/no format to record specific behaviors and physical arrangements pertaining to seven dimensions: indoor safety, health, nutrition, indoor play environment, outdoor play environment, interacting, and professional responsibility. The profile is completed by the provider and validated by a parent whose child is not currently in the provider's care and an NAFDC representative. The provider must be judged positively by all observers on at least 85 percent of the items on the profile, with at least 75 percent on each dimension, in order for the home to achieve NAFDC accreditation (K. Hollestelle, personal communication, July 15, 1991). It should be noted that this system is undergoing revision at the time of this writing.

3. *Family Day Care Rating Scale* (Harms & Clifford, 1989). The FDCRS consists of 32 items that are organized into six subscales covering space and furnishings for care and learning, basic care, language and reasoning, learning activities, social development, and adult needs. The range of items is compatible with the CDA functional areas. Three items are subdivided to allow separate scoring for infants/toddlers and children over two years old. The scale also provides eight supplementary items for use in homes where exceptional children are included.

Each item is scored on a 7-point scale anchored at scores of 1, 3, 5, and 7, with observable behavioral and environmental descriptors that denote four levels of quality: inadequate (1)—does not meet even custodial care needs; minimal (3)—meets custodial needs and, to some degree, basic developmental needs; good (5)—meets developmental needs; and excellent (7)—provides high-quality personalized care (Harms & Clifford, 1989, p. 1). The mean score for all items scored provides a global estimate of the quality of a particular home. The sources of information used in scoring are observation, notation of documents (e.g., schedules), and where necessary, teacher report.

The FDCRS and an earlier version entitled the Day Care Home Environment Rating Scale (DCHERS) (Harms, Clifford & Padan-Belkin, 1982) have been used as research instruments in Canada (Goelman & Pence, 1987a, 1987b; Stuart & Pepper, 1988) and in the United States (Fiene & Melnick, 1990; Fischer, 1989; Howes & Stewart, 1987; Jones & Meisels, 1987). However, the scale is also suitable for supervision and monitoring by agency staff as well as provider self-evaluation. Its format makes it particularly useful in self-assessment and for training.

4. *Family Day Home Observation Instrument* (Child Care Partnership of Dallas, 1987). This 109-item instrument, designed for use in the Family Day Home Accreditation Program in Dallas, Texas, covers the CDA's functional areas. In each of the eight sections of the Dallas accreditation instrument, a general statement of relevant child care goals (e.g., the importance of safety) is followed by specific items (e.g., "Has outdoor play area fenced"). A trained observer, who may examine documents or ask the provider about unobservable items, records whether the item was present, absent, or not applicable to the home.

To become accredited, providers must comply with at least 90 percent of the items concerning safety/health/nutrition; 80 percent of the items pertaining to physical, self/social, language/thinking, and creative development; and 50 percent of the items on child care as a business, working with parents/families, and the learning environment (N. Beaver, personal communication, July 12, 1991).

5. *Evaluating Home-Based Day Care* (Louise Child Care Center, 1988). The current version of the original Louise evaluation instrument, first published in 1976, is a 206-item checklist for recording the presence or absence of specific descriptors. The items, designed to be compatible with the CDA competencies, are grouped into nine categories. Within each category, items are subdivided to reflect three levels of quality: basic care—"a minimum standard of care which provides primarily for the physical needs of the child"; intuitively good care—"average good care, somewhat analogous to the concerned care the child would receive in his own home"; and informed care—"a sophisticated form of care which is possible when the intuitively good caregiver receives special training" (Louise Child Care Center, 1988, p. 1). Total scores, which are equated with the three levels of care, are calculated by subtracting negative scores from 206 to avoid penalizing the provider for criteria that are not observed in or not applicable to the home. However, this scoring procedure has the effect of giving credit for criteria that are not observed. The Louise evaluation instrument is designed to provide criteria for caregiver evaluation by professionals and to indicate areas in which providers require training, but its clear language makes it suitable for parental use and provider self-evaluation as well.

Because it was designed for use in conjunction with Pennsylvania's strict health and safety regulations, the current Louise Child Care instrument does not include basic standards in these areas. However, to permit wider usage, the center is currently working on a major revision of its measure, including health and safety requirements, which is expected to be available in the spring of 1992 (W. F. Hignett, personal communication, July 8, 1991).

6. *Family Child Care Program Quality Review Instrument* (California State Department of Education, 1988). The California instrument, which incorporates California state licensing standards for family day care homes, consists of seven program components: philosophy/goals/objectives, administration, identification of child's and family's needs, day care home environment, parent education and involvement, integration with community resources, and program evaluation. Using observation, interviews, and documentation, a review team assigns points to reflect compliance with each program component. Points are equated with descriptions of the family day care program as inadequate, adequate, good, or excellent.

Basic Dimensions Addressed

The six instruments described above are all designed to measure the quality of family day care, but their approaches to this task, as reflected in scale format and item content, differ markedly. In order to know whether beneath these surface differences these instruments are assessing similar aspects of day care quality, we need to determine whether their specific items are sampling from the same content areas and, furthermore, whether the items represent the same underlying dimensions of day care quality.

One straightforward approach to answering such questions is to develop a standard set of categories that represent generally accepted aspects of day care quality, sort the items from each instrument into the categories, and compare the number and content of items from each instrument within each category. For example, Modigliani (1991) presented a grid on which she sorted the items of the CDA credential (1985 version), NAFDC, FDCRS, Dallas, and Louise (1988 version) instruments into ten categories including cognitive development, safety, and professionalism. This qualitative approach is useful for summarizing the range of content covered by various instruments. In this instance, Modigliani found that the Louise Child Care instrument had fewer items dealing specifically with language and creative development than the other measures. However, this approach to determining the dimensions of quality that underlie each instrument is limited because there is no way to know whether any intuitively derived set of categories represents all the dimensions that define quality care or whether, on the contrary, the list includes some categories that are redundant or unimportant.

This approach also leaves open the question of how well each item tests the content in a particular category and which categories contribute most to day care quality.

An alternative approach to determining the dimensions of day care quality assessed by these instruments would be to factor analyze each one and to compare the factors that constitute each instrument instead of comparing the individual items themselves. To illustrate, a principal-components factor analysis of DCHERS (the 1982 version of the FDCRS) scores obtained from a combined sample of 236 day care homes revealed three oblique (i.e., correlated) factors accounting for 57.5 percent of the variance. The results of this factor analysis, presented in Table 14.1, was interpreted to mean that the 33 DCHERS items (excluding provisions for exceptional children) actually tapped three underlying dimensions of day care quality. The largest factor (Factor 1) comprised activities and arrangements of equipment and space to enhance learning activities. Factor 2 included items that reflected the provider's effective organization of both the physical environment and the children's activities in order to ensure safety, orderliness, and prosocial behavior. Factor 3, which was defined most strongly by informal use of language and tone of the interactions between caregivers and children, appeared to reflect interpersonal relations (Pellizzari, Pepper & Stuart, in preparation). A similar factor structure emerged when the DCHERS scores for only licensed providers within the combined sample were analyzed (Pepper, Stuart & Harms, 1988), except that a cluster of interpersonal items emerged as Factor 2 and some variations were observed in factor loadings.

In factor analyses such as the one described above were available for other measures, it would be possible to see whether these instruments sampled the same three dimensions assessed by the FDCRS (DCHERS) or whether one measure tapped dimensions not covered by others. Unfortunately, this important comparative work remains to be undertaken.

Usefulness for Different Purposes

Day care quality may be assessed for a variety of purposes: as a guide for parents seeking good quality care for their children, for licensing or certification of homes by government and social agencies, as a self-assessment/training tool for providers and their supervisors, and for research. The six instruments discussed above have been used in a variety of ways.

Accreditation or Credentialing. The CDA assessment instrument and the NAFDC profile were both designed to be used nationally with accreditation and credentialing systems. The Dallas instrument was designed for a more local accreditation system. The FDCRS was used as the assess-

Table 14.1. Factor Structure of the Day Care Home Environment Scale (N = 236)

ITEM	Factors		
	1	2	3
22. Dramatic play	**.82**	-.16	.02
19. Art	**.76**	.07	-.02
23. Blocks	**.75**	-.02	-.05
03. Child-related display	**.73**	.13	-.17
17. Helping children reason (using concepts)	**.72**	.07	.12
21. Sand and water play	**.69**	-.30	.17
15. Helping children understand language (receptive language)	**.68**	.13	.10
18. Eye-hand coordination	**.67**	-.03	.31
16. Helping children use language (expressive language)	**.66**	.05	.25
20. Music and movement	**.59**	-.04	.20
04. Indoor space arrangement	**.58**	.27	.05
29. Cultural awareness	**.56**	.26	-.33
02. Furnishings for relaxation and comfort	**.52**	.10	.11
25. Schedule of daily activities	**.49**	.38	.18
05. Active physical play	**.46**	**.46**	-.12
01. Furnishings for routine care	**.44**	.11	.29
06. Space to be alone	.32	.30	.26
12. Health	-.09	**.97**	-.13
31. Relationship with parents	-.11	**.81**	.18
28. Discipline	-.06	**.77**	.19
13. Safety	.10	**.76**	-.12
33. Opportunities for professional growth	.06	**.73**	.02
26. Supervision of play indoors and outdoors	.04	**.70**	.16
11. Personal grooming	.09	**.68**	.01
10. Diapering/toileting	.06	**.56**	.17
24. Use of T.V.	.31	**.45**	.04
14a. Informal use of language (infant/toddlers)	.04	.02	**.82**
14b. Informal use of language (3 years and older)	.18	.01	**.79**
27. Tone (general quality of interaction)	.09	.03	**.77**
07. Arriving/leaving	.09	.05	**.67**
32. Balancing personal and caregiving responsibilities	.04	.37	**.58**
09. Nap/rest	.09	.33	**.43**
08. Meals/snacks	.08	.26	**.40**
Eigenvalue	13.82	3.00	2.15
Percent of total variance	41.9%	9.1%	6.5%

Note: Oblique rotation of three principal components. Appreciable loadings ($\geq$.40) are bold. There were only 30 valid cases for item 30 (provisions for exceptional children); therefore, this item was excluded in the above analysis.

ment instrument in an accreditation system in San Antonio, Texas. (The acceptable quality level for a provisional accreditation was set at a minimum score of 3 for each item on the FDCRS.)

Regulation or Monitoring. The California instrument was designed for the purpose of state regulation. The FDCRS is used as part of the monitoring system for family child care homes on U.S. military bases.

Self-Assessment and Training. All the measures are suitable for assessment by a supervisor and for self-assessment. The NAFDC assessment profile is used in the accreditation process for self-assessment and also by the advisor. The Dallas accreditation procedure requires provider training as well. Similarly, the FDCRS, Louise, and California instruments explicitly state their applicability for provider training and self-assessment.

Research. Of key importance to researchers are the psychometric properties of an instrument, principally the reliability and validity. In this regard the six instruments vary greatly. A discussion of the psychometric properties of the instruments follow.

PSYCHOMETRIC PROPERTIES

Reliability

An important feature of any measure of day care quality is its ability to yield scores that are consistent across different parts of the scale or its subscales (internal consistency), consistent across observers (interrater reliability), and consistent over time (test-retest reliability). Available evidence regarding the reliability of each of the six measures is summarized below.

FDCRS. The internal consistency of the six FDCRS subscales, as measured by Cronbach's alpha statistic, was assessed by Howes and Stewart (1987) in 55 family day care homes in Los Angeles. Alpha coefficients were also computed for the DCHERS (the 1982 version of the FDCRS) and its subscales for 95 licensed homes tested by Stuart and Pepper (1985) and 55 unlicensed homes tested by Pepper and Stuart (1985) in Ontario.

The data in Table 14.2 indicate that the FDCRS has appropriate levels of internal consistency on all its subscales. The earlier version, DCHERS, displayed a similarly high level of internal consistency for the space and furnishings, language, and learning subscales and, in the Stuart and Pepper sample, the basic need subscale. The reliability coefficient for the social

Table 14.2. Internal Consistency of FDCRS (DCHERS) Subscales in Three Samples

	Scale and Sample		
	FDCRS *Howes & Stewart (1987) (*n* = 55)	**DCHERS** Stuart & Pepper (1985) (*n* = 95)	**DCHERS** Pepper & Stuart (1985) (*n* = 55)
Space and furnishings	.86	.87	.77
Basic care	.90	.81	.65
Language and reasoning	.90	.89	.90
Learning activities	.93	.90	.83
Social development	.83	.59	.32
Adult needs	.70	.68	.60
Total score	--	.96	.94

*Data not reported.

development scale was unacceptably low in the Pepper and Stuart sample, but Howes and Stewart's data indicate that this inconsistency has been corrected in the FDCRS. Similar findings of internal consistency for the DCHERS are reported by Pence and Goelman (1991).

Over seven available studies, the FDCRS's interrater reliability has been consistently high. Using the earlier DCHERS, Pence and Goelman (1991) found interrater agreement ranging from .79 to .89 over a sample of 46 homes in Victoria, British Columbia. Harms and Clifford (1989) had pairs of raters observe 19 homes in North Carolina and obtained an interrater reliability coefficient of .86. Eight items with reliabilities less than .50 were subsequently revised before publication of the FDCRS.

Using the FDCRS, Howes computed interrater reliabilities for the 55 homes tested by Howes and Stewart (1987) and an additional sample of 101 family day care homes in Los Angeles (C. Howes, personal communication, 1988). For both studies, the individual item median interrater agreements were all greater than or equal to .90. Jones and Meisels (1987) in Ann Arbor, Michigan, obtained a median interrater reliability of .83 on ratings of four homes tested before and after training. Nelsen (1989) reported 85 percent agreement between pairs of raters for 32 homes in San Antonio. Finally, in 62 registered family day care homes, Fiene and Melnick (1990) obtained interrater reliability of .90 or above.

Dallas Family Day Home Observation Instrument.   The interrater reliability of the Dallas instrument was assessed in nine homes chosen from a larger pool to represent good, moderate, and poor family day care settings. Two independent observers agreed in their ratings on 97.5 percent of the scale items (Mindel, 1988). Although it will be important to follow this initial study with larger samples, this preliminary evidence of interrater reliability is very promising.

Louise Child Care Instrument.   To assess the reliability of the 1976 version of the Louise instrument, Rodriguez (1982) measured the proportion of agreement between two observers in each of six homes. She reported that interrater reliability ranged from .74 to 1.00, with a mean over the 68 items of .88. Internal consistency and test-retest reliability were not tested. There are no data concerning the reliability or validity of the 1988 version of the Louise instrument, but assessment of the reliability and validity of the latest revision is currently under way (W. F. Hignett, personal communication, July 8, 1991).

NAFDC Assessment Profile.   Nelsen (1989) reported that this instrument was field-tested with 28 providers, but "information on validity and reliability is not currently available on this scale, although the authors state that they are monitoring interrater reliability among the three observers (parent, provider, and validator) as the instrument is used in accreditations and are finding over 97% agreement" (p. 5).

CDA Observation Instrument.   When discussing the CDA credentialing program (1984 version) as a whole, Modigliani (1991) asserted, without reference to the source, that "the CDA was field-tested extensively to achieve satisfactory reliability and validity" (p. 21). The CDA executive director indicated that no data on the reliability or validity of the CDA observation instrument (1991 version), which was reviewed here, are available. She anticipates that such studies might be undertaken after the instrument comes into use across the United States in the fall of 1992 (C. B. Phillips, personal communication, July 8, 1991).

California Instrument.   The published description of this measure (California State Department of Education, 1988) does not supply information on its reliability or its validity.

Summary.   There is now solid evidence supporting the internal consistency and interrater reliability for the FDCRS, but its test-retest reliability has not yet been investigated. The interrater reliability of the Dallas instrument and the 1976 version of the Louise instrument are each supported by one study based on very small samples of nine and six homes, respectively. Information on the reliability of the remaining measures is either indirect or absent.

Validity

In addition to showing that a measure yields consistent, reliable scores over different items, raters, and time intervals, it is important to establish that the instrument actually measures the content that its authors claim it measures. Three types of validity and current evidence of their applicability to the six quality assessment instruments are discussed below.

Content Validity.   One indication of the validity of an instrument designed to measure the quality of family day care is evidence that its content samples the entire range of activities and arrangements that are thought to contribute to the quality of home day care. The CDA observation instrument, the Dallas scale, and the Louise Child Care measure are all based upon the 13 functional areas of day care performance described in the CDA credentialing system. Harms and Clifford (1989) have charted the correspondence between each FDCRS item and the corresponding CDA competency. Thus, the CDA, FDCRS, the Dallas, and the Louise instruments support the content validity of one another. The apparent similarity in content between the FDCRS and the Dallas instrument was supported empirically by a correlation of .82 between scores on the two measures tested in 32 homes (Nelsen, 1989).

Moreover, the FDCRS was adapted from a well-established measure for assessing quality in day care centers—the Early Childhood Environment Rating scale (ECERS) (Harms & Clifford, 1980). An expert panel's ratings of the importance of the ECERS items for determining the quality of pre-school programs supported its content validity (Harms & Clifford, 1983) and, indirectly, the content validity of the FDCRS.

Our earlier discussion and Modigliani's (1991) review indicated that the NAFDC instrument also covers a comprehensive range of content that is relevant to day care quality. Nelsen (1989) found that this measure correlated less highly with the FDCRS and the Dallas instrument (.62, in both cases) than these measures correlated with each other. From these data, Nelsen concluded that her study failed to establish the concurrent validity for the NAFDC instrument. We would suggest, on the contrary, that the correlational evidence shows that the NAFDC shares substantial content with the other two measures.

With regard to the California instrument, our inspection indicates that it samples relevant content, but no empirical evidence on the degree of correspondence with other measures appears to be available.

Concurrent Validity. A measure of day care quality can be said to have concurrent validity to the extent that it is correlated with other currently available indicators of quality. Independent evidence that children are more competent or more developmentally advanced in more highly rated homes would support the concurrent validity of an instrument designed to measure family day care quality. Howes and Stewart (1987) examined the relation between children's behavior in 55 day care homes and a composite measure of quality that included the FDCRS. The validity of the FDCRS was supported by their finding that, with family characteristics statistically controlled, toddlers in more highly rated homes exhibited more advanced play with providers and objects. Girls in higher quality homes also played more competently with peers.

In the Victoria study, Goelman and Pence (1987a, 1987b) demonstrated that scores on the DCHERS (an earlier version of the FDCRS) were positively correlated with the level of children's language development. That is, the DCHERS total score and the score on the social development subscale were both correlated significantly (.33 and .51, respectively) with children's scores on the Peabody Picture Vocabulary Test. Scores on the Expressive One-Word Picture Vocabulary Test (EOWPVT) significantly correlated with total scores on the DCHERS (.32) and the subscales intended to assess learning activities (.33) and social development (.48), although somewhat surprisingly, the EOWPVT scores were not correlated with any of the DCHERS language items.

Goelman and Pence (1987a, 1987b, 1988) also reported that caregiver's activities that appear to foster language development were positively related to the DCHERS score. Specifically, when they coded interactions between caregivers and children, they found that the frequency of activities in which the provider conveyed information to the child was significantly correlated with scores on the DCHERS subscales on language development (.46), learning activities (.36), and social development (.41), as well as the DCHERS total score (.44).

Another criterion against which quality measures can be validated is the professional judgment of experienced day care supervisors or consultants. For example, to support the validity of the 1976 version of the Louise instrument, Rodriguez (1982) asked field representatives of the Louise Child Care Center to use "purely subjective, intuitive criteria" (p. 293) to judge day care homes that they knew well as below average, average, or above average. The representatives then completed the Louise instrument, which was found to correlate significantly (.72) with their professional judgments.

Similarly, Stuart and Pepper (1985) asked experienced supervisors employed by licensed family day care agencies in Ontario to use a 100-millimeter scale to rate the overall quality of each of 157 licensed homes compared with all others they had encountered professionally. These professional ratings correlated significantly (.64) with the DCHERS. Pepper and Stuart (1985) found that the professional judgments of two raters were correlated significantly (.75) with DCHERS scores for 79 unlicensed providers.

Because all three of these studies used the same professionals to provide global ratings and complete the quality instruments, it is likely that the estimates of the association between the quality measure and the professional judgment are inflated. Acknowledging this limitation, these studies do provide limited evidence of the concurrent validity of the instrument.

A more stringent demonstration of this type of concurrent validity was provided by Mindel (1988), who showed that observers' ratings on the Dallas instrument were correlated significantly (.68) with an independent expert's subjective ratings of nine day care homes.

A third approach to supporting an instrument's concurrent validity would be to demonstrate that it could be used to detect known changes in the quality of a day care home. For example, Jones and Meisels (1987) demonstrated that both FDCRS ratings and providers' knowledge about children with special needs increased significantly after the providers received training.

In summary, with the exception of one study that supports the validity of the Dallas instrument and one that supports the validity of the 1976 Louise measure, all other available research concerns the FDCRS/DCHERS. The evidence on this measure, although limited, indicates that children in homes with higher FDCRS scores are likely to play more maturely and have better language skills. Family day care professionals agree that homes that receive higher FDCRS ratings appear to be better child care environments. Thus, existing studies support the concurrent validity of the FDCRS and, to a more limited extent, the Dallas and the 1976 Louise instruments. Similar validation studies appear not to have been performed for the other three measures.

Predictive Validity.   When the predictive validity of a quality measure is assessed, scores on the measure taken at one time are correlated with an outcome criterion or a quality indicator that becomes available at a later time. Unfortunately, "there do not appear to have been any longitudinal studies of the impact of quality in family-based child care" (Doherty, 1991a, p. 19). Thus, the predictive validity of these six instruments is unknown at present.

The only data indicating potential predictive validity is that of Goelman and Pence (1987a, 1987b), showing signs of the relationship between quality as measured by the FDCRS, activities facilitating child development, and developmental status of children in care.

In the same sense that we want to know that sanitary inspections of restaurants reveal the major potential threats to the safe preparation and service of food, and that state medical exams appropriately and systematically measure a physician's ability to diagnose symptoms of disease and prescribe remedies, we want assurance that instruments used to reveal the quality of programs for our young children do so consistently and comprehensively.

In a somewhat unique and interesting approach, Pence and Goelman (1991) combined ratings from the DCHERS and the Caldwell and Bradley HOME (1984) to create an overall quality rating that included assessment of features more commonly associated with an individual family home and those of a more formal family day care home. Such combinations of measures may prove useful in assessing the broad range of aspects of family child care settings, even though the instruments may be highly correlated when used independently.

CONCLUSION

A number of issues in the assessment of family child care environments have been examined here. Four major questions were raised in the opening section of this chapter: Why is the assessment being undertaken? What is being assessed? Who is performing the assessment? How is the assessment being conducted? Responses to each of these questions are now reviewed.

The most pressing question is establishing the motive for the assessment. The answer is dependent in part on who will receive the assessment results. A family day care provider may be doing an assessment for her own information. She may be interested in improving the provision of care and thus see the assessment as an important step in the self-improvement process. Accuracy is important so that areas of weakness and strength are correctly identified. Care would be needed to be sure that the assessment was conducted in the same general manner from one time to the next, so that the improvement noted was real and not simply due to different interpretations. The caregiver's concern for reliability would be focused on test-retest issues as opposed to interobserver reliability.

In another situation, the caregiver may be seeking an assessment as part of the requirements for joining a family day care home association or support group. Here the results might be provided to a review committee of the association. The consequences of assessment are significant to the caregiver in a different sense in this situation, as well as being significant for the review team. It is particularly important here that the results are, in fact, comparable across the various family day care homes in the association. Thus, issues of interrater reliability are more significant, and training must be targeted to ensure fairness in the assessment process.

A third use of assessment may involve seeking official sanction by a licensing or registering agency of a local, provincial, or state government. Here, the results will be shared with a professional review group. Instruments used in this situation must demonstrate the ability to be used in a fair and unbiased manner. Adequate documentation of validity as well as reliability should exist for these instruments, and assessors should meet a high level of interrater reliability. It is critical to ensure the unbiased and fair assessment of family day care homes in this situation. The concern here is to maintain the emphasis on the quality of care provided to children while ensuring that the economic well-being of the individual caregiver is not inappropriately affected.

Finally, systematic assessment of family child care through research and evaluation is crucial to the goal of providing improved care for families and their children. Unless the status of quality is known, it is impossible to direct training and public policy in ways that maximize gains in quality. Similarly, it is impossible to determine the effect of new policies or of training efforts without some objective means of documenting changes in family day care in the field. Researchers and evaluators must be sensitive to all the issues of validity and reliability raised in the preceding sections of this chapter.

Once the purpose of the assessment is clear, the next question focuses on what is going to be assessed. The answer to this question depends on the theoretical framework and the prevailing concept of quality. Here, an ecological model was suggested, with family day care representing a microsystem encompassing the dual functions of the child care group and the provider's personal family responsibilities, mediated by a management function. We further suggested that family child care be reexamined as a unique child rearing/child care environment in light of the sparse but important research on the need for accommodation in home settings to meet the demands of caring for children.

The next question to face is who conducts the assessments. Should observers be child development specialists, or can untrained observers be used? All the instruments reviewed here require some training for observers. Most, however, do not require observers with extensive child development backgrounds. Training on observational methods is more important. Unfortunately, a number of the measures examined have relatively little data on interrater reliability. For those without such information, the people supervising the assessment have increased responsibility for documenting the training and reliability of assessors. Observational instruments are subject to rater bias. When teacher interviews are a part of the data-gathering process for rating questions, particular attention is required to avoid the use of leading or other inappropriate interview practices.

The issue of who should conduct the assessments relates back to the reasons for conducting the assessments. In a study in which settings were assessed after training was provided to caregivers, Berns (1978) found that when assessors were involved with the target of assessment, their built-in bias was hard to control. In particular, trainers were not reliable assessors of change in environments for young children when assessing settings with caregivers who had received training from the trainer's agency. It was impossible for the trainers to separate their own desire to see improvement from the real situation they were observing.

In the case of center accreditation by the National Academy of Early Childhood Programs, the issue is addressed in terms of conflict of interest on the part of assessors. People who have any form of personal interest in a program are not permitted to serve as validators in the accreditation process (National Association for the Education of Young Children, 1984). The Child Development Associate credentialing system has similar conflict-of-interest restrictions for persons involved in evaluation of a candidate's suitability for credentialing (Council for Early Childhood Professional Recognition, 1990).

The final decisions concern how the assessment should be conducted. Each of the instruments discussed in this chapter provides guidance on procedures for the assessments. Here we will return to one overriding concern. As described in the discussion of the theoretical framework, these settings are simultaneously the child care setting for children from several families and the private home of one family. They are, to a large degree, an expression of the people who make up that family. The home might contain religious symbols, expressions of ethnic culture, and many other items unique to that family. In other child care and early education settings, such symbols are often seen as potentially objectionable. The assessor must be trained to understand that family expressions of individuality must not be allowed to unconsciously influence the assessment.

The family whose home is being assessed will inevitably view the assessment, to some degree, as an evaluation of the family itself. Assessors must be sensitive both to the feelings of the family and to the needs of the children in care. Two groups of assessors are particularly subject to having a negative impact on the caregiver and her family. Researchers and their staff members are often perceived as being insensitive to the real-world situation of family care providers. Regulatory staff of licensing agencies are similarly seen as more concerned with the paperwork than with the real quality of care available to children. These two groups must be especially sensitive to the impact their visit may have on the caregiver, and to the changes in the normal operation of the family day care home that may result from their presence in the home. At the same time, the assessors must be careful not to react to potentially unhappy caregivers by giving ratings that are higher than warranted by the actual child care situation. Objectivity of rating should be coupled with sensitivity in behavior.

Recent advances in the ability to measure the quality of family day care settings give family day care providers, trainers, monitors, researchers, and public policymakers useful tools to assist in the establishment of a new professionalism in the care and education of our next generation. The availability of these new tools highlights the need for responsible and sensitive efforts to improve the settings where the majority of care and education takes place for children in child care in our society.

REFERENCES

Abbott-Shimm, M., & Sibley, A. (1987a). *Assessment profile for early childhood programs: Manual administration.* Atlanta: Quality Assist.

Abbott-Shimm, M., & Sibley, A. (1987b). *Assessment profile for early childhood programs: Preschool, infant and school age.* Atlanta: Quality Assist.

Abbott-Shimm, M., & Sibley, A. (1987c). *Assessment profile for family day care.* Atlanta: Quality Assist.

Berns, G. T. (1978). *Evaluation of the day care training network.* Raleigh, NC: Evaluation Section, Division of Plans and Operations, North Carolina Department of Human Resources.

Bowlby, J. (1951). *Maternal care and mental health.* Geneva: World Health Organization.

Bronfenbrenner, U. (1977). Toward an experimental ecology of human development. *American Psychologist, 32,* 513–31.

Bronfenbrenner, U. (Ed.). (1979). *The ecology of human development: Experiments by nature and design.* Cambridge, MA: Harvard University Press.

Caldwell, B. M., & Bradley, R. H. (1978). *Home observation for measurement of the environment: Administration manual*. Little Rock: University of Arkansas.

Caldwell, B. M., & Bradley, R. H. (1984). *Home observation for measurement of the environment*. Little Rock: University of Arkansas, Center for Child Development and Education.

California State Department of Education. (1988). *Family child care program quality review instrument*. Sacramento: California State Department of Education, Child Development Division. (ERIC Doc. No. ED 309 866)

Child Care Partnership of Dallas. (1987). *Family day home observation instrument*. Dallas, TX: Child Care Partnership of Dallas, Inc.

Council for Early Childhood Professional Recognition. (1985). *Child Development Associate assessment system and competency standards: Family day care providers*. Washington, DC: Child Development Associate National Credentialing Program.

Council for Early Childhood Professional Recognition. (1990). *Child Development Associate assessment system and competency standards: Family day care providers*. Washington, DC: Child Development Associate National Credentialing Program.

Council for Early Childhood Professional Recognition. (1991). *Advisor's report form*. Washington, DC: Child Development Associate National Credentialing Program.

Doherty, G. (1991a). *Factors related to quality in child care: A review of the literature*. Ontario: Ontario Ministry of Community and Social Services, Child Care Branch.

Doherty, G. (1991b). *Factors related to quality in child care: Annotated bibliography* (Document prepared for the Child Care Branch; Ontario Ministry of Community and Social Services). Toronto: Queen's Printer for Ontario.

Fiene, R. J., & Melnick, S. A. (1990, April). *Licensure and program quality in early childhood and child care programs*. Paper presented at the American Educational Research Association annual convention, Boston. (ERIC Doc. No. ED 317 320)

Fischer, J. L. (1989). *Family day care: Factors influencing the quality of caregiving practices*. Unpublished doctoral dissertation, University of Illinois at Urbana-Champaign.

Fosburg, S. (1981). *Final report of the national day care home study: Vol. I Family day care in the United States: Summary of findings*. Washington, DC: Department of Health and Human Services.

Gaunt, L. (1980). Can children play at home? In P. F. Wilkinson (Ed.), *Innovation in play environments*. London: Croom Helm.

Goelman, H., & Pence, A. R. (1987a). Some aspects of the relationships between family structure and child language development in three types of day care. In D. L. Peters & S. Kontos (Eds.), *Annual advances in applied developmental psychology. Vol. II: Continuity and discontinuity of experience in child care* (pp. 129–46). Norwood, NJ: Ablex.

Goelman, H., & Pence, A. R. (1987b). Effects of child care, family and individual characteristics on children's language development: The Victoria day care research project. In D. A. Phillips (Ed.), *Quality in child care: What does the research tell us?* (pp. 89–104). Washington, DC: National Association for the Education of Young Children.

Goelman, H., & Pence, A. R. (1988). Children in three types of day care: Daily experiences, quality of care and developmental outcomes. *Early Child Development and Care, 33*, 67–76.

Goelman, H., Shapiro, E., & Pence, A. (1990). Family environment and family day care. *Family Relations, 39*(1), 14–19.

Golden, M., Rosenbluth, L., Grossi, M., Policare, H., Freeman, H., & Brownlees, E. (1979). *The New York City infant day care study.* New York: Medical and Health Research Association of New York City, Inc. (ERIC Doc. No. ED 167 260)

Harms, T., & Clifford, R. M. (1980). *The early childhood environment rating scale.* New York: Teachers College Press.

Harms, T., & Clifford, R. M. (1983). Assessing preschool environments with the early childhood environment rating scale. *Studies in Educational Evaluation, 8*, 261–69.

Harms, T., & Clifford, R. M. (1989). *Family day care rating scale.* New York: Teachers College Press.

Harms, T., Clifford, R. M., & Padan-Balkin, E. (1982). *Day care home environmental rating scale.* Unpublished manuscript, Frank Porter Graham Child Development Center, University of North Carolina, Chapel Hill, NC.

Harms, T., Cryer, D., & Clifford, R. M. (1990). *Infant/toddler environment rating scale.* New York: Teachers College Press.

Howes, C. (1990). Can the age of entry into child care and the quality of child care predict adjustment in kindergarten? *Developmental Psychology, 26*(2), 292–303.

Howes, C., & Stewart, P. (1987). Child's play with adults, toys, and peers: An examination of family and child-care influences. *Developmental Psychology, 23*, 423–30.

Johnson, L., & Dineen, J. (1981). *The kin trade.* Toronto: McGraw-Hill Ryerson.

Johnson, L., Shack, J., & Oster, K. (1980). *Out of the cellar and into the parlour.* Ottawa: Canada Mortgage and Housing Corporation.

Jones, S. N., & Meisels, S. J. (1987). Training family day care providers to work with special needs children. *Topics in Early Childhood Special Education, 7*(1), 1–12.

Lewis, K. (1935). *A dynamic theory of personality.* New York: McGraw Hill.

Louise Child Care Center. (1988). *Evaluating home based day care.* Pittsburgh, PA: Louise Child Care Center.

Mindel, C. H. (1988). *Child Care Partnership family day home observation instrument: Reliability and validity.* Dallas, TX: Child Care Partnership of Dallas.

Modigliani, K. (1991). *Assessing the quality of family day care: A comparison of five instruments.* Hayward, CA: Mervyn's Public Affairs Office.

Moos, R. H. (1980). Evaluating classroom learning environments. *Studies in Educational Evaluation, 6*, 239–52.

Morgan, G. G. (1987). *The national state of child care regulation 1986*. Watertown, MA: Work/Family Directions.

National Association for the Education of Young Children. (1984). *Accreditation criteria and procedures*. Washington, DC: NAEYC.

Nelsen, M. J. (1989). *Concurrent validity of three family day care assessment instruments*. San Antonio, TX: City of San Antonio Children's Resources Division. (ERIC Doc. No. ED 312 036)

Olenick, M. (1986). The relationship between quality and cost in child care programs. In *Child and family policy renewal*. Los Angeles: University of California, School of Social Welfare.

Pellizzari, J., Pepper, S., & Stuart, B. (In preparation). *The structure of family day care quality*. Department of Psychology, University of Western Ontario.

Pence, A. R., & Goelman, H. (1991). The relationship of regulation, training, and motivation to quality of care in family day care. *Child and Youth Care Forum, 20*(2), 83–101.

Pepper, S., & Stuart, B. (1985). *Informal family day care: A study of caregivers*. Unpublished manuscript, Department of Psychology, University of Western Ontario.

Pepper, S., Stuart, B., & Harms, T. (1988). Assessing the quality of family day care. In B. Stuart (Ed.), *The human factor in day care: Proceedings of the National Guelph Conference on Child Care*. Ontario: University of Guelph.

Rodriguez, D. (1982). Assessment of home day care services. *Child Care Quarterly, 11*, 291–97.

Rossbach, H., Clifford, R. M., & Harms, T. (1991). Dimensions of learning environments. Paper presented at the annual meeting of the American Educational Research Association, Chicago.

Stallings, J., & Wilcox, M. (1978). Quality of day care: Can it be measured? In P. K. Robbins & S. Weiner (Eds.), *Child care and public policy: Studies of the economic issues* (pp. 103–32). Lexington, MA: Lexington Books.

Stuart, B., & Pepper, S. (1985). *Private home day care providers in Ontario: A study of their personal and psychological characteristics*. Unpublished manuscript, Department of Family Studies, University of Guelph.

Stuart, B., & Pepper, S. (1988). The contribution of the caregivers' personality and vocational interests to quality in licensed family daycare. *Canadian Journal of Research in Early Childhood Education, 2*, 99–109.

Whitebook, M., Howes, C., & Phillips, D. (1989). *Who cares? Child care teachers and the quality of care in America*. Final report of the National Child Care Staffing Study, Oakland, CA.

Winget, M., Winget, W. G., & Popplewell, J. F. (1982). Including parents in evaluating family day care homes. *Child Welfare, 61*, 195–205.

CHAPTER 15

Future Policy and Research Needs

Arthur Emlen
Elizabeth Prescott

Referred to in this book as "pioneers," we are two old Western frontier scouts who were brought out of retirement to reflect on where family day care has taken us since "the old days" when we were studying family day care. Back in the late 1960s and early 1970s, when we were exploring what was going on in family day care, Prescott, in Pasadena, California, systematically set about making detailed observations of family day care homes as a child-rearing environment, with all their spatial, physical, fuzzy-warm, socioemotional features and opportunities for learning. In Portland, Oregon, Emlen intensively interviewed mothers and caregivers over time to fathom the interaction and relative stability and instability of their informal neighborhood social arrangements.

Both of us studied family day care with wide-eyed wonderment much as one might observe the nesting behavior of birds in their natural habitat. We both viewed family day care as a product of realistic choices and social exchanges made informally by mothers and caregivers in a neighborhood environment that offered them minimal governmental support or relevant community programs. Both of us were impressed by the ingenuity, individuation, reciprocity, and diversity of these social arrangements, but we also recognized how unconnected and inaccessible they were to supportive networks or community mechanisms that addressed their needs. Both of us sought to devise community interventions designed to reach and improve this form of child care that was just beginning to gain public discovery if not recognition.

We do not claim to be the "pioneers" of family day care research. Indeed, one may question whether we blazed a trail or simply got lost out there in the wilderness. Nevertheless, both of us have followed with great interest the development of the rich body of North American research reported in this volume. Family day care has changed in many ways since we first looked at it closely. Yet many of the policy and research issues have persisted. Many of the early problems are still with us, though new policies and programs are emerging to solve them. We are only partway through the agenda of needed research.

Now we get to review what has been reported, to comment on where we think the field has taken us, and to say which of the remaining issues we think researchers should tackle.

THE IMPACT OF DEMOGRAPHIC TRENDS

First of all, we should recognize that family day care has changed since our day, because it has had to adapt to important demographic trends, which have been identified by Hofferth and Kisker and by many of the other authors. Maternal labor force participation has steadily, relentlessly increased since World War II, until two-thirds of the mothers of school-agers and over one-half of the mothers of younger children are in the labor force in both Canada and the United States. The result is an increase in the demand for family day care and a decrease in the potential supply of family day care providers. Family day care can occur only when a mother who enters the labor force finds a mother who has not, and this ratio, which was 40 to 60 when we were studying family day care in the late 1960s and early 1970s, is now 60 to 40. More mothers' relatives have entered the labor work force as well, and the trend is toward less care by relatives. For family day care this means that increasing demand chases decreasing potential supply. This trend lies behind the increasing attention to recruitment and retention of family day care homes by resource and referral services across the land. State initiatives to recruit a larger and improved supply of family day care are finding an increased diversity of backgrounds among new recruits, including those who dropped out of the labor force to become caregivers (Emlen, 1987). Pence and Goelman (1991) worry about the barrenness of neighborhoods, where the caregivers left behind may be increasingly isolated. Hofferth and Kisker report that group sizes of regulated family day care, as in center care, appear to have increased, although group sizes in the bulk of unregulated care probably have not. And the authors of this book point to evidence at least suggestive that high quality of care may not be universal.

Although there are more two-earner families, there are also more single mothers in the labor force—both never married and divorced—which has led to a two-tier work force in which low-income single mothers try to manage when three-fourths of their fellow employees have high household incomes.

The result is a marketing challenge for family day care as it tries to serve one group of consumers who can scarcely afford the already low market rates of family day care and another group of consumers who can afford considerably more than they are paying.

At the same time there is greater demand for caregivers to be flexible. There is more diversity in job opportunities for women, with different occupations, more diversity in job schedules, and a worse fit between work schedules and available care offered by child care providers. There is a greater burden on caregivers to adapt to the needs of employed parents, when the care providers themselves may wish to fix their caregiving schedules, and their greater flexibility may not make caregiving a more attractive job option. As Deiner pointed out in her chapter, children with disabilities add to the demand on family day care providers to be more accommodating. Part-time employment is an expanded option for women, and employee surveys suggest that perhaps 40 percent of family day care usage is for secondary arrangements by part-time employees, thus creating a demand for flexibility in fee-charging by caregivers.

THE INTERNATIONAL FOCUS OF THE BOOK

We are impressed by how much has been accomplished in both countries both in programs and in research on family day care. This volume demonstrates how valuable it is for researchers to share and integrate research findings across national boundaries. The book justifies the researcher's faith in the value of reliability and replications and makes a significant contribution to the literature, because we all have a lot to learn from one another. We salute the editors and the authors for a successful international tour de force.

Most of the authors met for the first time through this book. They had not been working together over the years. They had not even necessarily been following one another's research or attending the same conferences. In neither country has it been easy to sustain a career of funded research in family day care as a field of study. For the most part, therefore, these chapters reflect the fact that the book itself is part of an early stage in a possible recoalescing of the family day care research community. There have been periods in the past, often in connection with research centers, national studies, or conferences, when researchers have come together to become better acquainted with one another's work, but the communication has not been sustained over the years. These chapters are, however, a yeoman effort to bridge separate worlds, and they provide us with a first step in preparing for more sharply focused transnational studies. One is most impressed by the parallels between the two countries, including parallel national debates and divisions, but the chapters also reveal differences between Canada and the United States in national policy and in value assumptions about family support that may affect how family day care develops. It is likely now that these similarities and differences will become the focus of future research.

NEED FOR A HISTORY OF FAMILY DAY CARE

We would like to see a more complete history of family day care, especially in the years since World War II. We were absorbed by the historical perspectives presented in the chapter by Auerbach and Woodill,including their account of the Roman roots of caring for the children of others and the broad perspective that comes from reviewing the history of family day care jointly with the history of group care and early childhood education. But in a history of family day care, we were surprised to see perpetuation of Keyserling's conceptually and methodologically flawed portrayal of the abuses of center care as if they were about family day care as well as a 1918 description quoted by Tentler. Both citations obscured important distinctions about group size. This issue still needs to be clearly addressed in future research. The fact remains that average group sizes in family day care tend to be well below the usual licensing limit of six children, although research is scanty regarding the line and the differences between family day care, family group homes (usually licensed at from seven to twelve children), and centers that take more children.

There are other instances among the chapters that point to the need for an adequate history of family day care in order to shore up the researcher's sense of history. Authors in a number of chapters salute the flag of social ecology, which, we peevishly note, was dated as having been raised only recently. A history of family day care should also incorporate and expand the kind of material that both Perreault for the United States and Kyle for Canada included on the development of the various regulatory models, associations, resource and referral organizations, and support systems.

Mostly, however, our impression was that the authors strained to overcome a lack of history in the field of study they were trying to synthesize. Perhaps the grant-proposal process encourages too much emphasis on dramatically new studies that have never been done before, but we felt that the authors were summarizing findings from disjunctive studies that had not been built on the ones before them. Pollard and Fisher, in their chapter reviewing family day care research, faced the challenge of synthesizing quite separate streams of research that have developed out of diverse disciplines, and they succeeded in identifying gaps in application of the ecological framework. One stream of research that was somewhat overlooked was policy studies such as the National Day Care Home Study, which was detailed in design, well funded, and multifaceted in its findings. Many proposals and hypotheses came out of these different streams of research, providing a rich source of divergent ideas and approaches to understanding family day care. In the future, we would like to see more connections between past and present as well as stronger efforts to bridge the disciplinary streams. Each decade has produced important family day care research that tried to address different policy questions, but those findings tend to be lost when the questions change. A history of family day care in the United States and Canada, interwoven with a history of family day care research, would serve us all well in our research and our policy-making.

This brings us to some thoughts about the policy relevance of research about family day care. Perhaps the most useful commentary we can make from our review of the chapters is to pose and discuss research questions that we think still need to be addressed. In doing this, we dwell on questions that we believe are critical for establishing policy and developing programs. Sharper focus is needed on research issues of importance in formulating family day care policy.

ISSUES RELATED TO SUPPLY AND DEMAND

The book describes family day care in Canada and the United States in broad brush strokes and sometimes in useful detail. Barnett and others have raised significant questions about supply and demand. However, policymakers need to know much more about what the supply of and demand for family day care are really like. We need to know who uses it and how we reach parents in ways that are supportive, educational, and regulative and that might lead to their arranging better care for their children and relating better to the caregivers they use. Also, we need to know who the women are who become family day care providers and how we reach them in supportive, educational, and regulative ways that might lead to their providing better care for children and better support for the families they serve. But more important, we need to answer these questions at every appropriate level of policy-making and program implementation. It is not enough to think we know the answers as a matter of academic knowledge or even as a national or state-level generalization. We also need to know the answers county by county and city by city and neighborhood by neighborhood. Do we make it our business to look at family day care in its entirety community by community? Family day care is inherently a neighborhood phenomenon, though the families may be clustered densely or sparsely. Research on supply and demand must return to its neighborhood roots. The comparison of neighborhoods is a fruitful approach. What kinds of family day care providers make up the total supply that is being used by consumers and is being made accessible through resource and referral services and the array of community programs?

Both Kyle and Perreault described a rich variety of approaches that have been developed in Canada and the United States for intervening in the community to recruit caregivers, support consumers, or improve the quality of care. For each and every one of these approaches to intervention we should know and understand the characteristics of the special population that it is reaching. Special caregiver populations include those who participate in family day care associations, those who participate in training of various kinds, those who sign up for USDA food programs, those who seek to be licensed as group home providers with seven to twelve children as compared to various other group sizes, those who seek to be registered or accredited, and all those who are listed with resource and referral agencies as a community resource. Comprehensive family day care policy requires that we know who we are dealing with and how they are different in their backgrounds, their training needs, and their ongoing need for social support or regulative influence.

RECRUITMENT AND RETENTION OF CAREGIVERS

Everybody talks about the need for recruitment and retention of family day care providers because of their high turnover rates. But what do we know that is useful about how long caregivers of varying backgrounds and experience continue to provide care? How do the new recruits differ from the existing pool of providers? Who is being recruited? Who sticks with it? Are they the ones we need or want most as community resources?

In other words, to what extent are recruitment, retention, and turnover associated with key characteristics of family day care providers such as age, marital status, employment status of spouse, household income, stage of family development (age of youngest and oldest at home), number and ages of own children at home, ages and number of others' children usually cared for, continuity of care provided for children, prior employment and labor-force participation, continuity and regularity in the provider role, and other child care experience or relevant education, training, certification, registration, regulatory status, and affiliations with resource and referral services (R&Rs).

Knowing who is recruited, who takes more children than before, who stays, and who drops out—in other words, knowing more about our population in these terms—will help in developing our recruitment strategies and in assessing whether R&Rs are developing an adequate supply. Are our recruitment policies so coupled with a formal approach to training that they inadvertently have the effect of restricting the supply to only one kind of caregiver when we may need them all? What should recruitment policy be? Do you recruit a few caregivers who want to take many kids or many caregivers who want only a few kids? And are their training needs the same? Probably not.

We are not sure whether the demographic data from both Canada and the United States are enough for categorizing the types of caregivers. We would guess from our own research that there are still differences between young caregivers with their own small children, older caregivers whose children are all in school or grown, women who give some care to supplement social security or welfare payments but do not consider themselves full-time caregivers, and experienced teachers who stay home to be caregivers when they become mothers. Studies are not reported that have attempted to look at other differences that may be associated with caregiving types. For example, caregiving must vary from small towns—where even the most modest houses have fenced backyards—to inner cities—where apartments have no outdoor areas. Do results differ depending on whether studies are conducted in summer or winter? Are there differences in caregivers who specialize in before- and after-school care? It is difficult to evaluate studies that do not clarify the sample used or the context within which the caregiving occurs.

RESOURCE AND REFERRAL

There are questions that we need to know the answers to in order to evaluate the job that R&R agencies are doing. R&Rs represent the interests of parents as child care consumers by providing on-line information about the choices open to them along with referrals, advice, education, and social support for parents who are faced with difficult decisions, especially those whose child care needs are unusual or complicated. Likewise, R&Rs are in a favored position to reach out to the providers of family day care and furnish them with support and consultation and link them with the many other resources that could contribute to their capacity to provide care. Not enough research has focused on this process, despite the fact that many states and provinces are considering or are committed to a policy of establishing R&Rs in every area as a basic infrastructure for developing the child care system and for strategic planning regarding the child care needs of the communities.

Does an R&R's list of child care resources (i.e., its available supply) contain substantial, sufficient, or increasing numbers of providers in the geographic areas served by the R&R, assessed as a percentage of the population base of parents seeking child care? Do R&R services reach substantial, sufficient, or increasing numbers of children and parents who might be looking for child care in the geographic areas served by the R&R, again in relation to the population base of parents in or out of the labor force? The state of Oregon is estimating its child care needs in this way. How responsive are R&R services to parents' requests for the kinds of child care they seek; that is, do referrals correspond to requests with respect to type of care, age of child, hours of care, location, special needs, and characteristics that may be related to quality?

Nobody knows yet what are reasonable goals for R&Rs with respect to the proportion of the potential family day market they should be reaching on the consumer or the supply side. Many consumers find child care informally and successfully on their own without the need for R&R services, and there are complex community differences in kinds of families, stages of family development, kinds of employment, occupations, full- versus part-time labor-force participation, and neighborhood resources for family day care and alternative kinds of care. Nevertheless, R&Rs cannot be successful unless they address a large proportion of the child care market. Powell (1977) conducted an early study of the extent to which R&Rs were a factor in finding child care, but because so few are sufficiently well funded to undertake the needed magnitude of activity, the efficacy of R&Rs probably has never been put to an adequate test. R&Rs must be compared to one another and in relation to the relevant population base until we obtain a better sense of the range of services that communities should be getting from their R&Rs.

The reason that the role of R&Rs deserves attention by family day care researchers is that they are one of the few mechanisms in the community that is expected to reach consumers and family caregivers in large numbers. So it would be useful to compare communities where R&Rs have and have not operated in sufficiently large numbers. Surveys still point to the difficulty in finding child care as a dominant concern affecting one-half to three-fifths of employed parents across all income levels, though especially at low incomes.

THE QUALITY-OF-CARE ISSUE

Practical research that leads to sound programs and policies may also lead to resolution of an attitudinal impasse that remains a barrier to the development of well-informed, comprehensive family day care policy. Powell and Bollin, in their chapter, put their finger on a theme or at least a mood that permeates the book. They identify the ambivalent attitudes of idealism and suspicion about family day care and say, "The skepticism stems from the absence of reliable mechanisms for exerting professional influence on family day care providers." Perreault echoes this observation about the good and bad features of family day care, and many authors translate this evaluative ambivalence into their approaches to family day care policy. Some have such a strong vision of the early childhood educational potentialities of family day care that they are trying to make a silk purse out of a sow's ear. Others are so committed to developing the availability of resources for families in the context of their work that they focus too much on reality and become complacent about how much better child care systems can be. Both extremes overlook the benefits of a rich understanding of how family day care works and of how it may contribute to nurturing, learning, or unique family solutions. Professional skepticism about family day care is still based on assumptions, abstractions, generalizations, and general measures and needs to be channelled into research. The burden of proof is on professionals and family day care researchers to demonstrate that they can devise approaches to reach and favorably influence all the varieties of family day care that spring up in North American neighborhoods whether we like it or not.

Powell and Bollin noted that perhaps parents have a different definition of quality than professionals and that parents prefer a caregiver who has a child-rearing approach similar to their own. We think that parent definitions of quality should not be dismissed. Parents, like caregivers, are a very diverse group. If the care they are seeking is only part time, their requirements for quality may be quite simple, namely a safe, dependable, and accessible family day care home. Parents also judge quality by the criterion of making a good match for their own children. Individuation is paramount. A given home may be an excellent choice for a particular child, even though it is very limited in general terms. Often parents may look for a home that complements, in some way, the experiences that they themselves can provide. For example, a single mother may want a home where the provider's husband enjoys and interacts with the children, a parent may want a child to have the experience of being the oldest or youngest among children, or a young parent may want a grandmotherly person or caregiver from the same cultural background. These may be very different criteria from those viewed as important by the professional community, and we are not ready to dismiss the wisdom of parent choices.

We, like Golbeck, are not convinced that global ratings capture the quality of moment-to-moment interactions. For example, television is often left turned on in homes, but this phenomenon, on close observation, often looks quite different than first imagined. Unlike in group care, children are rarely required to sit and look. We have watched children in family day care weave bits and pieces of conversation from TV into wonderful play and have witnessed the making of connections from picture to real life in ways that are more effective than some of the structured teaching strategies common to group care.

Golbeck raises a question that we think is important to answer. Is the logic of home environments significantly different from that of group care? Are there important messages that are communicated by a setting where the adult is directly handling the tasks and problems of everyday living? Is it important that a child be surrounded by only child-sized objects, or is it perhaps important to experience all the variations that a home has to offer? We are beginning to understand that children begin to pick up subtleties of interactions much earlier than we had thought. Is it possible that they also absorb other meanings in home settings that are not found in the more contrived setting of group care?

Throughout these chapters we have sometimes felt that caregivers were not given much credit for the knowledge that they might have. The vocabulary in common use for child rearing is not precise. When mothers want a homelike atmosphere, or when caregivers say that they are like mothers or that the experience of mothering is valuable, there may be more precise meanings behind this. Hess (1981) examined a teaching task as executed by mothers and teachers and was able to describe differences. Perhaps we should be looking for ways to clarify some of these descriptions rather than dismiss them.

TRAINING

We think the issues we have discussed have relevance to training. Although caregiving cannot currently be considered a profession, as Kontos and others point out, the fact that there are now organizations, conferences, and an accrediting body seems promising. In most professions, any necessary preparation is given by those already in the profession. In the chapter on training, there was no description of the instructors. We would like to know if caregivers are beginning to take responsibility for training.

We worry whether the goal of promoting professionalism among family day care providers will lead to modes of training that ignore what caregivers bring to their roles from the learning experience of being a parent. Just because caregivers may think that being a parent is the best preparation for family day care does not mean that they actually perceive caregiving for others as mothering. We think they know that they are not the mothers. Rather, it is a transfer of learning to a new situation and role. The learning may be relevant and the experience may be valuable. People in the business of training providers should not assume that they are starting from scratch. Family day care providers may not have a "knowledge base" as professionals define it, but they indeed have some know-how that is a legitimate base on which consultation or training may build. In the rush to train, what has become of the art of consultation?

The training of caregivers still appears to be highly atheoretical. In other chapters, there have been discussions of caregiver status from a feminist viewpoint, and since child rearing has been at the heart of much of feminist literature, it seems important to consider this perspective. In *Women's Way of Knowing,* Belenky et al. (1986) suggest perspectives that are much more respectful of the reticence with which some caregivers view training and the resentment that older and very experienced caregivers feel at the prospect of being taught by a young, as yet unmarried, college graduate. We were also surprised to find no observational accounts of training such as were reported in Pasadena by Sale and Torres (1973) in the final report of their Community Family Day Care Project.

ASSESSING QUALITY IN FAMILY DAY CARE

The issues we raised above regarding quality of care are crystallized in the chapter by Clifford, Harms, Pepper, and Stuart on assessing quality in family day care. The chapter describes an impressive methodological achievement that is useful in measuring some favorable aspects of caregiving. Yet the chapter does a better job of describing the ecology of caregiving than it does the ecology of family day care as a social phenomenon, as the Canadians are trying to do in their National Child Care Study. We think researchers should be prepared to discover whether favorable outcomes for children depend on more than quality of care as defined and measured in the family day care home. The words "quality care" appear to refer to the supplemental care that is provided, and the measurement model seems to assume that quality of care resides almost totally in the supply side of the family day care equation. But is it not possible that any correlation of child outcomes with the care situation alone ignores the effects of parent selection and the population differences in the parents and children that children take to the care setting?

Whether or not quality of care actually occurs may depend very much on family life at home and on consumer attitudes, behaviors, preferences, values, and choices. We are inclined to think that the measurement of quality should make an effort to capture those unique selection factors and complementarities sought by parents as they consider the needs of their children and their own strengths or lacks to be supplemented.

We would like to see how these systematic research-based methods of assessment might relate to the ability of parents to assess quality of care as they consider their options or observe the care they are using. A research agenda might well include seeing how strongly the measurement methods and findings described correlate with or differ from parental assessments under a range of levels of consumer education about what matters and what to look for. Consumer understanding of what makes for quality care may have a long way to go, but so does research-based understanding of the conditions under which individualized quality of care occurs.

THE LINKS TO POLICY

The chapter on quality-of-care assessment discusses who does or would use the assessments and why. The why includes the obvious links to setting standards and to regulatory issues. However, we had hoped for new data on the effectiveness of various regulatory strategies. Does licensing effectively establish minimum standards? How much surveillance is necessary? Can registration or R&R accomplish the same objectives? There are excellent data on state and provincial limits on numbers of children, but no reports on other requirements such as specific safety features, TB tests, or background checks on providers for offenses considered dangerous to children.

In places where licensing requirements are regularly checked and enforced, do the number of violations found convince us that registration might have worked equally well, or that other systems should be tried? We would like to see information about parents' familiarity with regulatory requirements or reports of efforts to disseminate information about these issues. How effective can parents be as consumers or as regulators when those roles are reinforced by policy? Under the influence of which policies or programs—licensing, registration, certification, R&R services—do caregivers reach higher standards of care or do parents strengthen or abdicate their responsibilities and effectiveness as consumers? Answers to these questions are needed, and the policy alternatives have huge implications for costs.

In the 1970s, child care research had a strong focus on policy and program issues. This focus needs to be sustained in the future. This book reports a body of knowledge with important underlying implications for policy. If, as policymakers, we wanted to know what types of support services or interventions were most useful to parents or caregivers, or how money could best be spent to guarantee minimum standards, or how to retain experienced caregivers, or whether money is best spent in encouraging the development of more centers or family day care programs for infants and toddlers, we feel that the research reported would not always provide compelling evidence. As Kyle points out, economics is always an issue, consequently as provincial and state government budgets shrink, proposals that do not consider cost-effectiveness have little chance for serious consideration.

THE FUTURE

Research and policy must go hand in hand and include a broader scope of variables if quality in family day care is to be well understood and achieved for all children, and if effective systems of family day care are to be established and sustained in all communities. This book discusses important issues regarding the knowledge base for family day care in North America. There has been steady growth and a developing diversity in family day care research. We hope that the next phase of research will be informed by the range of work undertaken to date and will be shaped more determinedly by thinking through who wants to know and why, and how the information will be used. As a result of this book, future researchers are in a better position to build on what has been done before, and their research will be enriched by the mutual interests of a growing international research community working together on the issues in family day care.

REFERENCES

Belenky, M., Clinchy, B. M., Goldberger, N. R., & Tarule, J. M. (1986). *Women's ways of knowing: The development of self, voice, and mind.* New York: Basic Books.

Bruner, J. (1980). *Under five in Great Britain.* Ypsilanti, MI: High Scope Educational Foundation.

Emlen, A. (1987). Meeting the need for greater availability of child care services: A one-year evaluation of BankAmerica Foundation's child care initiative. *BusinessLink, 3*(2), 11–12.

Hess, R. D., et al. (1981). Different Roles for mothers and teachers: Contrasting styles of child care. S. Kilmer (Ed.), *Advances in child care.* New York: Basic Books.

Powell, D. R. (1977). *Day care and the family: A study of interactions and congruency.* Detroit: Merrill-Palmer Institute.

Sale, J., & Torres, Y. (1973). *Final report: Community family day care project.* Pasadena, CA: Pacific Oaks College.

Pence, A., & Goelman, H. (1991). The relationship of regulation, training, and motivation to quality of care in family day care. *Child and Youth Care Forum, 20*(2), 83–101.

About the Editors and Contributors

Judith D. Auerbach, who received her Ph.D. in sociology from the University of California, Berkeley, in 1986, specializes in research and social policy related to children, family, gender, aging, health, and science. She has taught sociology courses at Berkeley, UCLA, and Widner University. She is the author of *In the Business of Child Care: Employer Initiatives and Working Women.* She is currently Associate Director for Government Affairs of the Consortium of Social Science Associations in Washington, D.C. Previously she was Director of the Institute for the Study of Women and Men at the University of Southern California. During 1988–89 she was sponsored by the Society for Research in Child Development as a Congressional Science Fellow working with Congresswoman Pat Schroeder (D-CO) on issues of child care, family leave, and other family policy issues.

W. Steven Barnett received his Ph.D. in economics from the University of Michigan and has focused his work on the economics of early childhood care and education. Currently he is Associate Professor of Economics and Policy at the Graduate School of Education, and Senior Research Fellow at the Eagleton Institute of Politics, Rutgers University.

Gail Bollin is currently an Assistant Professor in the Department of Childhood Studies and Reading at West Chester University, West Chester, Pennsylvania. She previously taught at Rider College in Lawrenceville, New Jersey. In 1989 she received her Ph.D. in family studies from the University of Delaware. She has published in the areas of family day care provider job satisfaction and job stability, attitudes toward discipline among day care center providers, and maternal satisfaction with family day care arrangements.

Lois Brockman, Professor of Child Development in Family Studies at the University of Manitoba, obtained her Ph.D. in child development and family relations from Cornell University. Her basic research has focused on nutrition and cognitive development, competence and mastery motivation, and social interactions in infancy and early childhood. Her applied research concerns child care, including family day care. Currently she is investigating child care among Canadian one- and two- parent families, including those with children with special needs. Dr. Brockman has been extensively involved in the development of child care education programs in Manitoba and has been the recipient of several excellence awards in graduate teaching and service to the child care community.

Richard M. Clifford is Associate Director of the Carolina Institute for Child and Family Policy at the Frank Porter Graham Child Development Center at the University of North Carolina, Chapel Hill. He is also Clinical Associate Professor in the School of Education. His training is in educational administration with specialization in political science and research. He has had experience as a teacher and principal in the public schools. For nearly 20 years, he has been involved in studying public policies and in advising local, state, and federal officials on policies affecting children and their families. His work has focused on two major themes: public financing of programs for young children and the provision of appropriate environments for preschool and early school-aged children. Dr. Clifford has authored or edited several books and has had numerous journal articles published. He is coauthor of a widely used series of instruments for evaluating learning environments for young children.

Penny L. Deiner received her Ph.D. from Pennsylvania State University. She is currently a Professor of Individual and Family Studies in the College of Human Resources of the University of Delaware. Her research and writing have focused on the inclusion of children with developmental disabilities in early childhood settings and the empowerment of their families. She has been the principal investigator of two grants that trained center and family day care providers to care for children with or at risk for developmental disabilities. She is chairperson of the Delaware Developmental Disabilities Planning Council and the author of numerous articles and the book *Resources for Teaching Children with Special Needs*.

Arthur Emlen received his Ph.D. in social welfare from Tulane University. Before his retirement in 1989, Dr. Emlen spent 24 years on the Portland State University faculty in the Graduate School of Social Work and 16 years as Director of the Regional Research Institute for Human Services. From 1965 to 1972 he conducted pioneering studies of informal family day care arrangements and neighborhood referral services used by employed parents. He has done extensive research on issues of child welfare and foster care placement and has, since 1982, used employee surveys to study the impact of child care on the workplace, within the complex context of work and family life. He has received numerous prestigious awards for his research accomplishments, including, in 1987, the U.S. Secretary of Health and Human Services Award for his pioneering work in foster care permanency planning. He is currently engaged in the development of a national data base on work and family that so far includes survey data on 50,000 employees at 124 companies and agencies from more than 25 cities in 13 states.

Jan Lockwood Fischer received her Ph.D. from the University of Illinois at Urbana-Champaign in 1989. She is a member of the adjunct faculty at Bakersfield College and California State University, Bakersfield. Dr. Fischer previously taught preschool in Minnesota and kindergarten at the Oil Companies School in Tripoli, Libya. She is an honorary lifetime member of the Kern County Family Day Care Association, an advisor to the Kern County Family to Family Day Care Training Initiative, and serves as Administrative Vice President of the Junior League of Bakersfield.

Hillel Goelman is currently Coordinator of Early Childhood Education and Associate Director of the Centre for the Study of Curriculum and Instruction at the University of British Columbia. His research interests include the study of the effects of early childhood programs on children's emergent literacy and language development, as well as the social policy implications of the Canadian National Child Care Study. Dr. Goelman has written extensively in the areas of the effects of quality child care, the role of the family environment in family day care settings, and cross-cultural perspectives on child care.

Susan L. Golbeck is currently an Associate Professor of Early Childhood Education and Educational Psychology at the Graduate School of Education, Rutgers University. She received her Ph.D. in human development and family studies from Pennsylvania State University, where she also worked as a teacher in the laboratory preschool. Dr. Golbeck's research interests focus on children's cognitive development as well as the relationship between developmental theory and educational practice. She has written numerous articles on the development of spatial representation and children's understanding of their spatial environments. She served on the Board of Directors of the Jean Piaget Society from 1984 to 1990.

Sandra Griffin, B.A., M.A., is the founding president of the Canadian Child Day Care Federation and current president of the Early Childhood Educators of British Columbia. She has extensive employment experience in the child care field, including as a family day care provider, a teacher in a parent cooperative preschool, and director of a nonprofit child care center in Okanagan, B.C.. She is currently a visiting Assistant Professor in the School of Child and Youth Care at the University of Victoria. She has served on numerous provincial and national boards and advisory committees.

Thelma Harms received her Ph.D. in early childhood education from the University of California, Berkeley, where she served as head teacher of the Harold E. Jones Child Study Center Preschool. She is currently Director of Curriculum Development at the Frank Porter Graham Child Development Center, University of North Carolina, Chapel Hill. Dr. Harms is best known for her work in environmental assessment and curriculum development. She is coauthor of three widely used environmental rating scales (the Early Childhood Environment Rating Scale, the Family Day Care Rating Scale, and the Infant/Toddler Environment Rating Scale), numerous curriculum publications, and *Raising America's Children,* an early childhood education video training series.

Sandra L. Hofferth is a Senior Research Associate at the Urban Institute, in charge of major research projects on child care demand and supply. She received her Ph.D. in sociology in 1976 from the University of North Carolina, where she studied the contraceptive behavior of couples at the Carolina Population Center. Until 1983 she did research at the Urban Institute on teenage pregnancy and childbearing, children's family structure, and child care. From 1983 to 1988 she was at the Center for Population Research at the National Institute of Child Health and Human Development, where she oversaw research on these topics and coedited *Risking the Future: Adolescent Sexuality, Pregnancy and Childbearing (Vol. 2).*

Carollee Howes is Professor of Developmental Studies in the Graduate School of Education at the University of California, Los Angeles. She received her Ph.D. in developmental psychology in 1979 from Boston University. Her research interests include the antecedents and beginning constructions of peer friendships and social competence, as well as children's social development within infant child care. Her most recent books are *Peer Interaction in Young Children, The Social Construction of Pretend,* and *Forming Relationships: Children in Child Care.*

Ellen Eliason Kisker is a Senior Researcher at Mathematica Policy Research, Inc. She received her Ph.D. in foods research (applied economics) from Stanford University in 1983. Since joining Mathematica in 1986, Dr. Kisker has conducted research on the supply of and demand for early education and child care in the United States as well as on child care issues facing low-income families and teenaged parents.

Susan Kontos is Associate Professor in the Department of Child Development and Family Studies at Purdue University. She received her Ph.D. in child development from Iowa State University in 1980 and before that taught in elementary school and child care. She is author of a research monograph for the National Association for the Education of Young Children entitled *Family Day Care: Out of the Shadows and Into the Limelight.* She serves as Associate Editor of *Early Childhood Research Quarterly* and *Child and Youth Care Forum.* She was coeditor of the book *Continuity and Discontinuity of Experience in Child Care.*

Irene J. Kyle received her M.Sc. in family studies from the University of Guelph, where she is currently enrolled as a doctoral student working on research about Canadian family resource programs. She returned to the university after extensive work experience in child care, as a Senior Policy Analyst for child care with the Ontario Ministry of Community and Social Services, and as Executive Director of Mothercraft and of Cradleship Creche, both of which are multiservice child care agencies. She has been a board member of the Canadian Association of Toy Libraries and Parent-Child Centres since 1987. She is author of *The Role of Family Resource Services as a Child Care Support* and principal author of the Ontario Provincial Report of the National Child Care Study.

Donna S. Lero is an Associate Professor in the Department of Family Studies at the University of Guelph. Her involvement in the child care field dates from 1965, when she was employed as a Head Start teacher in New York City. Since 1980 she has been involved in several major studies of child care in Canada and currently is the Project Director of the Canadian National Child Care Study. Dr. Lero's publications include analyses of the factors that affect parents' preferences and choices among child care alternatives, parents' work schedules, work-family-child care tensions, and policy issues related to balancing work and family responsibilities. Her recent publications include a chapter, "Work, Families and Child Care in Ontario," coauthored with Irene Kyle, published in *Children, Families and Public Policies in the 90s,* and "Parental Work Patterns and Child Care Needs," to be published by *Statistics Canada.*

Sandra Machida received her Ph.D. in child development from the Department of Psychological Studies in Education, Stanford University, in 1983. Currently she is a professor in the Department of Psychology, California State University, Chico. Dr. Machida is also the Director of Policy Studies on Youth and the Family at CSUC. Her current research interests are in family day care, family and school factors associated with school achievement, and the efficacy of early childhood intervention programs.

Alan R. Pence (editor) is Professor of Child Care at the School of Child and Youth Care, University of Victoria. He has extensive experience in the field of child care, having worked as a child care worker, trainer, and program director before joining academia in 1981. Since 1981 he has been primarily involved in the development of Canadian early childhood care and education research. Dr. Pence was Co-principal Investigator with the Victoria and Vancouver Day Care Research Projects, Canadian Coordinator for the Childhood in Society Project, and he is presently Co-Director of the Canadian National Child Care Study. His most recent books include *Ecological Research with Children and Families: From Concepts to Methodology* and *Professional Child and Youth Care: The Canadian Perspective* (2d edition).

Susan Pepper is Associate Professor, Department of Psychology, and Associate Vice-President of Academic Affairs at the University of Ontario, London, Canada. She completed her B.A. in psychology at the University of Toronto and her Ph.D., specializing in personality psychology, at Stanford University. In addition to research on family day care, she has published articles on personality psychology, faculty development, and peer group entry among elementary school children.

Joe Perreault is currently Deputy Director of Save The Children/Child Care Support Center in Atlanta, Georgia. He is coauthor of a number of publications in family day care, including *Family Day Care as an Option for Rural Communities* and *The Child Care Food Program for Family Day Care: A How-to Manual*. He coordinates the Family Day Care Technical Assistance Conference, a national conference held annually in the United States.

Donald L. Peters (editor), who received his Ph.D. in educational psychology from Stanford University, is currently Amy Rextrew Professor of Individual and Family Studies at the University of Delaware. From 1968 to 1985 he was on the faculty of Human Development and Family Studies at Pennsylvania State University. He has done research and evaluation studies on Head Start, day care, and early intervention programs for young children with developmental disabilities and their families since 1966. He is the author of some 60 articles and author or editor of several books in the field of early childhood education. His most recent books include *Professionalism and the Early Childhood Practitioner* and *Continuity and Discontinuity of Experience in Child Care*.

June Pollard is Professor of Early Childhood Education at Ryerson Polytechnical Institute. Her teaching areas include child care policy, language development, and multicultural education. She has done international comparative policy research for the Ontario government on family and day care and is currently working on a study of political ideology and family day care policy in England, the Netherlands, Sweden, and Ontario. She is also managing a CIDA-funded four-year institutional linkage project with an early childhood education program in Rajasthan, India.

Douglas R. Powell is Professor and Head of the Department of Child Development and Family Studies at Purdue University. He conducted pioneering studies of relations between families and early childhood programs and has developed innovative programs of family education and support. He is editor of the *Early Childhood Research Quarterly* and is editor or author of numerous scholarly publications and four volumes, including *Families and Early Childhood Programs*.

Elizabeth Prescott was a member of the faculty of Pacific Oaks College for 24 years before her recent retirement. During that time she was the recipient of several pioneering federal grants to investigate issues of quality in day care settings. Of her numerous publications and presentations on this work, she is perhaps best known for *Planning Environments for Young Children: Physical Space,* published by the National Association for the Education of Young Children. She has served on numerous federal advisory panels and commissions and is currently on the editorial board of *Early Childhood Research Quarterly*.

Malcolm Read is Chair of the Early Childhood Development Department at Red Deer College, Red Deer, Alberta. He is currently completing his doctoral dissertation at the University of Alberta. He is coauthor with Annette LaGrange of *Those Who Care: A Report on Approved Family Day Care Providers in Alberta* and *Towards a Research Agenda on Child Care*.

Laura M. Sakai is a Postdoctoral Fellow at the UCLA Graduate School of Education. She received her Ph.D. in developmental psychology at the University of Southern California in 1990. Currently her interests include the study of individual differences, including how familial and child care experiences influence children's development. She is conducting both family and twin studies of parental child-rearing attitudes and attachment relationships.

Barbara Stuart is currently the Director of the Family Studies Laboratory Schools and an Adjunct Professor in the Department of Family Studies at the University of Guelph. Prior to managing and working in the Laboratory Schools, Ms. Stuart established and supervised a municipally operated family day care agency. She assisted in the development of and continues to provide consultation to an 18-week training program for women interested in becoming in-home caregivers in southern Ontario. She is currently part of a multidisciplinary team studying the stress on infants/toddlers, their parents, and caregivers associated with very young children's entry into three types of full-time child care.

Gary A. Woodill, Ed.D., is Professor of Education in the School of Early Childhood Education at Ryerson Polytechnic Institute, Toronto, Canada. He has worked in the field of education since 1971 and received his doctorate from the University of Toronto in 1984. He has produced several resource manuals on children with special needs in Canada and has written articles on the history of early childhood education and special education, on the applications of computer technology in early childhood education, and on new research paradigms in the social sciences. He is the senior editor of the forthcoming *International Handbook of Early Childhood Education.*

Index

Accreditation, of family day care providers
by National Academy of Early Childhood
Programs, 261
by National Association for Family Day Care,
193–94, 195, 237
and quality assessment, 251–53, 261
See also Credentialing, of family day care
providers; Licensing, of family day care
providers
Advocacy, 238–39, 241
AIDS, 134, 140
Alberta, Canada, 216, 217, 218
Alsace, France, 14
Altruism, parental, 80
American Journal of Psychology, 18
American Orthopsychiatric Association, Study
Group on Mental Health Aspects of Day
Care, 171
American Psychological Association, 18
Americans with Disabilities Act of 1990, 132
Andrew Fleck Child Centre (Ottawa), 23, 222
Associations, of family day care providers
in Canada, 223–24
development of, 23
and professionalism, 236–38
Atkinson, A. M., 176, 177, 182–83
Attachment theory, 103–4, 116, 122–24
Auerbach, J. D., 5, 9–27, 269
Autistic children, 132
Autonomy, 124–25
Aveyron, France, 17

Baby and Child Care (Spock), 18–19
Babyfarming, 12
Bailey, D., Jr., 135
BankAmerica Foundation, 235
Banzet, S., 14
Barker, R. G., 150, 151, 163
Barnett, W. S., 5, 72–91
Behavior setting, 150
Belenky, M., 276

Belief systems, 115–18, 125–26
Birthrate, 78
Bollin, G. G., 5–6, 170–87, 273, 274
Bowlby, J., 244
Bradley, R. H., 160
British Columbia, 173–74, 210, 214–15, 216,
218, 221, 226. *See also* Victoria (B.C.)
Day Care Research Project
Brockman, L., 5, 58–71
Bronfenbrenner, U., 148–49, 150, 244–45
Business model, of parent-provider
relationships, 179, 180–81, 183–84

Caldwell, B. M., 160
California, 136, 236
California Child Care Initiative, 196–97, 235
Calzavara, L., 96
Canada, family day care in
and day care public policy, 23–24
demographics of, 213–16, 225
and family day care provider training, 189,
190, 200, 202
and family day care provider turnover, 191–
92
models of, 209–28
regulation of, 209–12, 216–20
supply-and-demand of, 94–97
support services for, 210, 211–13, 220–24
See also specific provinces and programs
Canadian Association of Toy Libraries and
Parent Resource Centres, 216
Canadian National Child Care Study
demographic data of, 59–66, 214
implications of, 69–70
primary care data of, 66–69
and public policy, 58–59, 97
and socioecological context, 62–66, 68–70,
276
study design of, 59
Carew/SRI Observation System, 247
Caruso, G., 210–11

Child and Adult Care Food Program, 39, 45
Child care
    demand for, 74–75
    federal subsidies for, 29–30, 44–45, 81–82,
        210
    social attitudes towards, 192, 195
Child Care Action Campaign, 236
Child Care and Development Block Grant, 30
Child Care Food Program, 88, 231–32
Child care resources and referral programs
    (CCR&R), 211, 215–16, 221, 234–35,
    236, 237–38, 271–73
Child development
    and family day care, 103–6
    Freudian theories of, 17, 18
    See also Cognitive development; Ecology of
        human development; Linguistic
        development; Social-affective
        development
Child Development Associate Advisor's Report
    Form, 247–48, 250, 251, 255–56, 261
Child Development National Credentialing
    Program, 194–95
Childminding, 12, 20, 97
Children's Aid Society, 220
Children's Foundation, 235
Child-staff ratios, in family day care, 46–47, 52
Civic groups, involvement in family day care,
    235–36
Clarke-Stewart, K. A., 154, 155–56, 158–59,
    162, 164
Cleveland, G., 93
Clifford, R. M., 6, 243–65, 276
Cognitive development, 17, 19, 147–48, 155,
    158–61, 163
Cohen, N., 20, 201, 235
Columbia University, 16
Comenius, J., 13–14
Communication
    child-family day care provider, 159
    parent-family day care provider, 174–75
Community Family Day Care Project, 276
Connelly, K. J., 157
Corsini, D. A., 210–11
Cost, of family day care
    for disabled children, 134
    failure to pay for, 176
    fee structure of, 45
    increase of, 48–49
    and supply-and-demand, 76–89, 93–99

Council for Early Childhood Professional
    Recognition, 194–95
Credentialing, of family day care providers,
    193, 251, 253, 261

Dallas Family Day Home Accreditation
    Program, 249, 250, 253, 255, 258
Dame schools, 14
Day care centers
    in Canada, 61, 62–63, 64, 67
    comparison with family day care, 76
    parent-provider relationships in, 173–74
    physical environment of, 151–53
Day Care Home Environment Rating Scale
    (DCHERS), 249, 251, 252, 253–54, 257–
    58, 259
Day care networks, 22
Day Care Support Program, 221
Deaf and Dumb Institute (Paris), 17
Deiner, P. L., 129–45, 268
Delaware, 175, 176, 177, 179, 182
Delaware FIRST program, 136–37, 141
Demographics, of family day care, 28–57
    and availability of care, 39, 42
    and caregivers' wages and income, 46, 49
    and child-staff ratios, 46–47, 52
    and costs, 45–46
    and early childhood programs, 38–39, 40–
        41, 53
    and education/training of caregivers, 47, 49,
        52
    geographic distribution of programs, 38, 40
    and parental satisfaction, 52–53
    of programs for disabled children, 43–44
    of programs for low-income children, 44–
        45
    sampling of, 164
    of supply-and-demand, 47–52, 93–94
    trends in, 267–68
Disabled children, family day care for
    barriers to, 133–34
    benefits of, 134–36
    comparison with day care centers, 43–44
    and early childhood intervention, 130–31,
        132, 136–37
    health and safety concerns in, 134, 139–40
    individualized care planning in, 140–42
    need for, 129–30
    provider training for, 137–39
    social support for, 132–33

Doherty, G., 244
Doherty Social Planning Consultants, 96

Early Childhood Environment Rating Scale, 159, 256–57
Early childhood intervention
  legislative basis for, 132
  philosophical basis for, 130–31
Early childhood profession
  acceptance of family day care by, 239
  historical background of, 13–19
Early One-Word Picture Vocabulary Test, 160
Ecology of human development, 3, 104, 148, 163. *See also* Physical setting, of family day care
Economics, of family day care. *See* Cost, of family day care
Education, of family day care providers, 190. *See also* Training, of family day care providers
Education for All Handicapped Children Act of 1975, 132
Eheart, B. K., 100–1, 105, 120
Elder Life Plan, 222
Emlen, A., 6, 21, 99, 129–30, 266–78
Employers
  child care resource and referral services of, 234–35
  day care services of, 23
Evaluating Home-Based Day Care. *See* Louise Child Care Instrument
Exosystem, 244, 245
Expert advice, 115–16, 117–18
Expressive One-Word Picture Vocabulary Test, 257
Extended family model, of parent-provider relationships, 179–81, 183–84

Families and Work Institute, 239
Family Child Care Program Quality Review Instrument, 250, 256
Family day care
  criticisms of, 238–39
  definition of, 29, 70
  familial nature of, 118–22
  nonregulated, 29, 30, 38–54
  as percentage of all child care, 73–74
  regulated, 29, 30, 38–54
  social attitudes towards, 115, 117, 176–77, 239
  uniqueness of, 240–41

Family day care agencies, 232–33
Family Day Care Home Accreditation Program (Dallas), 249
Family Day Care Project, 136
Family day care providers
  attitudes towards child care, 192, 195, 204
  characteristics of, 100–1, 178, 180, 272
  hourly earnings of, 85
  motivations of, 119–20, 182
  number of, 82, 229
  recruitment of, 271–72
  social status of, 195, 225–26
  turnover of, 164, 190–91, 271
Family Day Care Rating Scale (FDCRS), 122, 136–37, 141, 158, 159, 160, 178, 199, 248–49, 250, 251, 253–55, 256–57, 258–59
Family Day Care Services (Toronto), 23, 222
Family Day Care Technical Assistance Conference, 235
Family Day Home Observation Instrument. *See* Dallas Family Day Home Accreditation Program
Family to Family Project, 236
Family Support Act of 1988, 30
Federal Interagency Day Care Requirements, 23
Fewell, R. R., 130
Fiene, R. J., 255
First-aid certification, 189
Fischer, J. L., 5, 92–112, 269
Fosburg, S., 178
Foster home care model, 220
France, 17, 197
Freud, S., 17, 18
Friends, as child care providers, 180, 181
Froebel, F., 16

Galinsky, E., 239
Geurin, Madame, 17
Goelman, H., 5, 58–71, 104, 159, 160, 162, 173–74, 176, 180, 200, 245, 254, 257–58, 259, 267
Golbeck, S. L., 5, 146–69, 274–75
Griffin, S., 6, 188–208
Group size, in family day care, 46, 52, 217–19, 220, 226, 269
Gruber, C. P., 155
Gump, P. V., 157

Hall, G. S., 17–18
Harms, T., 6, 243–65, 276

Hasegawa, P., 100, 101
Head Start program (United States), 30, 36, 81
Heft, J., 148, 150
Heinicke, C. M., 172
Helburn, S., 239–40
Hendrickson, J. M., 157
Historical perspectives, on child care
    in ancient Rome, 9–11
    and childhood education, 13–19
    during Industrial Revolution, 13–15
    during nineteenth century, 12
    during twentieth century, 18–19
Hofferth, S. L., 5, 28–57, 267
HOME Scale, 160, 178, 247, 259
Howes, C., 5, 104, 115–28, 156–57, 159, 161,
    199, 200, 239, 244, 247, 253, 255, 257
Hughes, R., 173, 175
Hunt, J. M., 148

Indiana, 136
Individualized family service plan (IFSP), 140–
    41
Individuals with Disabilities Education Act
    (IDSA), 132
Infant Care (magazine), 117–18
Infants, family day care for
    and belief systems, 115–18, 125–26
    demographics of, 38, 42
    developmental issues in, 122–25
    disabled infants, 138
    historical background of, 14
Infant School Society, 15
Infant school system, 15
Infant/Toddler Environment Rating Scale, 247
Infrastructure development, 235
International Business Machines (IBM), 234–
    35
Iowa, 176
Itard, J., 17

Johnson, L. C., 161–62
Jones, S. N., 255, 258

Katz, L., 120
Keyserling, M., 21
Kindergarten, 15–16, 29 61, 62, 64, 65, 67, 68
Kisker, E. E., 5, 28–57, 267
Kontos, S., 6, 104–5, 188–208, 239
Kopp, C. B., 124
Kyle, I. J., 6, 209–28, 269, 271, 277

LaGrange, A., 201
Lanark, Scotland, 15
Leavitt, R. L., 100–1, 105, 120, 174–75, 176
Lero, D. S., 5, 58–71
Licensing, of family day care providers
    in Canada, 61, 62, 64–65, 66, 67, 68, 210,
        211, 213–15, 216–20
    historical background of, 21–22
    and parent-provider relationship, 180
    providers' failure to comply with, 29, 193
    and providers' training, 189
Licensing agencies, as social support sources,
    231
Linguistic development, 158–61
Literacy development, 160
Lloyd, S. A., 101–2
Los Angeles, California, 21
Louise Child Care Instrument, 249–50, 255,
    256, 258
Low-income children, family day care for, 44–
    45

MacCaulay Child Development Centre
    (Toronto), 222–23
Machida, S., 6, 188–208
Macrosystem, 149, 244
Manitoba, Canada, 214, 216, 218, 220
Maryland, 133–34
Maternal belief system, 115, 116–17
Maternal employment
    in Canada, 58, 225
    and family day care demographics, 28, 33,
        34–35, 36, 42, 130
    and income tax, 79
    social attitudes towards, 115, 116–17, 118
    trends in, 73, 77, 130, 267
May, D., 15
McCartney, K., 117
McMillan, M., 16
McMillan, R., 16
Meisels, S. J., 255, 258
Merill-Palmer Institute (Detroit), 16
Mesosystem, 106, 244, 245
Michigan, 136
Microsystem, 106, 149, 150, 244, 246
Military, and family day care, 233
Mindel, C. H., 258
Minnesota, 236
Mitofsky-Waksberg primary unit, 31
Modigliani, K., 201, 239–40, 250, 255–56

Montessori, M., 17
Moos, R. H., 244
Multi-service child care/family support agency, 221–23

Nannies, 11, 116
National Academy of Early Childhood Programs, 261
National Association on Child Care Resource and Referral, 236
National Association for the Education of Young Children (NAEYC), 125, 172, 239, 240
National Association for Family Day Care (NAFDC)
  accreditation program of, 193–94, 195, 237
  Assessment Profile for Family Day Care, 248, 250, 253, 255, 257
  and Children's Foundation, 235
National Child Care Research Network, 96–97
National Child Care Study, 101
National Child Care Survey 1990, 30–47
National Council of Jewish Women (NCJW), 21, 197, 236, 239
National Day Care Home Study, 21, 84, 85, 119, 163–64, 179, 247, 269–70
National Family Day Care Association, 23
National Family Day Care Network, 224
National Family Day Care Project, 197, 236
Nelsen, M. J., 255, 257
Nelson, M., 12, 102
New Brunswick, Canada, 216, 218
Newfoundland, Canada, 216, 219
New Harmony, Indiana, 15
New Mexico Development Disabilities Planning Council, 136
New York City Infant Day Care Study, 164, 247
Northwest Territories, Canada, 219
Nova Scotia, Canada, 216, 219
Nurseries and Childminders Act of 1948 (United Kingdom), 20
Nursery schools
  in Canada, 61, 62, 64, 65, 67, 68
  and childhood development, 154, 155
  enrollment in, 29
  historical background of, 16

Oberlin, J.-F., 14
Ontario, Canada, 94–95, 96, 101, 106, 210, 214–15, 217, 221

Ottawa/Carleton Child Care Providers Association, 223
Owen, R., 14–15

Parent-caregiver relationships, 10–13
Parent-provider relationships
  business model of, 179, 180–81, 183–84
  disempowerment in, 102
  extended family model of, 179–81
  parents' attitudes towards, 101, 121, 175–76, 177–79, 182
  and provider's family, 181–83
  providers' attitudes towards, 101, 121, 175, 176–77
  research in, 171–74, 183–84
  types of relationships, 76, 174–75
Parents (magazine), 117–18
Pastoret, Madame de, 14–15
Peabody Picture Vocabulary Test, 160, 257
Pence, A. R., 5, 58–71, 104, 159, 160, 162, 173–74, 176, 180, 200, 245, 254, 257–58, 259, 267
Pennsylvania, 21–22, 136, 179–80
Pepper, S., 6, 243–65, 253–54, 258, 276
Perreault, J., 6, 23, 229–42, 269, 271, 273–74
Perry Preschool Program, 78–79
Pestalozzi, H., 14–15, 16
Peters, D. L., 1–6
Philadelphia, 21
Phillips, D. A., 117, 244
Physical setting, of family day care
  and child cognitive and linguistic development, 147–48, 158–61
  and child social-affective development, 153–158
  comparison with day care centers, 119, 146–47, 151–53, 154–55, 159–60
  and ecological framework theory, 148–50
  restricted areas in, 161–62, 182–83
Piaget, J., 19, 148
Play, 105, 156–58, 159
Play unit, 158
Plutarch, 11
Pollard, J., 5, 92–112, 269
Popplewell, J. F., 247
Portland, Oregon, 181
Powell, D. R., 5–6, 170–87, 273, 274
Preschool children
  in day care centers, 33, 34, 37, 38, 50–51, 74
  in family day care, 33, 34, 37, 38, 42, 50–51

Preschool children (*continued*)
  social development of, 103
  peer interactions of, 156–58
Prescott, E., 6, 21, 151–53, 154, 155–156,
    158, 159, 162, 266–78
Presser, H. B., 87
Prince Edward Island, Canada, 219, 220
Prince Edward Island Association for Early
    Childhood Education, 223–24
Professionalism, in family day care
  opposition to, 24
  and profession's entry standards, 193–95
  and provider associations, 236–38
  and training, 188, 198–203, 275
  and training regulations, 189–90, 195, 203
  and training sources, 195–97
Profile of Child Care Settings Study, 30–33, 47–
    52
Project Neighborhood Care (Pennsylvania), 136
Protestant Children's Home (Toronto), 23
Provider Connection, The (Windflower
    Enterprises, Inc.), 237–38
Public policy, for family day care
  historical background of, 19–24
  research base for, 269–70, 277–78
Purdue University, 239

Quality assessment, of family day care
  assessment instruments for, 136–37, 141,
      243–44, 246–59, 261
  and motive for assessment, 259–60, 261
  by parents, 178–79, 274, 276–77
  theoretical framework of, 244–46, 260–61
Quebec, Canada, 24, 96, 214–15, 216, 217,
    218, 220, 226
Quilitch, H. R., 158

Rapp, G. S., 101–2
Read, M., 6, 201
Registration, of family day care providers, 22,
    230
Regulation, of family day care
  in Canada, 209–12, 216–20
  economic effects of, 87–88
  government's role in, 19–24, 230
  and support services, 230–31
  types of, 211–12
Rehabilitation Act of 1973, 132
Relatives, as child care providers, 60, 61, 62–
    63, 64, 65, 67, 68, 73–74, 75, 84, 267

Research, in family day care
  developmental psychological studies, 103–6
  implications of, 239–40
  lack of, 1–3
  parent-provider relationship studies, 172–74
  problems of design in, 164
  recommendations for, 266–68
  sociological studies, 99–103
  supply-and-demand studies, 93–99
Resources and referral services. *See* Child care
    resources and referral programs
Respite care, 131
Risley, T. R., 158
Rodriquez, D., 255, 258
Rothstein-Fisch, C., 157
Rubenstein, J., 104, 156–57
Rubin, S., 176
Ruderman, F., 21

Sakai, L. M., 5, 115–28
Sale, J., 276
San Antonio, Texas, 21
Saskatchewan, Canada, 214, 216, 218
Satellite Family Day Care Home Project
    (Alberta, Canada), 217
Save the Children, 235
School-age children
  in center-based child care programs, 33, 34,
      35, 36
  in family day care, 34, 35, 36, 37
  trends in child care for, 74
School of Infancy (Comenius), 13
Schurz, M., 16
Security, 122
Seguin, E., 17
Self-assessment, 253
Self-regulation, 124–25
Sick children, family day care for, 44
Slaves, as child care providers, 10–12
Smith, P. K., 157
Snow, C., 201
Social-affective development, 153–58
Social Planning Council and Child Care
    Association of Winnipeg, Manitoba, 95–96
Social Security Act, Title XX, 22
Social Services Block Grant, 30
Socioecological context, of family day care, 62–
    66, 68–70. *See also* Ecology of human
    development
Sociology, 99–102

Special Care Outreach Project (California), 136
Spock, B., 18–19
State Grants for Dependent Care Planning and
    Development, 30
Stevens, J. H., Jr., 178
Stewart, P., 253, 255, 257
Stuart, B., 6, 243–65, 276
Subsidies, for child care, 29–30, 44–45, 81–82,
    210
Supply-and-demand, in family day care, 38–39,
    40–41, 47–52, 53, 76–89, 93–99, 267–
    68, 270–71
Support services, for family day care
    in Canada, 210, 212–13, 215, 220–24
    Child Care Food Program as, 88, 231–32
    child care resources and referral programs as,
        234–35, 236, 237–38, 271–73
    of civic and voluntary groups, 235–36
    for disabled children, 132–33
    family day care agencies as, 232–33
Synomorphy, 150
Systems theory, 181–82

Tacitus, 11
Task Force on Child Care in British Columbia, 210
Taylor, B., 235
Tennessee, 236
Three Essays on Sexuality (Freud), 18
Toddlers, family day care for
    and belief systems, 115–18, 125–26
    developmental issues in, 103, 122–25
    disabled toddlers, 138
    and peer interactions, 156
Toronto, Canada, 23–24, 94, 222–23
Torres, Y., 276
Training, of family day care providers
    in Canada, 189, 190, 212
    and children's attachment, 123–24
    demographics of, 47, 49, 52
    for disabled-child care, 137–39
    historical background of, 22
    and licensing agencies, 231
    and provider associations, 236–37
    and providers' behavior, 120–21, 199–200
    recommendations regarding, 203–4
    recruitment for, 201–3
    regulation of, 189–92, 195, 203
Travis, N., 23
Turnover, in family day care, 164, 190–91, 225,
    271

Unger, O., 157, 163
Unionization, of family day care providers, 225
United States
    family day care provider training in, 189,
        190, 200, 201–2
    family day care provider turnover rate in,
        190–91
    support services in, 229–42
    See also name of specific state or program
University of California at Los Angeles, 239
University of Colorado, 240
University of Toronto, 16

Vancouver, British Columbia, 223
Victoria (B.C.) Day Care Research Project, 173,
    178, 180
Vinovskis, M. A., 15
Vocabulary tests, 160
Voluntary groups, involvement in family day
    care, 235–36
Vygotskian theory, 124, 163

Washington (state), 236
Wattenberg, E., 99, 100, 200–1, 202
Werner, H., 148
Westcoast Child Care Resource Centre, 223
Western Canada Family Daycare Association,
    224
Wheelock College, 239–40
Whitebook, M., 244
Whitehead, L. C., 176, 177, 180–81, 182
"Wild boy of Aveyron," 17
Windows on Day Care (Keyserling), 21
Winget, M., 247
Winget, W. G., 247
Winton, P., 135
Wisendale, S., 210–11
Wohlwill, J., 148, 150, 163
Women's Ways of Knowing (Belenky et al.),
    276
Woodill, G. A., 5, 9–27, 269
Work/Family Directions, 234–35
Working Parents Day Care Assurance Plan,
    222

Young, K. T., 117–18
Yukon, Canada, 216, 219
Yverdon, Switzerland, 16

Zone of proximal development, 124